Dreams of disconnection

Manchester University Press

Dreams of disconnection

From the autonomous house to self-sufficient territories

Fanny Lopez

Manchester University Press

Published by Manchester University Press
Altrincham Street, Manchester M1 7JA

www.manchesteruniversitypress.co.uk

British Library Cataloguing-in-Publication Data
A catalogue record for this book is available from the British Library

ISBN 978 1 5261 4689 2 paperback

First published 2021

Typeset by
Servis Filmsetting Ltd, Stockport, Cheshire
Printed in Great Britain by
Bell & Bain Ltd, Glasgow

Contents

List of figures

Every effort has been made to obtain permission to reproduce copyright material, and the publisher will be pleased to be informed of any errors and omissions for correction in future editions.

Acknowledgments

I would like to express my gratitude to Nicholas Bullock for his involvement and warm welcome at King's College, Cambridge from the very beginning of this research in 2005. My gratitude also goes to Peter Cavanagh who permitted me access to the archives of Alexander Pike, as well as to Nona Pike for her trust, friendship and hospitality at Thorney Creek. Koen Stemeers, Director of Studies in Architecture at the University of Cambridge, facilitated my research through the practical resources made available to me at the Martin Centre.

I thank Dominique Rouillard – director of LIAT, the research laboratory where I have worked since 2008 – for her encouragement and her intellectual and amicable support. I would like to express my gratitude to Michel Rosell, John Frazer and Georges and Jeanne-Marie Alexandroff for having opened their archives, provided documents and devoted time to this project. I thank Ken Yeang, Peter Harper, Randall Thomas, John Litter, James Thring, Michael Jantzen, Michael Reynolds, Peter Cook, Richard Rogers, Emilio Ambasz and Yona Friedman for their availability and their invaluable personal accounts. I also thank all those who took the time to accompany me on site visits in New York, London, Barcelona, Copenhagen, Stockholm, Hamburg, Berlin, Hanover and Paris.

To my wonderful family and close friends, companions of research and thinking: Mady Cabrol, Julian Lopez, Marine Lopez, Elise Armentier, Alice Carabédian, Tony Côme, Cécile Diguet, Dominika Dolengiewicz, Brenda Lynn Edgar, Ilana Eloit, Capucine Fouga, Yasmine Fourdrinier, Doriane Hugues, Bérangère Mercier, Marianne Nicollet, Clayre Pitot, Emmanuelle Raoul-Duval, Michel Rosell, for their support, our happy discussions and adventures.

To my great researcher friends and colleagues, at the LIAT and elsewhere: Eric Alonzo, Paul Bouet, Valérie de Calignon, Alexandre Bouton, Olivier Coutard, Caroline Gallez, Margot Pellegrino, Antoine Picon, Eileen Powis, Paul Landauer, Frédérique Mocquet, Patrick Rubin, Mathias Rollot, Livier Venin, for the richness of our exchanges and collaborations, our friendships, our study trips and our seminars.

To my students at the architecture schools of Paris-Malaquais, Strasbourg and Marne-la-Vallée (Eavt) for our shared enthusiasm. To Amina Sellali and the Ecole d'architecture de la ville et des territoires in Marne-la-Vallée, to the Tuck Foundation,

Andreas Ehinger and Alexandre Rojey. To Estelle Dietrich, Véronique Dignac, Rachel Lemaire and Sandra Holgado for their help at the Eavt and at the Electricité de France archives.

To my French editors Marc Bédarida and, especially, Brankica Radic. At Manchester University Press, I thank David Appleyard, Thomas Dark, Lucy Burns, Alun Richards and Anthony Mercer for this publication in English, for their trust. To Eileen Powis, for the translation of the work and her involvement.

Fanny Lopez and the publisher warmly thank the Alexander Pike Memorial Trust, which supported the publication project from its very beginning. We would also like to express our deep gratitude to Karen Philipp and Melvyn Wallis for their contribution to this work's execution.

Introduction

In the future, housing will be completely independent of any main services (gas, electricity, water, drainage). The degree of autonomy is a practical question depending on the state of the art of modern urban technology and specific stages of socio-economic development.[1]

Alexander Pike, Cambridge, 1971

Alexander Pike's prediction on energy autonomy in 1971 is still valid today, resurfacing not only in academic discourse but among mainstream construction industry magnates. The French cement manufacturer, Lafarge, stated that "by the year 2050, new construction will no longer consume any energy from external sources [...], tomorrow's buildings will be autonomous,"[2] while the real estate developer Bouygues recently launched an "Autonomous Building Concept."[3] Although encouraging, the apparent consensus of these declarations is misleading: issues differ, and the only harbinger of autonomy or disconnection has been its repeated anticipation.

Since the beginning of the twenty-first century, the idea of energy autonomy for buildings and even cities has inspired innumerable architectural projects that have been widely disseminated in the press. Technically, economically and symbolically complex, autonomy defies the dominant paradigm of energy distribution that has been in place for over a hundred years. It is an industrial model of large-scale distribution networks that determined the scale of cities and entire territories, as well at the production modes of other utilities such as water, sewage and power (gas, electric and steam). While these distribution networks have undeniably improved the comfort and sanitary conditions of populations, they have also marginalized all other pre-existing or rival decentralized models.

Today, the rising demand for an energy transition and the resulting panoply of alternative models (energy living machines, self-sufficient cities, micro-grids and other eco-infrastructures) are tangible signs of the deconstruction of what historians of technology call the "large technical system."[4]

Architects' enthusiasm for energy issues has spawned a new imaginary repertory of infrastructural systems. Energy autonomy, however, is a technological utopia that has inspired architectural and urban projects for over a century. Beyond the realm of counter-cultural experimentation, conceptual antecedents can be found as far back as the late nineteenth century. Energy autonomy has been the dream of important historical figures in architecture, engineering and industry. As soon as the large-scale distribution and connection networks were imposed, disconnection projects appeared. The ambitions of protagonists for autonomy were twofold: first, to free consumers from the hold of the large utility monopolies to integrate a system into buildings that would provide a vital minimum of heat, water and electricity. How has this other aspect of the history of utilities developed over time? Who are the pioneers and what are the major projects?

The history of utilities is rich in surprising projects, such as John Adolphus Etzler's 1841 mechanical system or Thomas Edison's 1912 electrically self-sufficient house. Though theoretically and technically fragile, the major characteristics of this energy renewal were accentuated in the twentieth century. Driven by technological progress and the critical social context of the late 1960s, the energy autonomy movement reached a certain maturity on an international scale after the 1973 oil crisis. Led by the American counterculture, the autonomy movement quickly spread to other countries and contexts, becoming gradually institutionalized. The scale of projects also expanded, growing from individual housing units to cities and entire territories. Alexander Pike's autonomous house and Georges and Jeanne-Marie Alexandroff's self-sufficient city attest to the potency of a concept that combines technical virtuosity with social, political, economic and environmental spheres, in a critical inversion of the inherited technological order. Energy autonomy forged idealized rural and urban identities: a return to nature, self-generated vital necessities, everyday economies, as well as the relocation and cooperative management of resources.

Presented in terms of the relationship between connection and disconnection, the first part of this book provides a historical overview of autonomy from the origins of the sanitized, connected or cabled city in the early nineteenth century, to the moment when energy consumption became the object of governmental regulations and connection to urban utility networks became the generic model for power supply. Following this evolution of programs and scales, the second part of this book will analyze the decade of experimental architectural projects from 1970 to 1980, examining how they contributed to the fragmentation of the modern energy framework.

This book adopts a historical and pluralistic approach, situated between an architectural history that is oriented to energy, environment and climate and another that focuses on technology and infrastructure. While the former approach traditionally examines vernacular habitats and remains focused on passive relationships, as described in the work of Victor Olgyay and of Amos Rapoport, the latter approach is structured around the superiority of technology and its progress.[5] From the mid-1960s onward, engineering became an essential element in the relationship between architecture and the environment. James Marston Fitch, Leo Marx and the more radical Reyner Banham brought technology to the forefront of architectural history.[6] Although Banham examined the role of utilities in architecture in *The Architecture of the Well-tempered Environment*, he did not address the question of networks or energy autonomy.[7] Even though it constitutes a fundamental element of urban design and regional planning (in both real and theoretical projects), the relationship of architecture and cities to networks is rarely addressed in architectural history and theory. Technology historians, however, have sought to identify the expansion of network connections as the major phenomenon of modernity. In his influential theoretical work, *L'Urbanisme des réseaux: Théories et méthods*, Gabriel Dupuy analyzed the connection to the network space and the determining relationship between urban design and the evolution of networks, establishing the arrival of the "network city."[8] But the network system remains the model to defend and improve. Connection wins. Disconnection is never mentioned as a project and rarely in terms of positive values: disconnection perceived as undesirable, marginal and even punishable. To be "disconnected" is to be marginalized or excluded, to be deprived of access to the essential utilities and services that are the norm in modern society. Yet historically, the demand for autonomy has periodically surfaced in technical, architectural and political projects. Unlike an imposed autonomy (geographically isolated houses, for example, which must manage without networks), such projects proposed a desirable and planned autonomy. In this sense, being disconnected is not the same as being out of reach of a network. Planned disconnection is a modern societal project.

Today, environmental imperatives and the intensification of research and planning for post-carbon cities have encouraged different disciplines to re-examine themselves in regard to this legacy of network urbanism, causing problems once thought solved to resurface. Evolving lifestyles (energy savings, degrowth) and technological progress challenge the limits of the organizational management model of urban utility designed for industry-based growth. In recent years, critical thinking about distribution systems has developed significantly and researchers are increasingly considering the potential of decentralized systems.[9] This book presents a history of disconnection projects and theories which, despite current trends, have been lacking. Without attempting to be comprehensive, it analyzes some of the most significant and iconic cases, laying the groundwork for future reflection.

In examining this history of energy autonomy, one is forced to question the relevance of existing utility networks today. By changing their design and reinventing service systems at different scales, the autonomy project counters the very idea of infrastructure and thus constitutes a radical technical utopia. With the return of this theme in relation to sustainable development, many forgotten or overlooked experiments and plans have become relevant once again, underlining the importance of a new reinterpretation and critical reception of this movement for energy-focused architects in the twenty-first century. Sustainable development has become the battle horse of architects and builders who adopt the most advanced technologies and methods to this end. Progressive environmental standards now define the new constraints of the construction industry, bringing energy autonomy to the forefront in the urgency of an impending ecological disaster. The few forerunners who experimented with disconnection in the past have been joined today by a great number of architects and major international builders. In these times of crisis, government-sponsored ecological programs tend to smooth over the contradictions of a capitalist economy. However, the trivialization of the political and economic aspects of energy autonomy encourage us to more closely examine the history of a movement whose tenets were originally far more audacious.

Notes

1 Alexander Pike, "Social energy alternatives for urban human settlements" (November 1971), unpublished, p. 6, Archives of Alexander Pike (AAP).

2 Lafarge with the World Business Council for Sustainable Development and the United Technologies Corporation, "Concrétiser le rêve d'un bâtiment autosuffisant sur le plan énergétique," press release (March 2006).

3 Interview with Gaëtan Desruelles, vice-president, general innovation and sustainable construction for Bouygues Construction, "Dossier énergie-environnement," *Les Echos* (October 5, 2011).

4 Bernward Joerges, "Large technical systems: concepts and issues," in Thomas P. Hughes and Renate Mayntz (eds), *The Development of Large Technical Systems* (Frankfurt: Campus Verlag, 1988), pp. 9–32; Alain Gras, "Les réseaux, les machines et la mégamachine: sur l'origine des systèmes techniques contemporains," in Pierre Musso (ed.), *Réseaux et société* (Paris: PUF, 2003), pp. 141–152.

5 Victor Olgyay, *Design with Climate: Bioclimatic Approach to Architectural Regionalism* (Princeton, NJ: Princeton University Press, 1963); Amos Rapoport, *House Form and Culture* (Englewood Cliffs, NJ: Prentice-Hall, 1969).

6 James Marston Fitch, *American Building: The Historical Forces that Shaped it* (New York: Schocken Books, 1980); James Marston Fitch and William Bobenhausen, *American Building: The Environmental Forces that Shaped it* (New York: Schocken Books, 1999); Leo Marx, *The Machine in the Garden: Technology and the Pastoral Ideal in America* (New York: Oxford University Press, 1964).

7 Reyner Banham, *The Architecture of the Well-tempered Environment* (London: Architectural Press, 1969).

8 Gabriel Dupuy, *L'Urbanisme des réseaux: Théories et méthodes* (Paris: Armand Colin, 1991).

9 Cf. "Services en réseaux, services sans réseaux dans les villes du Sud," *Flux*, no. 56–57, April

(2004). Olivier Coutard, "Services urbains: la fin des grands réseaux?," in Olivier Coutard and Jean-Pierre Lévy, *Ecologies urbaines* (Paris: Economica, 2010), pp. 102–129.

Olivier Coutard and Jonathan Rutherford, "Vers l'essor de villes post-réseaux: infrastructures, changement sociotechnique et transition urbaine en Europe," in Joëlle Forest and Abdelillah Hamdouch (eds), *Quand l'innovation fait la ville durable* (Switzerland: Presses Polytechniques Universitaires Romandes, 2015), pp. 97–118.

Part I: Connection versus disconnection

1 Capturing territories through energy distribution

The family of territorial technical networks can be divided into three major categories: transportation (road, sea, rail, air); information and communication (telephone and information technology); energy and resources (water and sewage, gas, steam, electricity).[1] In the industrial countries of the northern hemisphere the organization of these basic services was gradually structured into large-scale networks and was central to the process of urbanization in the late nineteenth century. These networks became symbols of hygiene and convenience, representing transformed landscapes and lifestyles. Connection, which was a progressive ideal, became the norm. Supported by a group of laws, official documents, texts and ideas – including those of "public service," "network member" and "assistance policy" – wastewater treatment and energy supply technologies developed their basic forms in this period and have barely changed since. The history of the creation of the major networks is a web in which technical, financial and political choices were entwined. However, this was not without certain ambiguities: it was a battle of technical models, scales, movements and governance modes in which engineers and architects played a key role.

The network-web

The symbolism of the network system is based on a paradox: it simultaneously permits freedom of circulation, while its restraint creates both abundance and dependence. Etymologically, network comes from the Latin *nodus* or knot. It is the "net" used to capture certain animals in hunting or fishing (see Figure 1).

The vocabulary associated with this structure – "link," "hoop," "creel," "ramification," "web," "grid" – has always been part of the lexical field of captivity. For a long time, the network described a cluster of fibers, a fabric whose framework was linked to forms in nature. It was subsequently associated with the human body with the discovery of the circulatory system in the seventeenth century (see Figure 2).

The network materialized as a model that corresponds to the control of natural as well as artificial bodies.[2] It was not unusual to see these principles transposed from

Figure 1 Net for the capture of animals (1812)

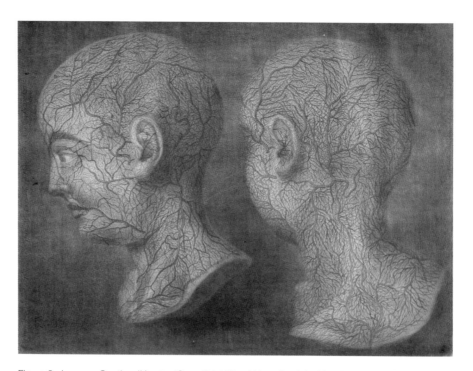

Figure 2 Jacques Gautier d'Agoty, "Superficial Blood Vessels of the Head and Neck" (1746)

Figure 3 Pierre Rousseau, map of the city of Nantes (1760)

the human body to the urban landscape in an attempt to solve circulation problems. For example, in 1760 Pierre Rousseau proposed organizing the city of Nantes around a heart-shaped boulevard (see Figure 3).

The analogy between the urban body and the human body tested the new rationality systems based on the circulation of flows. For the physician or the engineer, the networks distributed and ordered these flows. However, it was also a metaphorical figure that could be applied to politics and power relationships. Plato used weaving as a model for government: the king was a weaver who interlaced and crossed the threads of power.[3] The image of the network was subsequently more broadly used to designate a group of people or an organization, connected in order to act together.

It was not until the eighteenth century, however, with the advent of engineering sciences and the creation of a more autonomous discourse on technical domains, that the modern idea of the network emerged. Claude Henri de Saint-Simon, the philosopher of networks, conceptualized his "industrial system" based on his definition of the network organism, which used an analogy between the human body and the social body. Saint-Simon's approach "consisted in tracing on the body of France, that is, on its territory, networks to ensure the circulation of all of society's flows."[4] Barthélemy Prosper Enfantin, Saint-Simon's disciple and the creator of L'Union pour les chemins de fer de Paris in Lyon in 1845, and pioneer of the Suez Canal, stated: "We have enlaced the Globe with our railroads, gold, silver, electricity! – Spread, propagate by these new paths whose creators and masters you are in part, the spirit of God, the education of the human race."[5] Progress made it possible to see the network as a technical, economic and social system; it was the symbol of communion and universal association. Its gradual expansion can be read as an undertaking of territorial pacification and conquest: the network simultaneously frees and subjugates the spaces conquered by its ramifications. Scientific progress and the Industrial Revolution opened a new imaginary field of technology and the technical utopia led to social utopia.[6] In the mid-nineteenth century, the creation of urban service networks and the systemization of connections in urban territories were part of this dimension. The ambivalent notion of the network served both to connect, circulate and to mark out control. The railroad, the road network and the hydraulic system became reticular tools that channeled progress and freed men from the obscurantism of the past. The network was the technical and symbolic matrix of modernity; but its wired image of a conquering ascendancy did not fade.

The perception of the network as an ensemble that could imprison people and hinder their freedom would be accentuated in the twentieth century. Gilles Deleuze and Félix Guattari used weaving as a paradigm of the "royal science," that is, the art of governing people and using the machinery of state.[7] The authors strengthened the metaphor: the image of the link or web corresponds to that of "territorialization," which is the process of covering and infiltrating a territory through an alienation or a dependence. Deleuze and Guattari established the existence of two types of space: the "smooth," which has no obstacles, and the "striated," which is a marked-out space organized to allow the fixing and control processes function. The space is striated, they wrote, "through power, through energy, military-industrial, multinational complexities."[8] Deleuze and Guattari used a network-web rhetoric:

> The state needs to subordinate hydraulic power to conduits, pipes, banks that prevent turbulence, that make movement go from one specific point to another, make the space itself striated and measured, make the fluid depend on the solid, make flows follow parallel laminar sections. The state remains involved, wherever it can, in capturing flows of all kinds.[9]

If the energy network can be perceived as a territorialization, the terms "flows," "conduits" or "pipes" do not specifically refer to energy for the authors: these pipes and conduits describe power in general; they have a universal value.

From the net to the creel, the network simultaneously supplies and hems in. There is a type of semantic displacement happening here: the network, usually defined by the freedom of circulation and urban solidarity, can be connected to the vocabulary of captivity and the universe of the constraint. It becomes obligation, bondage, fixedness, blockage. These linguistic variations shed further light on a different history of resource distribution and management: conquest.

Conquering and controlling flows

The natural hydrographic network existed before the city, and since time immemorial the brilliance of irrigation systems, from qanats to aqueducts, has demonstrated a subordination of architecture and urbanism to these technical systems. The water network is the oldest. The study of ancient management procedures first raises the question of control and taxation, which is not the prerogative of our modern societies. In the earliest civilizations, there was often a master of water and "it was around and in regard to hydraulic problems that the concepts of social stratifications and political hierarchy emerged."[10] Whoever controlled water structured the organization of communities, thus it was at the moment that there was a centralizing state that the monopolistic administration of resources was organized. Karl Marx and Karl August Wittfogel showed that the rules of water distribution were among the first manifestations and prerequisites of the power of Eastern despotism in so-called pre-capitalist civilizations.[11] Wittfogel delved deeper into the study of the "Asian production method" showing that these ancient empires, notably China and Egypt, were founded on total control of water. With the creation of a broad centralized bureaucracy, these "hydraulic societies" or "hydraulic civilizations" controlled the rivers, the irrigation system and agriculture. This emergence of a state that managed resources using monopolistic methods corroborated Pierre Clastres's thesis, according to which political power preceded and founded economic exploitation.[12] The state would create the basis of interdependence and its duration through public management of water and seeds.

The question of taxes affected all of the large ancient cities. In the Roman Empire, the connection to the aqueduct and sewer system was a distinctive sign of the economic power of the owners, who had to pay a tax for cleaning and repairs. Vitruvius stressed the user's fiscal duties to the state for home economics management.[13] Any undertaking concerning planning and developing the water and sewer networks had to be supported by a general consensus or imposed by a sufficiently influential government. Moreover, the fall of the empires brought about the fall of these networks. Only the infrastructure remains, like the Pont du Gard, whose original aqueduct structure function has disappeared.[14]

Though there were large-scale water systems that structured the organization of vast empires, most territories' management method was self-sufficiency and the self-management of resources. Before the eighteenth century, water provision depended on local sources and an individual collection system in rivers, wells or public fountains. The medievalist Jacques Heers traced, in Italian villages like Bologna, the process that went from the old multicellular fabric with individuated resources to the birth of a so-called "public" space and shared services.[15] In the medieval city, different pockets of the community were self-sufficient to a degree with dual resource management: individual, from private properties; collective, from communal goods. In ancestral management systems, communal lands were based on self-regulation, sharing and the free use of certain resources: forests and grazing land, or water that the inhabitants of a locality could collectively use.[16] Heers evoked the princes' conquest of the public space, describing the birth of a communal power and the creation of administrative bodies to destroy the cells in place and make "the idea of public space triumph over the domain reserved for private use."[17] For better or worse, public service was born under the impetus of an authority. By the end of the fourteenth century, subsequent to a new demographic and economic boom in Europe, the number of those who benefited from communal lands was limited. In the fifteenth century, the gradual appropriation of these lands by private property or the state diminished these shared resources. The sovereign state–private property tandem reduced the management of water or land as common legacies.[18] It was only with the rise of environmental concerns in the late 1960s that the idea of a common heritage gained ground, questioning the foundations of this term and its possible regulatory changes.[19]

By the late eighteenth century, regulations had expanded to survey, control and sanction the self-management of resources. The sovereign enforcement power exercised by states in the name of planning rationality was indisputable. The dominant liberalism of the nineteenth century would seek to impose a model that set property against the state, leaving little legitimacy to intermediate management methods on the local scale.

The city as purveyor of services

The objective of this book is not to conduct a historical study on networks – there are already numerous reference texts in this area – but rather to examine the events that are consubstantial with the creation of the "cabled city" and to better grasp the emergence of the discourse on connection.[20]

From the mid-eighteenth century, the rationalist spirit of the Enlightenment favored the development of civil engineering and infrastructure. Architects like Pierre Patte joined the movement to modernize urban centers within the framework of improvement works. Greatly interested in the urban road system and mechanical engineering, Patte recommended a few techniques to improve the roadway. In *Mémoires sur les objets les plus importants de l'architecture* (1769), he proposed the reinforcement of salubrity through correct placement of sewers and water circulation and the combination of buildings' water distribution and disposal systems (see Figure 4).[21]

Patte's street section is recognized as "one of the very first of a type that will be subsequently popularized."[22] The standardization of access to water was improved and systematized; however, there was a rise in resistance to this standardization. The revolt of the water carriers of Amiens not only displayed this defiance, but the scope of the challenges of a fledgling public service:

> One observes in 1775 that several libertines, vagabonds, malicious people disturb, embarrass and insult daily the entrepreneurs, controllers and laborers employed in public works, notably at the fountains, whose creation, long desired, is as useful as it is necessary; they delay their prompt construction by degrading and tearing off the parts of the works completed; they throw sticks and stones to mutilate the facades of the water towers as well as the fountains and adjacent buildings, [...] they obstruct the pipes.[23]

No alternative, however, was proposed: the rowdy water carriers guild was opposed to both concessions or bringing their trade under municipal control, since it would make their guild disappear. The service system and the trades associated with it were rapidly changing, an evolution that was enforced by the police.

In 1782 in Paris, the first home water distribution service appeared, run by the Périer brothers. The 1850 framework of public works in Paris, and the creation of a general sewage plan undertaken by Eugène Belgrand and Baron Haussmann, the water and sewer director, offered the first major water distribution and disposal network. The first to be served were hospitals, military establishments and schools, but it was not until 1880 that water reached the upper floors of buildings. Whereas water distributed by tap stands was free, the individual concession was invoiced,

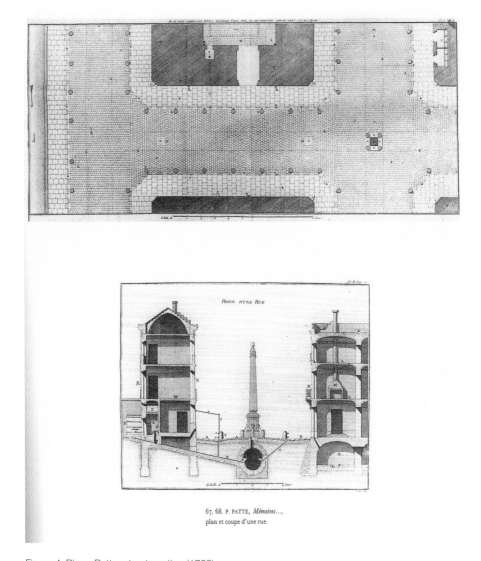

67, 68. P. PATTE, *Mémoires...*,
plan et coupe d'une rue.

Figure 4 Pierre Patte, street section (1769)

and this revenue was used to both maintain the network and pay the personnel. Initially, the network connection was minimal and the high cost of the service curbed demand. The civil engineer Henry Darcy wrote in 1856 that drawing water from tap stands had to be kept free for "the unfortunate class."[24] But this free access gradually disappeared: distribution to homes, linked to the development of water concessions, definitively put an end to the public tap systems, and individual wells and water carriers were replaced by "city water." The generalization and standardization of

distribution accelerated. As the mayor of Lyon recalled in 1843, any means could
be used:

> The municipal authority would use, with the aim of general utility, all the means of per-
> suasion and paternal coercion that are in its powers in the sphere of its legal attributions to
> have adopted in Lyon, as in Genoa, London and Edinburgh, the habit of water distribution
> to homes, by means of a moderate retribution, or at the very least, to have established in
> each house, for hygiene and public safety purposes, a fountain whose tap could be opened
> and closed at will.[25]

These changes led the public authorities to take complete charge of water distribution.
Concerned with maintaining equality of access and water quality, hygienists made
water distribution a major imperative.

In London, the engineer Joseph Bazalgette built a 1,750 km-long sewer system
that stirred the admiration of his contemporaries and influenced Belgrand in the
continuation of his work in Paris. In 1884, prefect of the Seine, Eugène Poubelle,
made it mandatory to connect to the sewer system. Across the Atlantic, in 1890, the
length of the sewer system was estimated at 9,662 km for all the American cities of
over 25,000 inhabitants; in 1909, its size increased fivefold for cities of over 30,000
inhabitants. That same year, 85 percent of the population of large urban centers had
a sewer system.[26] Simultaneously, heating systems were expanded. In Lockport, New
York in 1877, the inventor Birdsill Holly, who had already developed a pressurized
water distribution network, created the first urban heating system for fourteen buildings. Following this success, he installed fifty other small systems that he sold to a
group of investors. In the 1930s, his company equipped over 300 cities, including New
York, which had four heating plants, 61 km of conduits and 2,000 customers.[27] In
Europe, it was in Dresden in 1900 that the first steam system was put into operation,
supplied by an electric power plant that connected twelve public buildings. In the
1920s and 1930s, the growth of urban heating networks for domestic use continued
in Berlin, Brunswick, Hamburg and Kiel, but also in Budapest, Copenhagen, Madrid,
Milan, Moscow and Paris. These were initially decentralized and independent micro-
networks whose installation, management and maintenance were handled by the
companies that owned them.

Between 1850 and 1880, an urban planning cycle began that continued until
the First World War. Public health concerns intensified. The networks stretched
out and thickened into a spider-like system that provided each household with the
utilities needed for a new domestic life. If water, sewage and gas guaranteed a new
comfort, it was only in 1882 that wicks were blown out to give way to artificial light
(see Figure 5).

Figure 5 Sebastian Ziani de Ferranti, "The Modern Day Colossus" (1889)

It was with the specific conditions of the development of the electricity sector that the primary meaning of network took on all its significance. The electrification of Western society would create a technical rupture. A new generation of large-scale networks appeared. These networks popularized a more immaterial and complex invention whose know-how and technology, from production to transmission, would soon become the preserve of monopolies. From regional technical infrastructures to the domestic core, a complex supply system was created whose disconnection would reveal very great challenges.

Connection and coercion

In 1882, electrical energy was tamed by the American inventor and industrialist Thomas Edison. The world's first electric power plant was built by the Edison Electric Company in the Wall Street area in Manhattan (see Figure 6).

The power plant produced both heat and electricity for eight-five apartments and businesses. Other more powerful plants emerged in the United States, and London would rapidly follow. From 1882 to 1886, experiments showed that electricity could be transmitted; in 1886, the distribution of electrical current began in France. In Paris, the first subscriber was connected to the fledgling network in 1889, from the Les Halles plant. The press regularly reported on the economic upheavals of the new networks, and the elation and doubts that accompanied them in France and the United States. By the early 1880s, the question of managing and rationalizing utilities

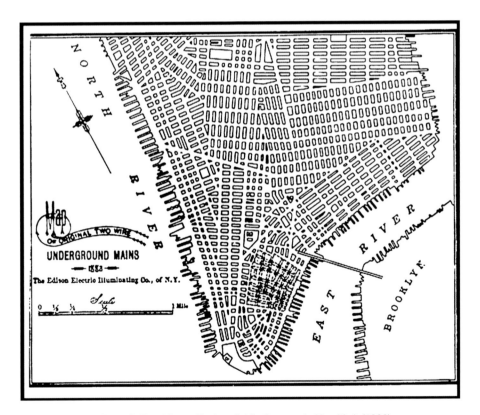

Figure 6 Thomas Edison's Pearl Street Station distribution area in New York (1883)

was openly raised, notably in the illustrious New York magazine *Harper's Weekly*. In an illustrated article, Uncle Sam fights over the control of cables in front of the Capitol (see Figure 7).

The authors called on the state on several occasions to put an end to the competitive, unequal concessions that caused variation in prices and destabilized new subscribers:

> The telegraph companies take possession of the streets, and line them from end to end on both sides with great towering poles, on which are carried a vast network of unsightly wires that are a disgrace to the metropolis of the United States.[28]

The gas companies were not "a whit better than either of the others."

> It is true, they do not lay their mains on the surface of the streets or sidewalks, nor do they suspend their pipes in mid-air, but they are quite unmindful of the rights of the people in other ways. They make just what gas they please, charge what they like for it, and slap the consumer's face, so to speak, if he dares to protest against either the quality or the price. If he does not like what he gets for the money, he may let it alone. And how can he help himself?

Governed by private interests, these supply systems played on competition to the detriment of consumers, subject to and "slapped" by its vagaries. If disconnection was suggested, it was nothing but provocation on the suppliers' part: as the customer did not have any other service offer, there was no future. The introduction of connection as a social norm was gradual, and in parallel to this revolution in daily life the question was raised as to the regulation of the market and costs.

In the late nineteenth century, the heads of the companies came to the conclusion that the largest profits would come from mass consumption, large-scale production and low prices. This massification led to development strategies and formidable sales campaigns, one example of which was the electrification of Chicago.[29] The investor Samuel Insull, Edison's secretary and agent, marked out and connected the city, and then the region, from 1890. Thomas Edison initially defended the reduced-size power plant and small networks, which were more practical from the perspective of technical maintenance. But Edison and Insull had to confront the fierce competition of another electricity giant: the George Westinghouse group, which developed a technology based on the distribution of alternating current invented by Nikola Tesla, a technology that efficiently solved the problem of large-scale electricity transmission.[30] Alternating current is economically superior since its cost is lower: the higher the voltage, the less loss on the line. An advocate of small-scale networks, Edison attempted to

Figure 7 William Allen Rogers, "US Monopoly of the Wires and Ropes" (1881)

demonstrate the harmfulness of alternating current, but he was soon forced to adopt it to stay in the race. Insull plunged in with conviction and merged the small companies into a single centralized organization:

> Right from the beginning, the inventors of electricity ensured the control of the monopoly by granting an operating license on their patents to local agents. The inventors were also given rights on their patents to consolidate control nationally. In 1895, only two competing companies remained: Edison General Electric (GE) and the Westinghouse Electric Corporation.[31]

The universal principles that enabled the production of direct and alternating current systems and the unification of smaller companies would be rapidly imposed by Westinghouse, later becoming the design and operating standard of electrical systems.

The corollary of the unification of energy systems was the installation of large-scale systems. In 1903, Insull offered the largest electricity consumers of Chicago the lowest possible prices. As the statutory connection price was minimal, the companies made up for it on consumption by encouraging demand. While expanding their market, the concessionaires' communication departments (not just those of Edison) created new consumer needs, such as the electric brush or cane, whose virtues were vaunted by the press (see Figure 8).

In an advertising offensive, General Electric distributed light bulbs and granted hundreds of families the free use of household appliances for several months. Groups of door-to-door salespeople vaunted the need not only to electrify one's home but to "be connected," through the network, to modernity. Non-subscribers had to be enticed by others encouraging them to keep their electric devices on for a longer time. The meters and accompanying consumption would create confidence, as argued by Louis Ferguson, head of sales at Edison General Electric:

> You have to get the future consumer to use electricity first, familiarize him with the advantages of your system, and do it in a very attractive way. When the tenant of the house is hooked up – more exactly connected – the increasing use of lamps or appliances by the family will soon exceed the break-even point. In this respect, the meter is useful: it creates trust and gives the user the impression that prices are justified. Whatever you may say about the counters, the average sensible man believes in them, he believes they are right.[32]

General Electric's intention was clear: "catch" and "connect" the population through attractive prices and popularize the meter. The capitalist primacy of supply

Figure 8 Publicity for "The Electric Brush" (1881)

and production over demand was thus established. Offering both technical challenge and a stake in power, the large energy networks and electricity sector structured a new energy market that was based "on technical systems that generate activity and new needs."[33] General Electric's strategy was very effective: the Great Depression did not stop the company's growth, and it remains one of the largest industrial conglomerates in the world. The accelerated development of energy distribution modernized sanitation in the capitals, quickly transforming the regions of the first Industrial Revolution into cities as purveyors of services that had to be logistically administered.

In the late nineteenth century, the government was the only entity capable of regulating the private interests of the rapidly expanding utility companies. A critical discourse emerged, the purpose of which was to permit industrial groups to influence politics and exert pressure on legislators: this was the birth of lobbies. The phenomenon of connection required two inseparable levels of analysis: the first examined the practical aspect of the supply system and the technical difficulty of coherently organizing it (production, storage, distribution, consumption); the second concerned the economic and political management that stemmed from it (costs for users, investment and profits for companies, supply and demand). Thus what emerged was a regime of instrumental energy systems, which sought to determine both the forms of appropriation and the creation of consumption modes. The economic and political sphere played a major role in the organization and expansion of the electricity system. In his brilliant historical study, *Networks of Power*, Thomas Parke Hughes examined the history of the electrification of Western society through the installation of the electricity network in three large cities: Chicago, Berlin and London. Looking at the mechanisms of decision-making, conflicts, mediations and concession contracts signed with the municipalities, Hughes demonstrates how, in each case, the energy networks were turned into economic and political instruments. It was not until the early twentieth century that the state's interventionism regulated and standardized these energy distribution systems.

Without challenging the beneficial social progress that resulted from introducing utilities, the feeling of dispossession and economic dependence caused by the stranglehold of the large groups on the populations must be stressed. The happiness of those connected to modern life was shadowed by questions and doubts over both the legitimacy of management methods and the mutations of the landscapes. These concerns were particularly noticeable in the urban representations of a few visionaries and caricaturists. The presentation of the anarchic invasion of distribution systems reflected the metaphoric apprehension of the web of the network as a new economic and social phenomenon.

Entangled landscape

As a technical monument, the infrastructure held an important place in the graphic production of several architects and engravers, the most illustrious of whom was Piranesi. He was known for having defended the legacy and supremacy of Roman public edifices, whose specific beauty he sought to depict in his many plates. The spatial saturation effects and the dark intensity of his prisons are especially noteworthy. Some historians have asserted that these prisons were inspired by the vast dimensions of the rooms of the first Roman sewer system, the Cloaca Maxima, which was linked to the Tullianum prison.

Sewers represent the underside of the city and have always inspired popular gloomy depictions. But from the nineteenth century, with the expansion of electricity connections among distribution systems, a new imaginary dimension of infrastructure appeared. Connection activated domestic practices and new urban representations. The extrapolations were equal to the revolutions of electrification and other inventions of this century conquered by energy. The city was swept along by the enormous connection project. The land was visually transformed by both transportation and energy infrastructures, in an accumulation of conduits, pylons and cables. Illustrations revealed underground or aerial entrails, popularizing in legend the descriptions of the city as "entangled," "cabled" or "tied up." Numerous cutaway street diagrams were presented in the press and the explanatory manuals of water or gas services, depicting the ground as the border that separates the city from its service frame (see Figure 9).

The engineers' rigorous and exact section drawings contrasted with the chaotic reality of the distribution systems, whose profusion ended up spilling onto the surface, as on a stormy day in 1914 on the rue du Havre in Paris, when the pipes were fully exposed (see Figure 10).

Fig. 3. — Amenée des eaux à Paris, pour les divers services publics et privés.

Figure 9 Arrival of water in Paris for the various public and private services

L'ORAGE DU 15 JUIN A PARIS —(1914)
Les Canalisations mises à nu rue du Havre

Figure 10 Pipes and networks on rue du Havre, Paris (1914)

If water, sewers and gas remained mostly buried under the opaqueness of the pavement, the arrival of electricity and its overhead network would intensify a feeling of disorder that the popular press would not fail to convey. From one issue to the next, the illustrators of *Harper's Weekly* depicted the new landscape of networks. The first electric telegraphs wove such astonishing webs in the streets (see Figure 11) that a passerby exclaimed, "I did not know there were such big spiders in the city."[34]

Rural territories and wild landscapes did not seem to be spared either, as can be seen in a caricature of the irremediably disfigured Niagara Falls hydraulic complex. This iconography can also be seen in Albert Robida's science fiction trilogy: *Le Vingtième Siècle* (1883), *La Guerre au vingtième siècle* (1887) and *Le Vingtième Siècle: La vie électrique* (1890). Robida reveals the first premonitions of the global transformations of the new network systems, plunging us into the fantastic machinery of the cities.

Robida's *La vie électrique* takes place in Paris in the mid-1950s, where both electricity and scientific progress have revolutionized the urban landscape. This futuristic tale of the electricity era begins with a description of the regulations and changes caused by this "marvelous conquest" that had, in many ways, modified the face of the world:

IN THE TOILS OF THE TELEGRAPH—TO THIS COMPLEXION WE MAY COME AT LAST.—[SEE PAGE 814.]

Figure 11 William Allen Rogers, "In the Toils of the Telegraph" (1881)

> Electricity is the Great Slave. Respiration of the universe, fluid moving through the veins of
> the Earth or wandering in spaces in dazzling zigzags scoring the immensities of the ether,
> Electricity has been seized, chained and tamed.[35]

From the very first pages, Robida reveals the power of electricity and those who
were able to tame it. Electric life conquered the land. The "view taken from an
aircraft at 700 m[etres]" offers us the vision of a rural landscape, striated by the
"Tubes" that transport electricity at a record speed and dotted with stations (see
Figure 12).

The picturesque nature of this landscape, crisscrossed by a river, rolling hills,
half-timbered houses and bell towers, contrasts with the rigidity of the imposing
infrastructure, whose tubular interlacing extended to infinity. The network and its
infrastructures are mostly invisible or hidden, their representation on the large scale
often a matter of territorial anamorphosis.[36] Their concealment, or the surprise on
seeing them, was equal to their monumentality.

In *La vie électrique*, between fascination and anxiety, Robida presented the technological obsessions of a century undergoing a mutation. If they were the backdrop of
progress, the energy networks were experienced as increasingly oppressive:

> A few areas appear veiled by a tightly woven trellis and tangled with electric wires that seem
> to envelope them with a gigantic spider's web. Too many wires! [And] networks going in
> every direction.[37]

Only a few preserved spaces, like the Armorique national park on the coast of
Brittany, remain. The park is protected under a law preserving "social interest." This
space, closed to industry and science's innovation, offers the calm of provincial life
in years past:

> [N]o tubes cutting up the landscape with an annoying and rigid line, none of those
> high buildings indicating electrified sectors, [...] not a trace of those electrical wires
> stretched like an enormous web with links crossed a thousand times over the rest of the
> land.[38]

With this evocation of "line," "web" and "links," the first significations of the network
and the feeling of captivity emerged. Robida contrasts bucolic landscape and mechanical utopia, times past and scientific progress, to describe the upheavals and mistakes
of the period. At the end of the book, the inventor Philox Lorris acknowledges, in a
discussion with the minister of public hygiene, that "modern science is somewhat
responsible for the poor general state of health" and that "the electric life [...] has

LES TUBES (VUE PRISE EN AERONEF A 700 MÈTRES

Figure 12 Albert Robida, "Tubes" (1890)

overtaxed the race and produced a sort of universal weakening." The "nervousness" produced by the surrounding electricity was just as worrying as industrial illnesses, polluted air and oversized urban areas. The scientist worried about air, water and subsoil pollution, observing that nature could not exist in the city and vegetation was gradually disappearing, sacrificed to the successive layers of asphalt and networks. The ground of Paris "no longer exists."[39]

> The real earth has disappeared from it, or nearly, replaced by an entangled maze of tun-
> nels, various pipes, metropolitan tubes linking the districts, outdoor expansion tubes,
> sewers, gutters, conduits for innumerable wires for TVs and various electricity services,
> power, light, theater, music, etc., intertwined through a bed of concrete and stones, where
> the roots of those poor devils of trees that their misfortune exiled in this rocky conglom-
> erate, saturated with diverse fluids, can, even by excessively lengthening and becoming
> entangled, only draw meager nourishment.[40]

The nineteenth century marked the arrival of the "machine street": the road was no longer just a line, but a flow-uniting element.[41] In his section drawings, Robida extrapolated the different natures of these flows: light, heat, food, music and package distribution (see Figure 13).

All that was needed was to push a button on the control panel from one's home. Robida evoked both fascination and fear. His phantasmagoric and burlesque warnings were a satirical take on the network and not only offered a remarkable imaginary view of these transformative infrastructures, but bore witness to the new landscape. The infrastructures introduced by the energy network imposed a new territorial order. Directly associated with modernity, without having "an intention of a clear action on the visible," these energy objects were ambiguous and difficult to classify.[42] During the twentieth century, burying or concealing telephone and electricity networks would become an essential challenge of landscape policy. By striating the subsoil and the skies, the taming of flows and fluids radically changed both the organization of land and the lifestyles of populations. If the network seemed to be a necessary evil, urban planning in the late nineteenth century would work hard on improving accessibility to the network, despite other energy possibilities.

A structuring element of urban and regional planning

The expansion of the new energy landscape gave expression to deep civilizational mutations. Rationalizing utilities in the name of hygiene and modernity was an emerging urban planning priority. The transportation, information-communication and energy networks were a structural element in urban planning, and there were

LE SOL DE PARIS.

Figure 13 Albert Robida, "The Soil of Paris" (1890)

many signs of their importance in urban thinking. Gabriel Dupuy analyzed the conception of the network system as a founding phenomenon of modern urbanism. In *L'Urbanisme des réseaux*, Dupuy encouraged contemporary urban planners to pursue urban connection. Dupuy defined connection as the circulation of people, goods and fluids, as well as that of information. Connection was a prerequisite of economic activity, urbanity; it was the networks – all the networks.

> What urbanism has not understood is the generalization of relations ensuring, in brand-new space/time relationship, the circulation of people, goods, information point by point, until the connection to the network, the urban connection takes on the meaning of a new urbanity. It is this urbanism, forgetting what constitutes human life, economic activity, in short, today's city that declares that it is in a crisis, and wonders why.[43]

Dupuy rehabilitated urban network theories by examining the global visions of those he considered pioneers: Ildefonso Cerdà, Frank Lloyd Wright and Maurice-François Rouge. He stressed the typological and kinetic dimensions and the adaptability of the road system in Wright and Cerdà. The approach is less sector-based in Rouge, who apprehends the networks as a structural and territorial, even infinite, phenomenon.

The place of the road system and the car was essential to the culture of development. Unlike road networks, utility and energy networks were not specifically studied in the history of architecture. Starting in the twentieth century, railroad clusters, axes and highway hubs were thought of and built as architectural and urban objects.[44] In many ways, the road replaced the conduits and pipes of the urban planner; it was observed that the energy network would most often be housed in the density of the road network, following its path and expansion model. Cerdà's road system, presented for Barcelona in 1867, planned for drinking water, waste and energy utilities, while the same was true for Arturo Soria y Mata's linear city, designed in 1882. The totality of the utilities are brought together in the density of the railroad axis, which created an extensive and territorial concept of urban development (see Figure 14).

Despite his reticular concept, Soria y Mata did not provide many details on either the wires and cables, or the type of energy used. Rather, the operating principle of the linear city was to expand the transportation and energy distribution systems. Inversely, Cerdà devoted much of his plans to the technology, management and governance of services. Overlooked or forgotten in architectural and urban theory, utility networks must be considered separately. They are a founding element of any project, be it large or small scale, realistic or utopian.

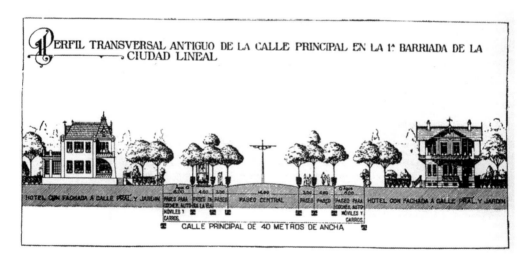

Figure 14 Arturo Soria y Mata, "The Linear City" (1882)

Reorganizing the street and ensuring connection

Ildefonso Cerdà, the first theoretician of urbanism and the designer of the plan to extend the city of Barcelona, was above all a network engineer. In his celebrated *Théorie générale de l'urbanisation* (1867), he was enthusiastic about adapting the materiality of the city to the technical and scientific progress of modern civilization. Cerdà described how urban infrastructures and energy were a key factor in the advent of the twentieth-century city:

> Placed in the hands of the new civilization and considering its possible applications still unknown today [electricity] must hasten events and accelerate the course of the transformations begun so powerfully by steam applications.[45]

As unknown as the civilized world's energy destiny was, the engineer's previsions were full of promise. In his analysis of "urban roads or streets," Cerdà imagined an in-depth section drawing of the street that revealed the pipes through which the city's fluids flowed.

> One would say at first glance that these different elements form the venous system of a mysterious being with colossal dimensions [...]. This group of tubes constitutes nothing other than a system that maintains the functioning of human life.[46]

This specific consideration of utilities is partially explained by the fact that Cerdà was a specialist on these questions; in the early 1840s, he directed the installation of the pipe and water distribution system in the city of Valencia. In the passage describing "the house considered the family's home or an elementary *urbe*," Cerdà wrote that civilizations inaugurated by steam and electricity "tend to visibly and powerfully meet and ensure the needs and convenience of the greatest number of people." Convenience then, invariably aligns with connection. Like the human body that covers its vital necessities, the house also enters into a biological relationship of circulation, consumption and excretion of flows with the exterior. The house exercises "genuine vital functions," wrote Cerdà:

> If it [the house] was philosophically analyzed, one would find all the organs in it or, better still, all the material elements corresponding to the functions of the organs of human life: organs corresponding to motor functions, such as doors and domestic paths; organs corresponding to the eyes and ears, such as balconies and windows; organs corresponding to all the food intake, digestion and excretion functions, such as the pantry, water pipes, the kitchen with its outbuildings, the toilets, the waste pipes for fecal matter, etc.[47]

The house therefore had to be surrounded by an "operations field," or urban infrastructure matrix, which enabled the management of fluid inflows and outflows on the site. Each house or block had to be connected to this matrix.

Cerdà's anthropomorphic approach highlights the mechanics of vital functions like food intake, digestion, excretion, which concerned vital needs that were not only technical but legal. The public administration had to suitably organize this "field of operations" as there was a nascent sanitary need for the connection. For Cerdà, once the infrastructure and conduits were in place they "simply" had to be connected. And if, under urban development pressure or overpopulation, new constructions were built, one only had to link them to the pipes and dispatch "the whole thing" underground. That was easy: "connect the pipes."[48]

Reconstituting the history of the human habitat, Cerdà noted that if each individual has a real home, families "cannot function without the help of means and instruments common to all these elements that form the neighborhood."[49] Among these were interior courtyards, wells, water tanks, fountains, pipes, chimney flues, toilets and lighting. Citing these elements, Cerdà formulated a request for collective facilities that went hand in hand with the rationalization of space expressed in the middle of the century. But if the public administration endeavored to reconcile general and individual interests, he recognized that:

> [W]ith time, the municipal administration became that of the states, absorbing, absolute and monopolizing. Since the individualism of the Middle Ages, we have arrived by degrees at a constant, active, predominant supervision, which makes itself felt down to the slightest details of urban life.[50]

The plan presented for Barcelona gave impetus to a movement that would affect a large number of cities in Europe in the decades that followed. The confidant solicitation of state power for the facilities of technical modernity was part of a project to transform society.

Cerdà proposed a functional and hygienist construction plan. The municipalities were called on to install sanitary facilities that guaranteed what were considered to be basic needs. The sewer system remained precarious, however, wastewater purification and disinfection and urban waste management being subjects of growing concern.

> The ensemble of wells, fountains and water tanks causes frequent quarrels and ongoing vexation. The ensemble of wastewater pipes is an ongoing cause of dampness, dirtiness and repulsive spectacles. One could still address numerous criticisms to the ensemble of smoke, water and gas conduits.[51]

Moreover, Cerdà raised the problems caused by discharges from pipes outside the city. If the fast-flowing rivers of certain cities carried away these "repulsive" liquids without leaving a trace, he was very much concerned about the issues this would cause for those close to the sea:

> The waves bring the refuse onto the shore and the beach becomes a center of infection. Where there is neither river nor sea, one can only rarely prevent the evaporation of liquids damaging salubrity.[52]

In fact, liquid and solid urban waste increased at the time, as the sanitary facilities of cities improved.[53] Cerdà recognized the weaknesses and complexity of the organization of the domestic infrastructure, which was a central focus of planning. The home, the street and facilities were key elements of urbanization, thus Cerdà proposed a plan of utility networks connected to buildings and detailed the underground gallery that would bring together different urban utilities. Decidedly modern, Cerdà's concept of the energy network was very advanced, whereas it was barely present in traditional urban theories.

Eugène Hénard was a key proponent of these energy concerns. In "Les villes de l'avenir" (1910), Hénard dealt with the chaotic burying of the networks, formulating a reorganization proposal in a section drawing that is now famous.[54] The architect-urban planner counted the conduits and pipes that were entangled under the road: in addition to the first water conduits, those of gas were added, then pneumatic tubes for mail, telegraph and telephone wires, then electrical cables, constantly requiring new excavations. Hénard regretted that this group of pipes was "superimposed, juxtaposed without and order or method."[55]

> When it is necessary to work on them, each enterprise, belonging either to different companies or administrations, works without any master plan, on a day-to-day basis. This is why, for the last 10 years – I am speaking for Paris – the city has been constantly turned upside down and car and pedestrian circulation has become increasingly difficult.[56]

Hénard acknowledged that underground space was saturated and that it was impossible to include new distribution systems in it. A project was needed to reorganize these systems. To illustrate his proposal, he compared the section drawing of a street from the previous century to that of the future (see Figure 15).

Hénard proposed expanding the current street by creating a utilities street under the road that would contain all the street service systems. The upper part would be for car and pedestrian circulation, while the lower part would allow for the installation of pipes, evacuation systems and the transport of heavy goods. This underground

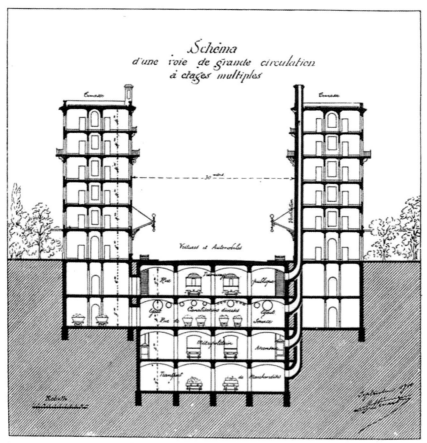

_Eugène Hénard, « Plan et coupe de l'habitation future », 1910.

Figure 15 Eugène Hénard, "Plan and Section of the Future" (1910)

reorganization plan came with an estimated budget, the expenditures of which were spread out over a hundred years, but Hénard remained cautious about "the possible multiplications of these distribution systems, that later scientific discoveries could further increase."[57]

Bringing together and organizing distribution management is a fundamental economic and technical principle. In Cerdà as in Hénard, political arguments were called on to strengthen the management of common services. In each of these cases, the energy network linked but was interiorized; it was a non-extensive urban concept. In a different manner, the proposals of the Brazilian Saturnino de Brito, the Spaniard Soria y Mata, as well as the Russian disurbanists raised the question of large territories and available resources. Energy was tamed on an expansionist mode and the network became the support of spatial, economic and social projections on a very large scale.

A large-scale reticular utopia

The engineer Saturnino de Brito was a major figure of South American urban planning. He initiated the first sewage plans for dozens of Brazilian cities, presenting several of his concepts in *Notes sur le tracé sanitaire des villes* (1915).[58] In one of the rare articles devoted to him translated into French, Carlos Roberto Monteiro de Andrade sheds light on the itinerary of this engineer, who criticized architects for not sufficiently taking the technical nature of the modern city into account. Brito was a true connoisseur of the Brazilian territory, whose climate, rainfall pattern and underground water and vegetation he studied. He believed that a city's regulatory plan should be based on the natural flow of water and its management. Influenced by Camillo Sitte, Brito formulated an organicist vision of the urban milieu and initiated a vast program to reorganize the hydrographic networks in order to attain "the ideal city of sanitary utopia – the city as a beautiful and healthy body."[59]

In the late 1920s, faced with the repeated floods that occurred in Rio de Janeiro, Brito proposed building a network of drainage channels in the streets, rather than underground galleries. He also defended, in Paraíba do Sul and Santos, the separator model for city sewage. The aim of this plan was to simplify the problem, intensified in a tropical city, of rainwater that did not need to be purified and could be discharged into waterways, whether the water was natural or collected. Brito proposed a landscape marked by an open-air channel network carrying this water, bordered by lateral avenues, planted promenades and market gardens. For São Paulo, he solved the problem of water supply in the capital and the flooding of the Tietê, the river that crosses the entire metropolitan region, by building a system of dams and storage zones in 1926. As floods were consequently stopped, the capital's drinking water supply was ensured and hydroelectric power plants were built. Brito's "sanitary utopia" was a macro-territorial concept of the hydraulic resource, emphasizing flow, irrigation, drinking water supply and hydroelectricity.

Brito worked on the adaptability of a huge network that highlighted the environmental, economic and social potential of the city. However, his viewpoint was still that of a large-scale connection. The arrival of mass production of electricity and the possibility of transmitting it by cables would give impetus to a new perception of regional development. This was particularly obvious in the proposals of the Russian disurbanists, for whom electrifying the country and building a broad centralized network represented the renewal of the urban project and a genuine vehicle of utopia.

In 1920, the urbanization of the Soviet territory depended on the electrification program. The Goelro plan proposed the construction of about thirty regional electrical power plants over fifteen years to concomitantly ensure industrial development and the creation of new towns. One of the most powerful hydroelectric

LA CENTRALE ÉLECTRIQUE DU DNIÉPR. CE GRANDIOSE MONUMENT ÉLEVÉ À LA MÉMOIRE
DE LÉNINE, EST L'INCARNATION DE SON IDÉE DE L'ÉLECTRIFICATION DU PAYS

Figure 16 The hydroelectric dam at Dnieper (1934)

stations was that of the Dnieper in Ukraine, whose dam and adjoining buildings were designed by the constructivist architects Viktor Vesnin and Nikolai Kolli in 1927 (see Figure 16).

At this point, the enormous Soviet territory was sparsely populated and under-electrified. Under the impetus of a state-planned economy, everything seemed possible to the regional development actors. In the late 1920s, the urbanists–disurbanists debate not only revealed the technical issues surrounding the creation, density and form of the new socialist lifestyle, but problems concerning the location of industries and agricultural zones. The disurbanists envisaged the dissolution of cities as a regional development project that would allow for dispersion. The first question raised was that of transportation and energy resources. The vision of the new socialist city, called *Sotsgorod*, was that of a federation of small-scale industrial and agricultural communities that would be grafted and connected to the electrical links of a centralized regional network.[60] Electrical power was to play a leading role in their proposals, since it was the major tool of the conquest of the territory and its low-cost transmission made it accessible throughout the country. The question of resources and climate was no longer raised as each point of the territory became equally viable. It was proposed that connecting all of the electric power plants in the USSR would create a single large network, whose service could be extended to make the entire territory exploitable: "We must be able to connect to the network at any moment and in any location as natural resources are discovered and new industries are created," Anatole Kopp explained.[61] As paradoxical as it may seem, the centralization of electrical energy was the prerequisite for the decentralization of the historic city and dispersion. As the theoreticians of the disurbanist movement, Leonard Sabsovich and Mikhail Okhitovich, would assert:

> The network will supplant the center. It is not so much the energy centers themselves that are important as the interconnection of the smaller centers into a single energy network. The shift from the use of energy centers to that of a network totally changes the problem of the exhaustion of energy sources in the world.[62]

The energy produced by each isolated plant had to be connected to this single loop. The electricity network was planned as both a foundation and a regulating element of the territorial system, enabling productivity to be optimized.

The proposals of Nikolay Milyutin, Mikhail Barsch, Ivan Leonidov and Moisei Ginzburg showed the application of these principles, sharing a treatment via linear strips structured around an infrastructural axis that was close to Arturo Soria y Mata's concept.[63] The English garden cities movement also proved influential, as did the model of the German *Siedlungen*, whose architects, such as Bruno Taut and Ernst May, were used by the Soviets. Ernst May would lead, among others, the Magnitogorsk mining city project. It was one of the first times that a discipline linked to regional development laid claim with so much determination to electricity as an explicit support for architecture and urban planning. With this macro-territorial perception of energy, the Russian disurbanists took part in the construction of a

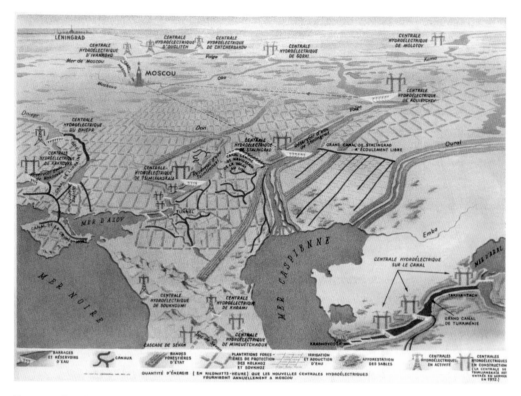

Figure 17 Stalinist plan for the transformation of nature (1948)

large-scale energy model, the "technical electricity macro-system," which would be exported to China under Mao, who would continue to take inspiration from this Soviet energy-territorial conquest. It was a concept on the scale of the territory. In this regard, Stalin's Transformation of Nature (1948) plan was emblematic (see Figure 17).

It was a schematic map that showed irrigation systems as well as the large buildings of communism. Architecture, infrastructure and territory were merged. Architects and urban planners certainly favored local initiatives (like food self-sufficiency, individual heating, water reserves and collection, and septic tanks), but a centralized electricity network that could transport domestic energy was the source of every hope. We are a very long way from the small self-sufficient colony: the electricity network unified the new Soviet territory and was the prerequisite for the dispersion of human and industrial settlements, in a city–country merger.

In 1929, the Soviet authorities launched a competition for a green city with 100,000 inhabitants outside Moscow. However, this green idea bears no relationship to how we think of it today in terms of environmental concerns or energy savings. The idea was to found a garden city devoted to leisure activities and rest for workers, who could consequently recover during their vacations or at the end of the workweek. In fact, in the majority of the projects presented, nothing obvious was put forward except the "green" of the landscape setting, with the exception perhaps of Melnikov, who stressed the concept of solar pavilions and introduced the use of wind as "the principal energy source needed for the city's functioning."[64] Melnikov's hypothesis of wind as an energy resource, and the concept of a building that could optimize rest conditions, would make his proposal renowned.

Contrary to Frank Lloyd Wright, who focused on decentralization through the multiplication of small self-managed production centers, among the Russian architects the state-run centralized electricity network was the framework of regional development. The network was a structural element of urban and regional planning, and its infrastructures were the system's visible nerve centers. The architects were careful to treat them as full-fledged architectural objects, in the same way as Tony Garnier had envisaged a promenade on the hydroelectric power plant of his industrial city. But it was Herman Sörgel, influenced by the Russians' fascination with electricity, who would push to expand the infrastructural project of modernity. In 1928, with Atlantropa, the German architect went as far as wondering if one could produce enough concrete to build a hydroelectric dam across the Strait of Gibraltar, composed of a lock surmounted by a 400 m² building and a belvedere. Atlantropa appeared as the paroxysmal project of a generation dedicated to the cult of grandeur and the power of energy. Hoping to merge the entire continent of colonial Africa with a united Europe, technology and engineering were at the foundation of this racist project. It aimed to partially dry up the Mediterranean to free up arable land, transform the Congo into an artificial lake, and build a network of hydroelectric power plants and road links, including one over the Strait of Gibraltar, and railroad connections linking Berlin, Rome and Cape Town (see Figure 18).

The ambition of this expansionist and colonial "supercontinent" project was to respond to the threat of the exhaustion of coal and oil resources. Europe would thus possess the means of energy production and guarantee its self-sufficiency. Atlantropa marked the apogee of a new technical generation of project that "coincides with the development of the second Industrial Revolution: apart from the expansion of chemistry, it is characterized above all by the massive electrification of the industrialized countries."[65] The twentieth century confirmed the industrial model of large networks and the cult of large infrastructure. Technical modernity saw energy in terms of centralization, expansion and connection. But it was also ordinary architecture, the home environment in its mechanical core, that was turned upside down by the new services available. Channeled in the city's underground depths, cables and

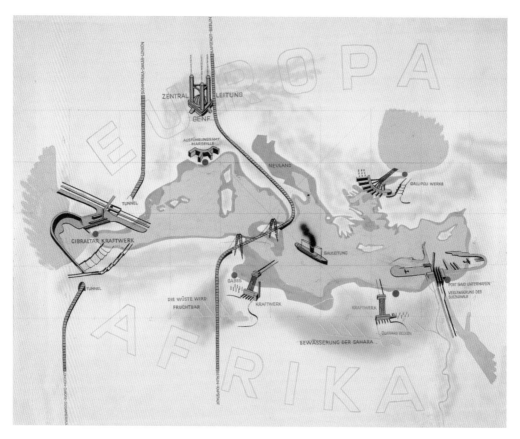

Figure 18 Herman Sörgel, Atlantropa (1928)

conduits assailed buildings and interiors. Acclaiming or criticizing these channels, the world of architecture and industry set to work organizing this energy that was finally tamed.

Rationalizing the mechanical core

Following the end of the First World War, mechanization invaded the home sector, affecting the kitchen, the bathroom and laundry. The use of mechanical controls of the home environment generated a number of technical, energy and aesthetic problems. In *Mechanization Takes Command*, Sigfried Giedion highlighted the advent of the automation industry and presented mechanization as a phenomenon. Fascinated by the introduction of these new conveniences in architecture, Giedion analyzed the effects of mechanization:

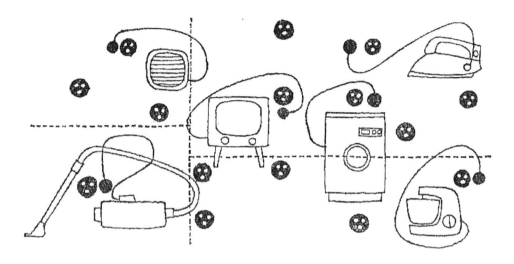

Figure 19 Electric socket outlets, Ministry of Housing and Local Government (1961)

What had been in preparation for a century and a half and especially what had been germinating since the second half of the nineteenth century suddenly ripened and hit human life hard.[66]

The degree of modernity within the home was henceforth measured by the number of electrical outlets and its household appliances (see Figure 19).

The electrification of daily life was a founding element of the American way of life. The ideal of grouping together utilities into a prefabricated unit would strongly mobilize the industrial world (see Figure 20). If this mechanical core originated in the work of Catharine Beecher, Giedion reintroduced the question of compactness and management: how should heating, plumbing and electricity systems be reassembled?[67] This challenge would raise a number of issues in the world of industry, as that of architecture, with each shifting the responsibility for the untamable from one to the other:

> Industry, whatever it does, is not fit to solve the problem of the mechanical core, too closely linked to the deep organization of the home. It is, in truth, the task of American architects. [...] What is important is knowing how to control mechanization rather than letting it tyrannize the entire home.[68]

Management problems were accentuated by the seldom crossed barriers between the disciplines. Few architects examined the innervation buildings in depth, and when

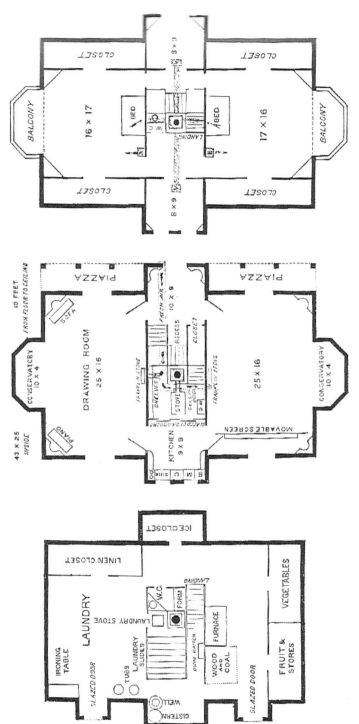

Figure 20 Catherine Beecher, "Heart Unit" (1879)

attempts were made to rationalize and improve this core through prefabrication and industrial assemblage, dealing with architectural issues remained unsatisfactory. This gradual introduction of utilities into the home became a challenge for industrialization.

Starting in the late nineteenth century, a number of prefabricated houses were made, but it was not until the 1930s that this industry genuinely developed in the United States. The Second World War activated state control at every level of industrial output. The enormity and urgency of the need for housing could not be met by traditional construction techniques; large-scale industrial production appeared as the logical solution to fill such an enormous demand. Postwar American architecture adapted the techniques and materials developed by the military industry to home use.[69] The efficiency of industrial production under the pressure of war conditions had to be extended in peace time to meet new needs. At the heart of the war, buoyed by the potential and acceleration of industrial techniques, the house became the object of unprecedented enthusiasm and hope. But what provided domestic bliss and vital necessities was not so much architecture in itself as the equipment in the utility unit. Most of the prefabricated proposals made the rationalizing of the mechanical core the basic requirement of their success. This explains the compositions of the photographer and graphic artist Herbert Matter, published in a special issue of the *Arts & Architecture* journal, titled "Prefabrication" (1944). On the first page, a transparent human body reveals its internal organs and its nervous, blood and muscle systems from three angles; the correspondence between this anatomical image of the body and the first representations of the network can clearly be seen (see Figure 21). This vital network is directly analogous to that produced by atoms, the sun or the electricity circuit, the whole forming a single large network. On the other page, the question "What is a house?" offers an assembly of mechanical cogwheels as a response (see Figure 22).

As it was the most expensive part of the house, simplifying the production of the utility unit was a priority. However, though proposals reached a peak in evolution with the arrival of prefabrication techniques, most of them remained prototypes.[70] With a view to rationalizing and simplifying this unit, the idea of combining all the elements (kitchen, bathroom, toilet) into a centralized and standardized room that could be easily connected developed. Thus designed, this ideal "heart" could become the starting point of a new home production strategy. The mechanical core, developed as a wall of utilities, illustrates this movement in the United States, as well as in Europe.

The phenomenon of trailers and mobile homes, whose industrial production took off in the 1930s and 1940s, also shows the particularities of the viewpoint of the home space and the miniaturized utilities core. Initially intended to be a temporary house for seasonal use, they would be partially adopted and adapted as permanent housing. If the mobile kitchen-bathroom-bedroom unit encouraged a great

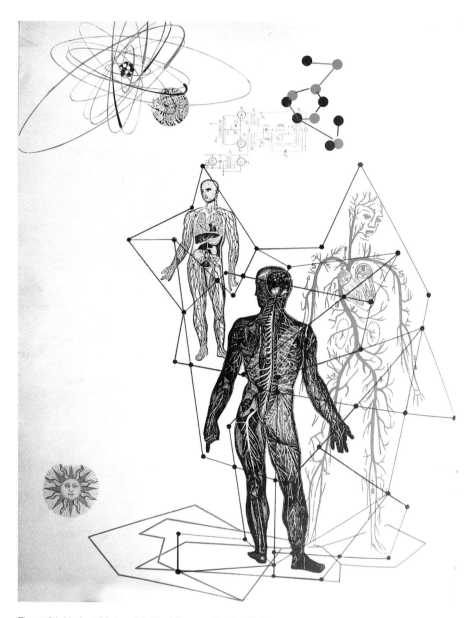

Figure 21 Herbert Matter, "Untitled Composition" (1944)

many experimentations, the search for a utilities unit for fixed and supposedly durable housing greatly increased constraints. The first examples came from the United States. The Pierce Foundation proposed a mechanical core prototype for an experimental house. It was composed of a back-to-back bathroom and kitchen connected by a vertical plumbing panel. Separate units developed alongside research on utility walls:

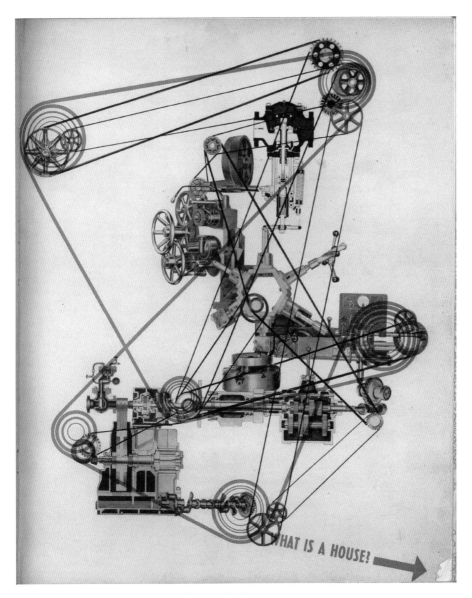

Figure 22 Herbert Matter, "What is a House" (1944)

the integrated kitchen or integrated bathroom. These partitions with interchangeable elements could be adapted and connected to each other, like the *Arcode Kitchen* or the bathroom and toilet partitions by the American designer George Sakier. Among the large number of utility walls proposed, the kitchen-bathroom package designed by Charles E. Elcock, or that of the American architects Ralph Rapson and David B. Runnells for their *Fabric House*, are worth noting (see Figure 23).

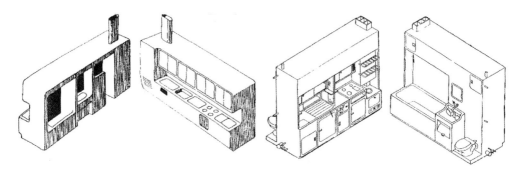

Figure 23 Left: Charles E. Elcock, "Package Kitchen Bathroom" (n.d.); Right: Ralph Rapson and David B. Runnel, "Kitchen and Bathroom, Fabric House" (1939)

Also available on the market was the *Two Storey Unit A. Howard* built in Datchet, Berkshire, which was quite close to the principle and form of the *Denham Plumbing and Heating System Unit*, produced by W. N. Froy & Sons, and created by S. J. Gravely and S. C. Warren, both planned for a two-story house (see Figure 24). In this example, the mechanical core clearly appears as an independent unit around which other rooms would be arranged. In 1946, the Borg-Warner Corporation produced the *Ingersoll Steel Utility Unit*, which contained a particularly complete unit with equipment and settings for electricity, water and gas, with a forced-air heater, thermostats, an automatic water heater, conduits and drainpipes incorporated into the prefabricated unit.

In Europe, one of the production successes of the immediate postwar period was the *Ministry of Work Unit*, produced by the Arcon company[71] in the United Kingdom, which would become the utility wall unit of the British Temporary Housing Programme (THP): the *Arcon Service Unit.*[72] This program marked a significant step in the industrialization of the utilities core in Europe. Following the halt in construction during the war years and the damage and destruction that the UK suffered, the urgent need was for governments, urban planners and architects to provide housing that offered an appropriate and inexpensive standard of living for hundreds of thousands of people, in a very short period of time. With its utility wall, the THP encouraged a revival of interest in mechanical cores. Created in spring 1943, Arcon promoted experimental constructions equipped with a utilities wall that could be mass-produced. These temporary or permanent houses that met the immediate postwar demand had two parts: the structure, or covered space, and the services, or mechanical core. One of Arcon's successes was linked to the development of the back-to-back bathroom-kitchen combination unit. In 1944, the production of 86,000 Arcon temporary houses was launched and different models began to appear on the market, including *Arcon Mark II* (see Figure 25).

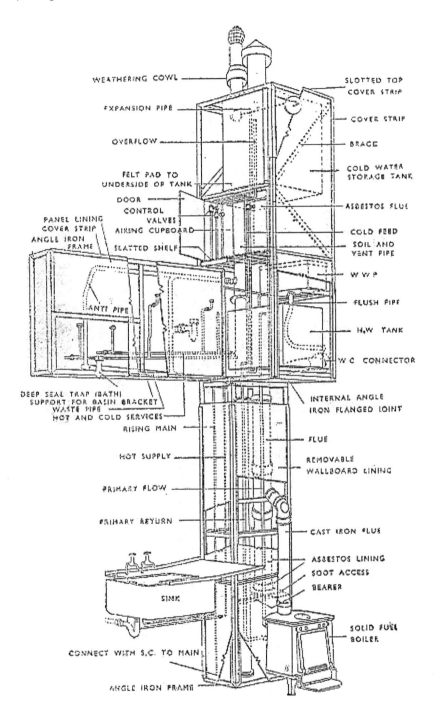

Figure 24 William Nathaniel, Froy & Sons, "Denham Plumbing Unit" (1946)

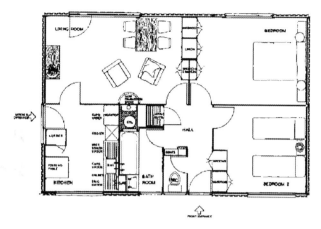

Figure 25 Arcon Temporary House (1948)

Despite their poor aesthetics, the cheap, temporary Arcon houses inaugurated the mass production of the kitchen-bathroom mechanical core for a minimum domestic space. These houses were favorably received at first, though they were subsequently heavily criticized by their occupants. The public's prejudices and the negative connotation of prefabrication eroded the basis for mass production. In spite of a certain disappointment with this adventure and its forms, the prefabrication of the 1930s, 1940s and 1950s would strongly mark and influence the attitudes of later generations, who – while submitting new proposals to the industrial world – would never acknowledge its debt. Warren Chalk, in issue 6 of *Archigram*, devoted to the 1940s and 1950s, brought together a few of the most iconic productions (see Figure 26). Chalk commented on the *Arcon Mark V*: "Everything is there: the central module, the fully equipped kitchen and other goodies to connect that still look new twenty-five years later."[73]

In France, Jean Prouvé would, in numerous projects, bring forward the mechanics of the vital functions. He developed the principle of the loadbearing utility core in the *Maison Alba*, which included a kitchen, a bathroom, heating and a toilet. The principle was reused and improved, notably in the dismountable and inexpensive *Maison des jours meilleurs* prototype in 1956, following Abbé Pierre's celebrated call for affordable housing. Built on the quai Alexandre III, the technical block in the center of the volume was structural. But the project would remain in the prototype stage as it was never officially certified. The history of the evolution of the mechanical core since the interwar years illustrates the "utilities problem." The creation and prefabrication of a high-performance mechanical core was a basic ambition that was the focus of in-depth studies by manufacturers and engineers. The examples mentioned above make it possible to not only determine a few layout complexities, but to grasp

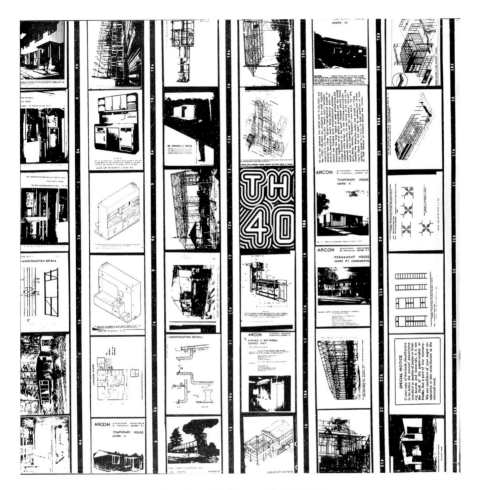

Figure 26 *Archigram 6*, p. 17: "The Forties" by Warren Chalk (1965)

how connection was pursued in architecture, as a vehicle of modernity. Most of the architects in the Modern movement – as fascinated as they were by home mechanics – generally remained silent about its relationship to the network.

Modernity means being connected

Hygiene was the "supreme act" of the modern project; however, the requirements for producing energy flows, from infrastructures to housing units, were rarely brought up.[74] Of course, one notes a shared fascination for the objects of mechanization and its techniques as well as for nature (green spaces, the sun and pure air). Nevertheless, questions on energy resources and fluid circulation outside the home were rare. The network model did not have opponents in the architects of the Modern movement and very few ventured into the channels of home mechanics. In the late nineteenth century, connection to basic services was perceived as the guarantee of modernity and a common culture, as is shown in "Les plombiers" by Adolf Loos. The Viennese architect wrote that he could easily imagine the nineteenth century without finish carpenters and stonecutters but that, without the plumber, there would not have been a nineteenth century.[75] He acknowledged the pre-eminence of the English, the Americans and the French in areas of sanitary installations. Loos urged Austrian and Viennese plumbers to come up to the level of the other Western countries to reach the front of the pack in the race to modernity:

> Only the people who come close to the English in water consumption will be capable of rivaling those in the economic order, only the people who surpass them in this domain will surpass them in the hegemony they exercise on the world. The plumber is the pioneer of cleanliness. He is the first artisan of the state, the guarantee of culture, of the dominant culture today. [...] The increase in water consumption is one of our most urgent cultural tasks.[76]

Every English bathroom sink, every bathtub connected to the sewer system, every stove to gas and even every electricity bill, was a sign of progress. The Modern movement would celebrate the arrival of fluids by presenting bathroom sinks or chandeliers of growing splendor: they were the only visible points in the network. The place given to sanitary fixtures in the vestibule of the Rufer House in Vienna (Loos, 1922), in the Villa Noailles (Mallet-Stevens, 1923) and in the Villa Savoye (Le Corbusier, 1929) attest to the modernist cult of liquids and cleanliness (see Figure 27). For Colin Rowe, the Savoyes' guest sink represented "the triumph of running water."[77]

Though they were a recent development, utility networks were generally considered an asset and their rapid development was implicitly supported by architects, who seemed as carried away by this facilitated access to utilities as they were by the car or the plane. Their expansion and improvement aimed at modern comfort. Le Corbusier, in his *unités d'habitation*, gauged all the importance of utilities and recognized connection as an efficient system established by engineers. This technical revolution, however, encouraged a new architectural concept:

> [I]f one admits that these pipes should be able to freely rise from the bottom to the top of the house and go back down and that they *should, under the effect of the most elementary common sense*, be able to reach their origin in or outside the city visible for surveillance and accessible for repairs, one will understand that the traditional wall, the bulky foundations are so many obstacles, and that burying pipes in the ground is the most incredible nonsense of modern times.[78]

Figure 27 Le Corbusier, Villa Savoye, Poissy (1929)

The frame and the open plan that Le Corbusier proposed as a new construction principle for vertical garden cities would enable simplified utility management. "The city's pipes will be installed as the organs of a machine in a factory," he added, "accessible, able to be visited, repairable." Le Corbusier recognized the importance of collective utilities: water, electricity, gas, telephone, that had been established as the most indispensable elements of modern life (see Figure 28).

The arrival of innumerable pipes, cables and conduits radically changed the ground, and the architect used the term "artificial terrain" to describe this new state of the landscape. The ground became artificial. Le Corbusier felt that the small single-family house was economically blameworthy because its artificial terrain was, in many ways, for single use. With the *unités d'habitations*, he proposed expanding this artificial terrain, multiplying it by thirty, fifty or even more to show the financial benefits for the community and the municipality.[79] The extension of the availability of utilities consequently enabled 200 or 300 apartments to be equipped (see Figure 29). Creating and operating production centers and connection remained the business of engineers, but Le Corbusier recognized the architect's role in the management of the inflows and end distribution in the building.

With more or less this exception, very few architects ventured into home mechanics. If channeled energy was a new urban element, it was not very perceptible in representations. The concerns were of a logistical (technical and circulatory) nature but were still not architectural, as would later be the case with solar urbanism, for example, in which the energy source would typologically and morphologically mark the building. In modern architecture, the walls and floors seemed to create an opaque frontier with the world of machinery. A rather widespread invisibility of utilities could be seen. Artifice-technology and nature-ornament became complementary. Acoustical insulation, air-conditioning and electricity systems were encased, as though by magic, in floors or hung ceilings. Two emblems of architectural modernity, the *Glass House* by Philip Johnson (1946–51) and Farnsworth House by Mies van der Rohe (1945–51), displayed this trend. Heaters and mechanical cores were hidden in this game of illusions, while nature could be seen through the glazed surfaces, at the same time producing pockets with unparalleled thermal conductivity. Georges and Jeanne-Marie Alexandroff, in the critical evaluation they drew up on the period's energy ambitions, wrote:

> The thick *anticlimactic* towers now interest manufacturers and are revolutionizing urban architecture; then the growing dissemination and miniaturization of equipment enable their insertion into domestic architecture. This is the end of the last American regionalisms, and the house *for everywhere* is already emerging, connected to its network and no longer taking the natural environment into account.[80]

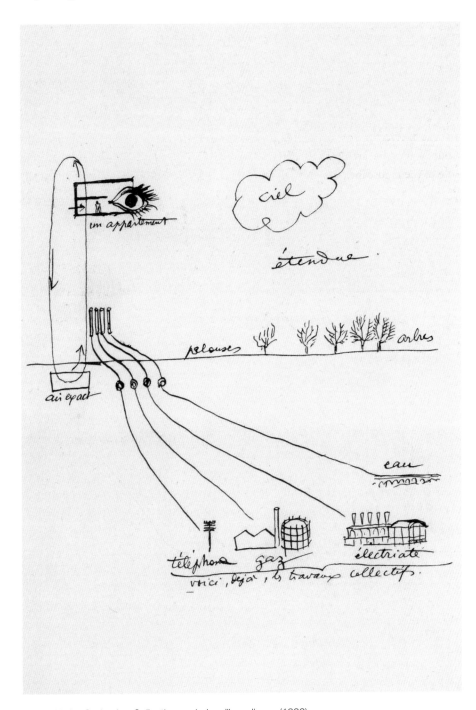

Figure 28 Le Corbusier, Collective work, La ville radieuse (1933)

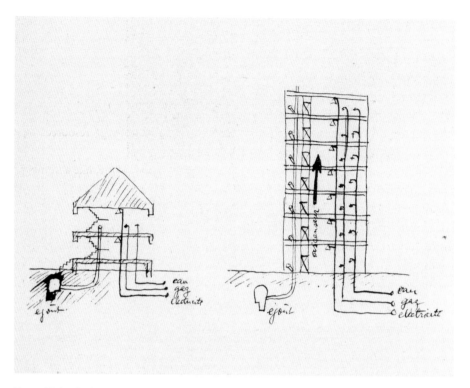

Figure 29 Le Corbusier, The artificial ground, La ville radieuse (1933)

Only a few fragments of vernacular architecture (sun-screens, solarium, roof garden, natural air-conditioning) subsisted. The nourishing link with nature, in the sense of a subsistence economy, had definitively disappeared. For most architects, connection was an obvious marker of progress. The architecture-technology-environment relationship was relatively weak; the manufacturing process and energy supply was globally ignored to the benefit of formal values. The masterpieces of the Modern movement would moreover be criticized by Fuller, who stated:

> [They] never went back of the wall surface to look at the plumbing, never dared to venture into 'printed' circuits of manifoldly stamped plumbings. They never inquired into the over-all problem of sanitary functions themselves. They settled upon the real estate's sewers like hens on glass eggs.[81]

In *The Architecture of the Well-tempered Environment*, Reyner Banham evaluated the impact and innovations of technological modernity on household equipment, criticizing the separation between architecture and technology in the Modern movement and highlighting the energy advantages offered by the immediate environment. Utilities and sanitary facilities in the home were an accepted convenience, indispensable to the success of the modern dwelling. Apart from the plastic and symbolic interest in the new industrial design objects – sinks, bathtubs and faucets – there was no desire to intervene in the traditional distribution system. As for "nature," the vehicle of hygiene and well-being, it was one of the ingredients of the global revamping of the industrial city, without the question of energy resources being raised.

In his essay "Le vert dans la grande ville" (1908), Camillo Sitte, like a number of his contemporaries, asserted that "if it didn't have recourse to nature, the city would be nothing but a fetid jail."[82] Léon Jaussely similarly observed in 1922 that "modern urbanism tries to bring the urban man closer to nature, to better put him in contact with it, to better associate his life with it."[83] The Modern movement took hold of this question and the production of a return-to-nature ideology could be seen. But if these architects made a major effort to bring pure air, water, sun and greenery back to the city, nature was mainly a source of landscapes or leisure activities. In Le Corbusier, it was a frame, a decisive plastic and sensitive element:

> The conditions of nature should provide a sound counterweight to the artificial factors born from the machine, it is therefore timely to make an inventory of the available *nature capital*, to keep accounts on *nature stocks*: nature intervenes in an essential fashion in the *inhabiting* function (sun, space, greenery), it is also present in the *working* function (greenery and sky). It plays an eminent role in the *cultivating the body and mind* function (sites and landscape), it accompanies circulation (sites and landscape).[84]

The green policy became a collective requirement that responded to a reconciliation of the contradiction of the city and its functions, notably the *work* function.[85] For this purpose, Le Corbusier proposed the creation of new green zones in order to promote a spirit that encouraged work. "Green workshops," "green factories" were initiatives "incumbent on the authority and informing the urban planner and architect to have the landscape element enter into the constituent data of the work unit."[86] A desire to create an amalgam of the work–leisure functions was at work in this decor that embellished the reality principle. The production of green spaces and parks intensified, but the city–country and work–leisure separation nonetheless remained. Of course, the garden cities could be surrounded by vast areas of land that could be reserved, according to the demand, for individual kitchen gardens, but nature represented a pleasure space more than a domain providing nourishment.[87] Moreover, Le Corbusier rained sarcasms down on the image of the traditional farm and urban horticulture.

The Alexandroffs analyzed these contradictions in their reference work *Architectures et climats*, demonstrating the conceptual confusion of the idea of nature:

> Modern architects, like all those who will follow or impugn their principles, no longer have anything in common with vernacular builders: not really living in nature, they go there by choice, not by necessity. [...] The open spaces with which they will enrich their architecture will always be leisure spaces, whether for sports or meditation. Lastly, their relationship to materials, in the same was as to natural energies will remain more of an ethical or aesthetic type than materially and objectively necessary.[88]

If the Alexandroffs examined the respective ambiguities of a few of these architects, they considered Frank Lloyd Wright one of the most influential in terms of "climate architecture." The break in the direct link between the living environment and the resources of the natural milieu was consummated. Amenity gradually replaced necessity. Nature became sterile in the sense that home economics was not dependent on using energy directly derived from natural resources. The relationship still seemed passive: there were very few who went beyond these contradictions. The energy network was an invisible and nutritive conduit that served the inhabiting function and corresponded to a new consumption ideal. A decrease in the feeling of dispossession and economic exaction corresponded to the increase in comfort. State interventionism was a fundamental element of the process that led to the completion of the utilities-for-all project.

The subscriber city: from private monopoly to public service

Most networks owe their existence to private initiatives and the interests they represent. Initially, competition between operators prevailed, until the creation of the first monopolies and the birth of the idea of "universal service." It is important to examine this term and the claimed benefits of the monopoly for subscribers. "Universal service" was invented in 1907 by the American Theodore Vail, president of the American Telephone and Telegraph Company (AT&T). The existence of competing networks specifically for the telephone was a loss for users, who had to take out several subscriptions to be able to communicate throughout the country. The idea of the "natural monopoly" then emerged: it was based on the idea that a large company could produce at lower costs. For Theodore Vail, "the duplication of infrastructure is a loss for the investor and the duplication of costs is a loss for the user."[89] Vail showed that it was economically advantageous for subscribers to have a single network, held by a single company, rather than several networks held by competing companies. With this demonstration of the decrease in costs and the stability of rates, AT&T obtained a near monopoly thanks to the agreement of the state, which recognized that the company's policy served public interest.[90] If the public authority encouraged this monopoly, it demanded the right to exert a regulatory control over it in exchange. The extension of intervention and supervision procedures was the counterpart to the freedoms granted to companies.

In the 1920s, state interventionism proliferated. In addition to telephony, it would spread to all the sectors considered essential for the population, including sewage, drinking water, gas and electricity distribution. Several countries would accompany monopolizations through independent commissions, which regulated the cost of services and offered measures to extend the networks into unprofitable areas. With the boom in liberalism, the economic and social protection of the populations became a concern for the public authorities. Due to certain abuses of the laws of the market and the development of this "public interest," in the early twentieth century, major industrial groups were subject to a strong state interventionism. Legal frameworks and regulations varied from one country to the other according to the respective power of local, regional and central authorities. There were very large disparities depending on the networks.

Diversity initially characterized the production of electrical equipment in Europe as the private monopoly and municipality system coexisted. In France, at the very beginning of the twentieth century, the first wave of the extension of public services was linked to the development of municipal socialism. Independently of the state and the market, communities promoted municipalization for local management. A host of local networks without any common voltage standards supplied different sectors. Consequently, the interconnection of electricity networks was a technically and economically difficult project before the early twentieth century. In the first decades, the action of American and European governments would accompany the creation of large networks and their management by the administration.

In the United Kingdom, the Central Electricity Board was created in 1926 and its public funds were earmarked for the purchase of units that were not very profitable in order to unify production and distribution. From the 1930s, a general regulation of public interest services could be seen. The welfare state was extended in Britain, and in the United States the economic and social programs of the New Deal were created by Franklin D. Roosevelt in 1933. Threatened by the economic crisis, a certain number of freedoms concerning healthcare, consumption, work and business seemed fundamental.

In France, state intervention was systematized with the appearance of powerful state-owned companies. Electricité de France (EDF) was created in 1946 after the assets of over a thousand electricity production, transport and distribution companies were nationalized. The establishment of public service was a slow regularization process aimed at both lowering production costs, harmonizing rates, ensuring service continuity and solidifying the points served. The advent of public service helped remodel the state's image by giving it new legitimacy. The French concept of public service – based on the idea of public interest – was theorized in the 1920s. Public service appeared as:

> the genuine keystone of state construction: it is what permits enclosing the state space on itself, by tracing a firm demarcation line between public and private, but also by integrating the different elements of the theory of state, by combining them through a strange alchemy into a unified and coherent conceptual whole.[91]

The idea of a public service responsible for the major collective functions and structured into a network explains why the monopoly had been considered one of its prerequisites. There is a complex ideological configuration induced by the very term public service. For Jacques Chevallier, it "sculpts the myth of a welcoming, generous state, concerned about everyone's well-being; public service is the 'axiological' principle that is supposed to command public management."[92] The ideology of public service moves between a project entirely focused on meeting collective needs (public services would only, in the end, ensure the public interest) or a factor of state subjection (giving the public authority legitimacy in principle to dictate its law to subscribers).

Reticular and mono-centered structures emerged as the unification of the energy space accelerated. The codification and standardization of equipment, voltages, meters and installations for reasons such as compatibility, safety or profitability constituted an *ideal-type*.[93] Hygiene and service regulations and subscriptions provided the new framework of urban life. A licit city subjected to an organization and biological orchestration of needs was created.

A biopolitical mechanism

The upheavals of the nineteenth century, such as the industrialization and massification of society, were accompanied by the development of sanitary and healthcare policies. In this framework, the large utility networks became one of the most important mechanisms for regulating vital necessities. It is in light of Michel Foucault's concept of "biopolitics," formulated in the late 1970s, that this new form of power, whose aim was the management of life itself, must be envisaged.

Foucault rejected a purely negative vision of power by demonstrating that the control of physiological life permitted the social body to be regulated. If the disciplinary technique was directly applied to individualized bodies, biopolitics acted on the population's multiple body, on its environment, through assistance mechanisms like access to treatment and services and assistance for the poor. Foucault described the appearance of this power:

> [I]n the second half of the eighteenth century technologies [appeared] that did not aim at individuals as individuals as such, but that aimed on the contrary at the population. [...] At this moment what I will call biopolitics, as opposed to anatomopolitics, [...] was invented. It is at this moment that we see problems appear such as those of the habitat, living conditions in a city, public hygiene, the relationship between the birth rate and the death rate. [...] And starting from this point, a whole series of observation techniques, among them statistics, obviously, but also all the large administrative, economic and political bodies, were responsible for regulating the population.[94]

Foucault believed that it was the development of liberalism that favored the structuring of this coverage as of the late eighteenth century, the specificity of the liberal art of governing being to measure and limit the "complex game between individual and collective interests, social utility and economic profit, between market balance and the public power regime, [...] between fundamental rights and the independence of the governed."[95] In a society in which exchange determined value, the state henceforth had to ensure that the interests of some did not comprise a danger for others. Liberalism would favor interventionism to arbitrate the freedom and safety of individuals around the ideas of danger and need. Liberalism was the general framework of biopolitics. By considering power as an instrument for the regulation of the behaviors and basic needs of individuals, the urban technical networks appeared as one of its mechanisms. The development and absolute necessity of energy distribution stemmed from the health policy that constituted biopolitics: the idea was to organize society "as a milieu of physical well-being, optimal health and longevity."[96]

Health and hygiene were the priorities of nascent urban planning. In the framework of sanitary reforms, a genuine "urban medicine" was implemented, in which doctors, engineers, urban planners and architects participated. Supervised by a series of proactive interventions, energy services developed as an assistance policy. From the late nineteenth century, the obsession of a healthy and vigorous body went hand in hand with a ventilated, electrified space connected to the network. If biopolitics corresponded to the state's gradual consideration of the population's life, then the state energy apparatus was a mechanism of its control. Life was administered by creating an institutional sphere that produced a body of law regulating vital necessities: energy consumption became the object of a carefully thought-out governmentality. The management methods of this progress could therefore also be considered the threat of a new power. The citizens' economic relationship, the physiological dependence and the passivity in respect to the energy system ensured a submission to its mechanisms and their renewal. The deployment of a broad power over the life of the populations, service was a concrete materialization of the application of this system in a given area of social and biological life. However, despite the strong impact of this critical approach, the world of architecture and urbanism validated the city of networks, without questioning its ideological foundations.

In 1953, the urban planner Maurice-François Rouge confirmed the meteoric growth of networks and their decisive role for urbanism. He set forth the advent of a cabled universe and, more broadly, the coverage and dependence of the territories by and toward the networks.

> Maps thus increasingly become network plans: networks of all sorts, which are multi-plying, crisscrossing the land, intersecting in every direction, being superimposed and covering the surface of a frame that seems to fix the surface and even lock it in under their grids. These networks fill, in an increasingly dense manner, an ecumene that is constantly being extended; it moreover overflows on what was not a part of it, on the deserts and the poles. Man's hold seems to be especially established through networks.[97]

Rouge raised the question of the role of large infrastructures in the organization of space, wondering what economic life would be without their existence. Aware of the "immense profits and no less immense risks that they bring to humanity," he considered that urbanism had to intervene in and through the network to dominate, control, organize and coordinate these irrepressible mechanisms.

The connection ideal won over the twentieth century, and it would be appropriate here to better define the responsibility of the countries of the northern hemisphere in this model's establishment. Electrifying one's house, benefiting from gas and water at home, represented "being connected" or "subscribing" to modernity, through the network. The shared arrival of the connection as a model and the network as a system could be observed in the scientific approach to the analysis of urban technical services. Dupuy brought up the insufficient consideration of this phenomenon by the development disciplines:

> [W]hat urbanism has not understood is the generation and generalization of relations ensuring in a brand new space–time relationship the circulation of people, goods, informa-tion from point to point, up to the connection to the network, urban connection, takes on the meaning of a new urbanity. [...] A new urbanism is obviously being sought in France. It is being sought, sometimes in a reactionary manner, but often on the right track, that of the urban connection.[98]

Dupuy nonetheless raised the problems stemming from the political, economic and technical "perversions" of the network on the operator level. However, connection remained the right path: its progression bore witness, in a certain way, to its triumph.

The constancy of this sense of the network as an *ideal-type* that could be improved had few detractors. We can observe a history of services that were created in line with this objective of connection and the generalization of access to the service. The acceptance of the fascination of the urban planners' milieu for the connection system gives the impression that the history of architecture and urban planning of the twentieth century gave its imprimatur to the city of networks. However, one area has largely remained unmentioned in architectural and urban theory: disconnection. When disconnection is mentioned, it is generally marginal:

> [T]here are still indigents who cannot pay the minimum required for connection: holdouts who, for different reasons, reject the service. There can be disconnections and subscription cancellations that remain marginal but prevent the totality of the population from being reached. Above all, the connection costs of the last to be connected are considerable because the network first had to be built where there was the greatest demand, where it was easiest, the least expensive.[99]

But these "indigents" and "holdouts" were rare, since, from the start, the objective remained to connect everyone. The political project of universal access to services of basic necessity was also an economic project, because being connected did not systematically mean having access to the services. Physical accessibility (the connection) was distinct from financial accessibility. Citing different European and American cases, Douglas D. Anderson explained how the operator could favor users compared to those who only consumed the strict minimum (the elderly, the disadvantaged), and how subscribers had to accept new services and new rates unless they wanted to see their subscriptions cancelled.[100] But it was perhaps especially the operators who had trouble taking other energy distribution modes into account.

Non-connection or disconnection is generally understood as an acceptance of exclusion from the network, echoing a state of precariousness, of poverty. Disconnection always leads to marginalization. Marguerite Duras's story about the water-cutter illustrates this situation. She recounted the tragic tale of a water company employee who had come to cut off the water of very poor people who could not pay their gas, electricity or water bill. People who, she pointed out, were "a little apart, a little different from the others, let us say backward."[101] In the process of generalizing access to the networks, not being connected was not belonging to the territory-network; it was being doomed to survival or death. The disconnection one was subjected to was constraint, failure, punishment; it was rarely evoked as resistance or the invention of other energy possibilities.

Notes

1 The energy concept was defined in the seventeenth century by physicists based on the idea of mechanical work; it was extended to heat in the nineteenth century. See Jean-Claude Debeir, Jean-Paul Deléage and Daniel Hémery, *Les Servitudes de la puissance: Une histoire de l'énergie* (Paris: Flammarion, 1986). See also the new revised and expanded edition, *Une histoire de l'énergie* (Paris: Flammarion, 2013).

2 See in particular André Guillerme, "L'émergence du concept de réseau, 1820–1830," *Cahier / Groupe Réseaux*, Ecole nationale des ponts et chaussées, no. 5 June (1986), pp. 30–47; André Guillerme, *Genèse du concept de réseau: Territoire et génie en Europe de l'Ouest, 1760–1815*, research report, TMUPD/URA CNRS 1244 (Champs-sur-Marne: Laboratoire Théorie des mutations urbaines: Institut Français d'Urbanisme, 1988); and more recently Pierre Musso, "De la mythologie grecque à l'idéologie d'Internet," in P. Musso (ed.), *Réseaux et société* (Paris: PUF, 2003), pp. 15–41.

3 Plato, *Le Politique* (Paris: Garnier-Flammarion, 1969), p. 194.

4 Pierre Musso, "La symbolique du réseau," *Quaderni*, no. 38, Spring (1999), p. 81.

5 Cited by Gaston Pinet, *Ecrivains et penseurs polytechniciens* (Paris: Paul Ollendorff, 1898), p. 165.

6 Antoine Picon, *Les Saint-Simoniens: Raison, imaginaire et utopie* (Paris: Belin, 2002); Dominique Rouillard, "Utopie," in Antoine Picon (ed.), *L'Art de l'ingénieur: Constructeur, entrepreneur, inventeur* (Paris: Centre Pompidou/Le Moniteur, 1997), pp. 527–529.

7 Gilles Deleuze and Félix Guattari, *Mille plateaux: Capitalisme et schizophrénie 2* (Paris: Minuit, 1980).

8 *Ibid.*, p. 480.

9 *Ibid.*

10 Cited by Jean-Louis Gazzaniga and Xavier Larrouy-Castera, "Le droit de l'eau et les droits d'eau dans une perspective historique," in Olivia Aubriot and Geneviève Jolly (eds), *Histoires d'une eau partagée: Irrigation et droits d'eau du Moyen Age à nos jours, Provence/ Alpes/Pyrénées* (Aix-en-Provence: Publications de l'université de Provence, 2002).

11 "There have been in Asia, generally, from immemorial times, but three departments of Government; that of Finance, or the plunder of the interior; that of War, or the plunder of the exterior; and, finally, the department of Public Works […] As in Egypt and India, inundations are used for fertilizing the soil in Mesopotamia, Persia, &c.; advantage is taken of a high level for feeding irrigative canals. This prime necessity of an economical and common use of water, which, in the Occident, drove private enterprise to voluntary association, as in Flanders and Italy, necessitated, in the Orient

where civilization was too low and the territorial extent too vast to call into life voluntary association, the interference of the centralizing power of Government. Hence an economical function devolved upon all Asiatic Governments, the function of providing public works." Karl Marx, "The future results of British rule in India," *New York Daily Tribune*, 8 August 1853.

12 Pierre Clastres, *La Société contre l'Etat* (Paris: Minuit, 1974).

13 Cf. Hélène Dessales, "Le prix de l'eau dans l'habitat romain: une étude des modes de gestion à Pompéi," in Ella Hermon (ed.), *Vers une gestion intégrée de l'eau dans l'Empire romain* (Rome: L'Erma di Bretschneider, 2008), p. 57. See volume II of the colloquium proceedings "La gestion intégrée de l'eau dans l'histoire environnementale: savoirs traditionnels et pratiques modernes," Université Laval, Quebec (October 27–29, 2006).

14 Virginie Picon-Lefebvre, "La question de l'obsolescence des infrastructures. Destruction ou transformation," in Claude Prelorenzo and Dominique Rouillard (eds), *Le Temps des infrastructures* (Paris: L'Harmattan, 2007), pp. 113–121.

15 Jacques Heers, *Espaces publics, espaces privés dans la ville: Le Liber Terminorum de Bologne (1294)* (Paris: CNRS, 1984).

16 Maurice Bourjol, *Les Biens communaux: Voyage au centre de la propriété collective* (Paris: LGDJ, 1989); Nadine Vivier, *Propriété collective et identité communale: Les biens communaux en France, 1750–1914* (Paris: Publications de la Sorbonne, 1998).

17 Heers, *Espaces publics*, p. 22.

18 Jean-Louis Gazzaniga and Jean-Paul Ourliac, *Le Droit de l'eau* (Paris: Litec, 1979); Jean-Louis Gazzaniga, "Droit de l'eau, le poids de l'histoire," *Etudes foncières*, 52 (1991).

19 The specific characteristics and principles of the communal management system have a few equivalents today that once again openly question this idea and its foundations in the framework of the shared governance of certain resources on the scale of communities of inhabitants in a few contemporary eco-districts. See in particular: Arjan Van Timmeren et al., "Sustainable urban decentralization: case EVA Lanxmeer, Culemborg, The Netherlands," communication at the international colloquium, Sustainable Urban Areas, organized by the European Network for Housing and Urban Research, Rotterdam, 25–28 June 2007.

20 Abraham Moles, "La cité câblée: une nouvelle qualité de vie?," *Les Annales de la recherche urbaine*, "Cités câblées, conversations, communications," no. 34 (1987); Xavier Lacoste, "La ville du service" (PhD thesis, University of Paris XII, 1991).

21 Pierre Patte, *Mémoires sur les objets les plus importants de l'architecture* (Paris: Rozet Libraire, 1769).

22 Antoine Picon, "Pierre Patte et la ville rationnelle," in Antoine Picon, *Architectes et ingénieurs au siècle des Lumières* (Marseille: Parenthèses, [1988] 2004), pp. 176–190.

23 Père Féry (André Rémi), *Mémoire sur l'établissement des fontaines publiques dans la ville*

d'Amiens (Amiens: Caron Hubault, 1749). Cited in Guillerme, "L'émergence du concept de réseau," p. 39.

24 Féry, *Mémoire sur l'établissement des fontaines publiques*. On free water, cf. the work by the English architect and historian Colin Ward, *Les Voleurs d'eau: Les déboires marchands d'un bien commun* (Lyon: Atelier de création libertaire, 2006) and Colin Ward, "Les voleurs d'eau," *Réfractions*, "Privés, publics, communs, quels services," no. 15, Winter (2005), pp. 55–65.

25 Jean-François Terme, *Des eaux potables à distribuer pour l'usage des particuliers et le service public* (Lyon: Imprimerie de Nigon, 1843).

26 Joel A. Tarr, "Perspectives souterraines. Les égouts et l'environnement humain dans les villes américaines, 1850–1933," *Les Annales de la recherche urbaine*, no. 23–24 (1984), p. 65.

27 Michel Raoult, *Histoire du chauffage urbain* (Paris: L'Harmattan, 2008), p. 63.

28 "The tyranny of monopolies," *Harper's Weekly*, 14 May 1881, p. 314.

29 Harold L. Platt, "La ville électrique. Les réseaux régionaux d'énergie et la croissance de Chicago, 1893–1933," *Les Annales de la recherche urbaine*, no. 23–24 (1984), pp. 202–217.

30 Thomas P. Hughes, *Networks of Power: Electrification in Western Society, 1880–1930* (Baltimore, MD: Johns Hopkins University Press, 1983), pp. 106–139.

31 Platt, "La ville électrique," p. 204.

32 National Electric Light Association, *Proceedings* (1898), p. 331. Cited in Platt, "La ville électrique."

33 Jean-Claude Debeir, Jean-Paul Deléage and Daniel Hémery, "L'expansion du système énergétique capitaliste: l'âge des réseaux," in Debeir, Deléage and Hémery, *Les Servitudes de la puissance*, pp. 176–212.

34 Peter Newell, "The Telegraph Spider," *Harper's Weekly*, 12 November 1881, p. 768.

35 Albert Robida, *Le Vingtième Siècle: La vie électrique* (Paris: Engel, 1890); Adamant Media Corporation, "Elibron Classics Series" (2006), p. 3.

36 Luc and François Schuiten, "Centrale d'énergie," in L. and F. Schuiten, *Les Terres creuses* (Paris: Les Humanoïdes associés, 1980), p. 21.

37 Robida, *La Vingtième Siècle*, p. 129.

38 *Ibid.*, p. 83.

39 *Ibid.*, p. 8.

40 *Ibid.*

41 Eric Alonzo, "La rue machine," in Eric Alonzo, "L'architecture de la voie: histoire et théories" (PhD thesis, University of Paris-Est, 2013).

42 Gildas Baudez and François Béguin, *Critique du paysage de l'énergie* (Paris, Roux-Bauer & Associés, 1980).

43 Dupuy, *L'Urbanisme des réseaux*, p. 182.

44 Eric Alonzo, "Dessiner la voie pour l'automobile," in Eric Alonzo and Sébastien Marot (eds), *Marnes, documents d'architecture*, vol. 2 (Paris: Editions de la Villette, 2011), pp. 19–83.

45 Ildefonso Cerdà, *Teoría general de la urbanización y aplicación de sus principios y doctrinas a la reforma y ensanche de Barcelona* (Torija: Imprenta Española, 1867). French translation, *La Théorie générale de l'urbanisation*, presented and adapted by Antonio Lopez de Aberasturi (Paris: Seuil, 1979), p. 73.

46 *Ibid.*, p. 119.

47 *Ibid.*, p. 139.

48 *Ibid.*, p. 142.

49 *Ibid.*, p. 151.

50 *Ibid.*, p. 159.

51 *Ibid.*, p. 152.

52 *Ibid.*, p. 157.

53 In *La Ville délétère*, Sabine Barles underlines the inexistence of waste and wastewater in the eighteenth-century city and demonstrates, in *L'Invention des déchets urbains*, that it was starting at the moment when spatial links between city, agriculture and industry were unwoven, at the end of the nineteenth century, that one can observe a decrease in the treatment and recycling of urban excretions, which continued to increase. Cf. Sabine Barles, *La Ville délétère: Médecins et ingénieurs dans l'espace urbain, XVIIIe–XIXe siècle* (Seyssel: Champ Vallon, 1999), p. 256 and *L'Invention des déchets urbains: France: 1790–1970* (Seyssel: Champ Vallon, 2005).

54 Eugène Hénard, *Etudes sur les transformations de Paris, et autres écrits sur l'urbanisme (1903–1910)* (Paris: L'Equerre, 1982). Republished as *Etudes sur l'architecture et les transformations de Paris* (Paris: Editions de la Villette, 2013). Cf. "Les villes de l'avenir," pp. 326–336.

55 *Ibid.*, p. 328.

56 *Ibid.*

57 *Ibid.*

58 Francisco Saturnino Rodrigues de Brito, *Notes sur le tracé sanitaire des villes* (Paris: Imprimerie de Chaix, 1916). Written in 1915–16, this work was published in French for the Cité reconstituée exhibition, which was held in Paris in 1916 on the initiative of the Association générale des hygiénistes et techniciens municipaux, of which Brito was an honorary member.

59 Carlos Roberto Monteiro de Andrade, "Le pittoresque et le sanitaire. Sitte, Martin, Brito, traductions et métamorphoses de savoirs professionnels (1889–1929)," *Genèses*, vol. 22, no. 3 (1996), pp. 64–86.

60 Nikolay Milyutin, *Sotsgorod: Le Problème de la construction des villes socialistes* (Paris: L'Imprimeur, [1930] 2002).

61 Anatole Kopp, *Changer la vie, changer la ville: De la vie nouvelle aux problèmes urbains, URSS 1917–1932* (Paris: UGE, 1975), p. 298.

62 Mikhail Okhitovich, "Remarque sur la théorie du peuplement," *CA (L'Architecture contemporaine)*, no. 1–2 (1930).

63 Selim O. Khan-Magomedov, *Pioneers of Soviet Architecture: The Search for New Solutions in the 1920s and 1930s* (London: Thames & Hudson, 1987).

64 Konstantin Melnikov, cited in S. Frederick Starr, *Melnikov: Solo Architect in a Mass Society* (Princeton, NJ: Princeton University Press, 1978), p. 179.

65 Wolfgang Voigt, "Le plus grandiose projet des temps modernes," in Hubert Damisch and Jean-Louis Cohen (eds), *Américanisme et modernité: L'idéal américain dans l'architecture* (Paris: EHESS/Flammarion, 1993), p. 378.

66 Sigfried Giedion, *Mechanization Takes Command* (New York: Oxford University Press, 1948).

67 As James Marston Fitch highlighted in 1947, then Banham in *L'Architecture de l'environnement bien tempéré*, it was in *A Treatise on Domestic Economy* (1842) and *The American Woman's Home* (1869) that Catharine Beecher presented for the first time the concept of a central axis of grouped utilities, around which each level was deployed. Considering that the smooth functioning of home economics was expressed in the position of the kitchen, she developed reflections on the layout and place of the core in a series of comparative plans. In *Principles of Domestic Science* (1870), a major evolution appeared since it eliminated chimneys and proposed a central domestic pole equipped with a "modern" plumbing system.

68 Giedion, *Mechanization Takes Command*, p. 17.

69 "Manufacturers were turning wartime industry to peacetime productivity, going from missiles to washing machines." Beatriz Colomina, *Domesticity at War* (Barcelona: Actar, 2006). Also see Jean-Louis Cohen, *Architecture en uniforme: Projeter et construire pour la Seconde Guerre mondiale* (Montreal/Paris: Centre canadien d'architecture/Hazan, 2011).

70 John Gloag and Grey Wornum, *House out of Factory* (London: Allen & Unwin, 1946). Also see Rudolf Doernach, *Vorgefertigte Installationen für den Wohnungsbau* (Stuttgart: Forschungsgemeinschaft Bauen und Wohnen, [1970]).

71 Arcon, for "Architecture Consultants." The Arcon, Chartered Architects company was created in the spring of 1943 by Edric Neel, Raglan Squire and Rodney Thomas, with the support of industrial groups. In 1952, the company became A. M. Gear & Associates, before being dissolved in 1967. Cf. A. M. Gear & Associates, *The Arcon Group, 1943–1967*, (London: AMG Press, 1967), p. 29.

72 Arcon, Chartered Architects, "The design, organization and production of a prefabricated house," study report (March–June 1948).

73 Warren Chalk, *Archigram 6* (November 1965). *Rent a Wall* (1966) by Mike Webb came directly out of the utility walls of those years. Cf. *Archigram 7* (December 1966).

74 Nadir Lahiji and Daniel S. Friedman (eds), *Plumbing: Sounding Modern Architecture* (New York: Princeton Architectural Press, 1997).

75 Adolf Loos, "Die Plumber," *Neue Freie Presse*, 17 July 1898; Loos, "Les plombiers," in Adolf Loos, *Paroles dans le vide – Malgré tout* (Paris: Ivréa, 1979), pp. 51–56.

76 *Ibid.*, p. 55.

77 Colin Rowe, *The Architecture of Good Intentions: Towards a Possible Retrospect* (London: Academy Editions, 1994), p. 60.

78 Le Corbusier, "Analyse des éléments fondamentaux du problème du logis minimum: Rapport présenté par Le Corbusier et Pierre Jeanneret," in Le Corbusier, *La Ville radieuse* (Paris: Vincent, Fréal & Cie, [1935] 1964), p. 29.

79 *Ibid.*, p. 56.

80 Georges and Jeanne-Marie Alexandroff, *Architectures and climats: Soleil et énergies naturelles dans l'habitat* (Paris: Berger-Levrault, 1982), p. 183.

81 Fuller cited by Banham, in John McHale, "Richard Buckminster Fuller," *Architectural Design*, vol. 31, no. 7 (1961), pp. 295–296.

82 Cited by Monteiro de Andrade, "Le pittoresque et le sanitaire," p. 71.

83 *Ibid.* Cf. Raymond Unwin, *Town Planning in Practice: An Introduction to the Art of Designing Cities and Suburbs* (London: T. Fisher Unwin, 1909).

84 Le Corbusier, *Manière de penser l'urbanisme* (Paris: Gonthier, 1947), p. 83.

85 Birth of a genuine green space policy: 1956 decree for Paris, the Lafay law, which instituted the obligation to develop green spaces. This law permits the building of housing developments on the Paris green belt with a compensation system aiming at the creation of green spaces in the center of Paris.

86 Le Corbusier, *Manière de penser l'urbanisme*, p. 69.

87 *Ibid.*, p. 63.

88 Alexandroff and Alexandroff, *Architectures et climats*, p. 160.

89 AT&T, *Annual Report 1907* (Boston, MA: Alfred Mudge & Son, 1908), p. 18, cited in Maxime Tourbe, "Service public *versus* service universel: une controverse infondée?," *Critique internationale*, no. 24, July (2004), p. 3.

90 Kenneth Lipartito, *The Bell System and Regional Business: The Telephone in the South, 1877–1920* (Baltimore, MD: Johns Hopkins University Press, 1989).

91 Jacques Chevallier, *Le Service public* (Paris: PUF, 1987), p. 5.

92 *Ibid.*

93 Max Weber, *Essais sur la théorie de la science*, trans. Julien Freund (Paris: Plon, 1965).

94 Michel Foucault, "Les mailles du pouvoir" (1981), in Michel Foucault, *Dits et écrits II, 1976–1988* (Paris: Gallimard, 2001), pp. 1012–1013.

95 Michel Foucault, *Naissance de la biopolitique: Cours au Collège de France, 1978–1979* (Paris: Gallimard/Seuil, 2004), p. 65.

96 Michel Foucault, "La politique de la santé au XVIIIᵉ siècle" (1976), in Foucault, *Dits et écrits II*, pp. 13–27.

97 Maurice-François Rouge, "L'organisation de l'espace et les réseaux," in *Eventail de l'histoire vivante: Hommage à Lucien Febvre* (Paris: Armand Colin, 1953). Republished in *Flux*, vol. 5, no. 3 (1989), p. 87.

98 Dupuy, *L'Urbanisme des réseaux*, p. 183.

99 *Ibid.*, p. 41.

100 Douglas D. Anderson, *Regulatory Politics and Electric Utilities: A Case Study in Political Economy* (Boston, MA: Auburn House Publishing, 1981).

101 Marguerite Duras, *La Vie matérielle* (Paris: Gallimard, [1987] 1997), pp. 115–116.

2 Being disconnected: genesis of a new technical utopia

At the very moment when the dream of connection was becoming a reality, transforming each city-dweller into a network-subscriber in a very short lapse of time, a new technical utopia emerged: disconnection. Whereas connection became a principle, its relevance was questioned. The criticism of the network's accessibility for the largest number of people was based on both economic and environmental issues. Faced with the depletion of non-renewable reserves and the pollution of the industrial city, the self-management of energy derived from the natural milieu appeared as an alternative. If the inventions intended to promote hydroelectric, wind and solar energies continued throughout the nineteenth century, energy autonomy and/or autarky was emerging as a phenomenon and a full-fledged project. Starting in the nineteenth century, discussions in the United States, France, Germany and the United Kingdom began in favor of energy decentralization and self-production, which could not only free the landscapes and ground from the web of flows, but users from the monopolies. However, the wish for energy autonomy was often expressed in the future tense. For this program to carry the day, it required such a high degree of technical improvement and socio-economic evolution that its development was constantly postponed to a later date.

Autonomy and autarky

Autonomy appeared in the early nineteenth century as a vehicle of technological utopia, sometimes arising from mechanical narratives and political and economic idealism, while at other times emerging from scientific pragmatism. A few engineers, chemists and theoreticians considered decentralization – free use and self-sufficiency in a connected and complementary manner, without any clear priority – though others treated them separately. The terms self-sufficiency, autonomy and autarky define projects with different ambitions. Here, the terminology conceals deeper questions whose issues must be brought to light.

The idea of autonomy was part of a tradition of philosophical and political thought. The word "autonomy" (from the Greek *auto*, "oneself," and *nomos*, "law) designated the right to be governed by one's own laws. First applied to political relations, autonomy initially referred to the self-government of particular states and communities. Until the nineteenth century, the self-government of certain cities was a civic model, in countries such as Germany, for example, where municipal power was strong.[1] Starting in the late sixteenth century, autonomy became one of the attributes of the individual, who determined his or her own rules of conduct vis-à-vis an external authority. Kantian philosophy thus gave primacy to the thinking subject who, emancipated from his guardians, made use of his understanding and became freer. Subsequently used to describe a political and social struggle phenomenon, in the twentieth century, the word took on a radical meaning: it designated all of the political practices, outside the parties and union organizations recognized by the state, which aspired to self-institution and self-emancipation.

The word "autarky" comes from the Greek *autarkeia* (from *auto* and *arkein*, "protect, save, suffice"). Autarky initially referred to material independence: it is the economic system of self-sufficiency. Widespread in wartime, autarky and *autarchy* (a government or group practicing a closed economy) commonly refer to isolationism. Often confused, autonomy and autarky designate the situation of a country or group that can subsist without needing anything from beyond its borders. Saint Thomas Aquinas and the medieval scholastics brought these two ideas together in the term "sufficiency."[2] In the nineteenth century, "autarchy" reappeared in the writings of economists, but its use was not widespread and the French retained "autarky" to designate economic independence. Autarky describes the economic system of a community that is sufficient unto itself. It is the result of a deliberate policy, or one forced on it by war. The national autarky (or autarchy) doctrine would subsequently be assimilated to totalitarian countries that had little or no trade with the exterior. In 1936, Hitler pronounced, for example, in favor of autarky: the "four-year plan" launched under Hermann Göring aimed at creating the Reich's independence to avoid the shortages of the First World War.[3]

In this book, local energy autonomy refers to the capacity of a local group of actors (like a cooperative or a municipality) to define their energy project, as well as the energy production and supply conditions. Energy autonomy can be divided into two types. The first is secessionist autonomy: this refers to the radical independence project and is related to the community isolationists, including certain communities of the 1970s and some gated communities. It is the result of a deliberate policy of a group of individuals practicing a closed economy. Secessionist autonomy can be likened to autarchy. In a different way, the second type, which we will call cooperative or generative autonomy, can put forward the potentialities of pooling and interconnection of the local links according to a political project shared by the actors of the "connectable places." Today, in institutional architecture and urbanism, the term self-sufficiency refers to a balance between production and consumption without economic consideration.

If the self-sufficient colony was initially the material system for conquering virgin or foreign soil, it was also used as a tool for territorial, social and industrial reforms. Looking back at the myth of the first human settlement, it was a way to make a clean sweep and start from zero again.

From populating the colony to planning large-scale agro-industrial complexes

The popularity of the independent and self-sufficient community theme was first observed in the United States, with the settlement of the first British colonies on the East Coast of the New Continent: "The American society was founded, from its origins, on [the] myth of small communities of individuals working their own lands and emancipated from any bondage."[4] The vastness of the territory favored the emergence of a host of agricultural colonies, from the Plymouth Colony to the Shakers. Confronted with the dense cities of the "Old" Continent, the young nation claimed "the unalienable right of every American to own his plot of land that he can cultivate as he likes and on which he builds his house [as well as] the total liberty he is offered to constantly recreate his own activity horizon," that is, individual freedom and ownership as guarantees of a genuine democracy.[5] Without energy autonomy being an objective or a project, this organization model encouraged it, since it was founded on the strengthening of independence on every scale: of the individual, the community and the country. In 1809, Thomas Jefferson asserted this tendency: "a balance between agriculture, manufacturing and trade has certainly become essential to our independence."[6] Thus, the American pioneer tradition was perpetuated. Faced with technological and industrial acceleration and the inexorable growth of the city and its urban grid, a large number of texts emerged like *Nature* (1836) and *Self-Reliance* (1841) by Ralph Waldo Emerson and Henry David Thoreau's *Walden* (1854), which bore witness to the American idealism that John Adolphus Etzler or, in another fashion, Frank Lloyd Wright, would attempt to turn into a reality.

Autarky, which concerns the question of resource decentralization and self-management, equally became the anarchist intellectuals' favorite theme, notably in France. Pierre-Joseph Proudhon denounced the economic and political structuring of agricultural and industrial centralism, as well as that of the railroad. For Proudhon, the principle of the large centralized network was monarchical, and the decentralized network was a more democratic and equalitarian organization. While the subject of self-management and federalism was raised, energy and food self-sufficiency appeared, in Proudhon, as a leading topic. It first of all permitted vital necessities to be ensured and a support base to be reconstituted. Next, by raising the question of energy ownership and its governance, self-sufficiency marked the search – between the individual and the state – of an intermediate level for the management of a "common good." If Proudhon repudiated both collective and individual ownership in *Qu'est-ce que la propriété?* (1840), he subsequently rectified this:

> Ownership is the greatest revolutionary force that exists and that can counter power. […] Serving as a counterweight to the public power, balancing the state, by this means ensuring individual freedom: such will therefore be, in the political system, the principle function of ownership.[7]

This "counterweight" echoed Peter Kropotkin's "rear base," in which Kropotkin called for the strengthening of the individual's autonomy. Energy held a central place in these arguments; it was a necessity as fundamental as bread. Solving the "question of foodstuffs" was primordial for Kropotkin because it was what made men secure. To do so, a rear base had to be ensured without charge: housing, water, electricity, food and clothing, because the power knew, he wrote, that "a people that did not go hungry and that slept in a heated house would be very difficult to control."[8] He therefore proposed to organize "the enjoyment of foodstuffs in common" via self-management:

> As long as pumps are enough to supply the houses, without people fearing a lack of water, no company would think of regulating the use of water in each household. Take as much as you like! And if one fears that water would be lacking in Paris during the hottest months, the companies know very well that only a simple warning is needed, four lines printed in the newspapers so that Parisians reduce their water consumption and do not waste too much of it.[9]

The most political intention of autonomy is evoked here as clearly as it would be by several counterculture actors: the guarantee of vital necessities, abundance and self-management comprise the basis of a political or revolutionary future. The management and structure of the energy network is not directly mentioned as such, and renewable energies and the environment are not discussed. Rather, it was the revamping of the agricultural and industrial system that would make it possible to meet social needs such as consumption, production and mutual protection. This is what Kropotkin would point out in *Champs, usines et ateliers*, published in 1899.

These writings clearly influenced the urban theories of the century's transformations, notably those of the radical fringe of the garden city movement in Germany and one of its most ardent representatives, Leberecht Migge. In the late nineteenth century, criticism of the dense and compact industrial city, amassing demographic, hygiene and management problems, intensified. An international anti-urban current was organized; it constantly referred to the myth of the self-sufficient colony, one of whose incarnations was the modern project of urban dissolution, in a leap in scale.[10] The planning of autonomous houses, of agrarian communities or garden cities, attempted to establish an alternative built framework in the United States and Europe.

The mechanical Eden of John Adolphus Etzler

An American engineer of German origin, John Adolphus Etzler, imagined a complex machine in 1833 that would offer a "new Eden" in which self-sufficiency and abundance would reign by using energy derived from nature.

> I promise to show the means for creating a paradise within ten years, where everything desirable for human life may be had for every man in superabundance, without labour, without pay.[11]

Prophetic in tone, Etzler's work is halfway between a technical manual and a philosophical treatise. In an ideal of energy abundance, the interplay of sound and visual ambiences and varied settings, the author depicted a controlled and adjustable environment. For Etzler, nature, through machines, could supply all the energy needed and replace fossil energies that were rare, expensive and polluting. He proposed using wind power, water movements, the amplitude of tides and the sun's heat. Etzler reminds us that these innumerable and boundless energy sources, even if they were underestimated, would be largely sufficient to free people from all "the domestic constraints." Etzler presents a series of chapters on these different resources: "The power of wind," "The power of steam," "The power of the waves," "Burning mirrors," developing their potential in turn. Using Archimedes' heat ray or dazzling mirror principle, he described, for example, how steam could be produced and seawater made drinkable:

> The steam engines, used for their propulsion and other mechanical functions, will also be used for the distillation of water which, once collected in the basins, can be diffused through channels throughout the island; while, where necessary, it can be artificially refrigerated and changed into iced water.[12]

Without providing further details on technical processes, the author reinvented a whole energy production system that, thanks to "perpetual motion machines," would produce a paradise.

As in Robida or, later, Archigram, it is the dream of facilitated access to technology that meets all of our needs through the push of a button or the turn of a crank. Amenity and facility are brimming with this fantasy in which nature and technology coexist: Etzler was both an engineer and a utopian.[13] His intention was to build a universal machine that could do everything, but no design or diagram supported the descriptions of this new enchanting world where domestic needs would be filled by a simple movement of a connecting rod. Etzler's work garnered some success when it was published, though it also attracted criticism. Thoreau would lose no time in condemning this mysterious use of natural forces: "Unfortunately, the ten years in question have already passed, and there is not the slightest sign of any Eden."[14] Thoreau blamed the engineer's mechanistic dreams and wondered about the moral values that stemmed from the illusion of technical progress. He distrusted Etzler's vision of production and technology, which could harm nature, criticizing his lack of abstraction and pragmatism out of the sense that Etzler was more of a materialist than a utopian.

Etzler reacted, in 1841, with *The New World; or Mechanical System to Perform the Labours of Man and Beast by Inanimate Powers, That Cost Nothing, for Producing and Preparing the Substances of Life*, which was published with illustrations. He described and presented plans for the "satellite," a "complex and autonomous" machine that could draw its energy from the sun or the flow of water: the "core or central sun" was connected to other machines, belts, gears and levers handling energy distribution and transformation. With its extensions, the satellite would accomplish all the work on a farm: leveling, working the soil, planting, digging canals, water tanks; its form defined, according to the author, that of the farm that is organized around it. The satellite was composed of several electrical circuits, each enclosing an energy point in its center (see Figures 30 and 31).

> Each circuit is to have, at its centre, a stationary power, which may be a secondary one, derived from a distant reservoir through a canal or pipe [...] supplying the centre of each Circuit with water power driving a water wheel. It's the *Dominion* [...] each hexagon of it a Circuit, to the number of 55, each may be about 1,400 acres, in all about 80,000 acres. The lines from centre to centre of each circuit indicate the feeding canals or pipes, to be conducted between the Orbits, in a serpentine direction in consequence, to avoid needless obstruction to the tracks of the Satellite. As one Satellite may cultivate 20,000 acres, such a Dominion would then require four Satellites.[15]

Etzler had invented a micro-network based on renewable energies. However, the energy descriptions are convoluted, even unrealistic, and the technical drawings are difficult to read to determine how the Dominion functioned. But Etzler was

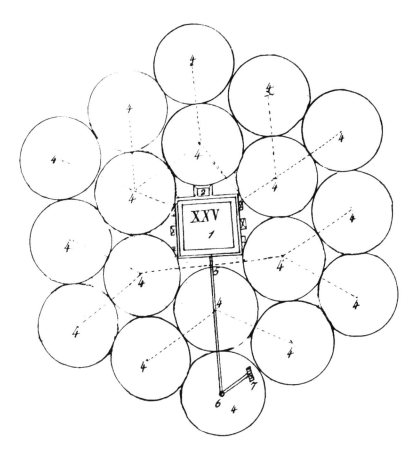

Figure 30 John Adolphus Etzler, "Circuit" (1841)

enthusiastic about his "Universal Machine," which would be the counterpart of the "Universal Republic": "How to clear the land, uproot trees, move stones, fill or dry swamps, make dams and canals, ditches or roads, build houses and provide all the necessary energy from natural resources at any point on these 20,000 acres, all with one system?"[16] With the universal autonomous machine! Etzler replied.

Formulated in the 1840s, Etzler's dream of self-sufficiency was accompanied by great technical abstraction. Its anticipatory nature, however, should be stressed. The first electric power plants were only built in 1880. The German engineer would have a few modest successes, such as his patent filed in 1842 for the "naval automaton" or his mechanical forerunners of planes, ocean liners, farm equipment, public transportation and air-conditioning. His contributions were not limited to his prophetic abilities; Etzler had above all introduced a few energy decentralization and autonomy principles. Despite his pomposity, one cannot neglect his anticipatory genius, which,

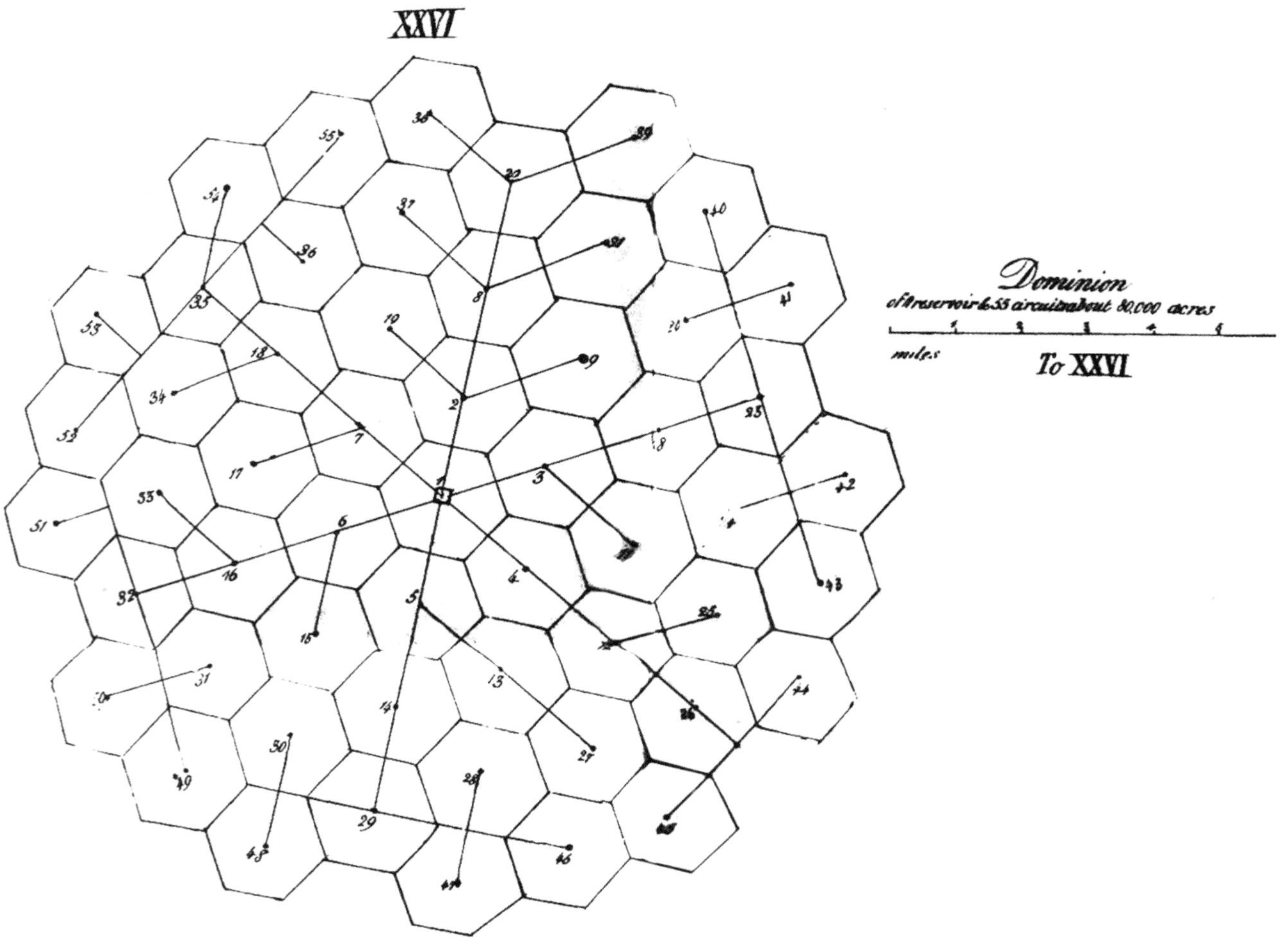

Figure 31 John Adolphus Etzler, "Dominium" (1841)

having grasped all the potential of energy, whether hydraulic, wind or solar, ran the risk of formulating the maddest predictions.

Etzler's mechanical utopia contrasted with Thoreau's "ethical transcendental-ism."[17] His solitary adventure in Walden was unlike Etzler's agrarian communities. Thoreau's naturalist individualism, his rejection of technology, his antigovernment ideal and his mystical taste for untouched nature was fully shown in *Walden; or, Life in the Woods* (1854), which stemmed from his experience living alongside the epony-mous pond in Massachusetts. He built a house with his own hands that corresponded to the mythic figure of the cabin, close to the hut or wigwam, and devoted himself to cultivating a hectare of beans. In Etzler, technology was prominent and autonomy was clearly used as a vehicle for a utopia and abundance, whereas in Thoreau, it was implicit in his quest for self-sufficiency and association with the natural milieu. In the context of the deep mutations of American society, different technological antic-ipations emerged: Etzler's mechanical and abstract undertakings, Thoreau's more literary and philosophical ones, while Edison's scientific pragmatism would add the first prototype of an electrically autonomous house in 1912.

Thomas Edison's attempts

The two electricity pioneers, Thomas Edison and George Westinghouse, had defended their contrasting concepts for distributing current that had begun the industrial conflict. Whereas Westinghouse considered that electricity should be conveyed to the house via cables, Edison maintained that decentralized electricity production in each household would be more advantageous for its occupants. In 1901, the press described how Edison's recent invention of electric cells and batteries could modify the question of the electricity supply (notably in the countryside) and increase energy autonomy. "With a wind turbine coupled to a small electrical generator," Edison wrote, a household would have enough current.[18] The first house that used wind-generated electricity was built in Cleveland in 1888 by the inventor Charles Brush, but for Edison, this type of experimentation had to be extended to mass housing. In 1901, he designed a wind turbine capable of generating electricity for a group of six houses. In 1912, he announced the result of a decade of research: a house whose energy was independent of the networks. The first electrically autonomous house was that of its designer, Edison himself: his manor in Llewelyn Park, New Jersey (see Figure 32).

In September 1912, an article acclaimed its performance:

> The powers of Darkness have suffered another rout. [...]. For Mr. Edison has perfected
> a combination of gasoline engine, generator, and storage batterie by which, for a modest
> expense, every man can make his own electricity in his own cellar, utterly and for all time

EDISON'S LATEST MARVEL—THE ELECTRIC COUNTRY HOUSE

Any One May Now Have an Electric Plant in His Own Cellar at a Comparatively Small Cost Which Will Light and Heat It and Make Housework Easy.

Kitchen Equipment, Including Washing and Wringing Machine and Electric Iron, All Run by a Cellar Electric Plant.

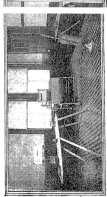

Automatic Voltage Adjuster, the Crux of the Invention

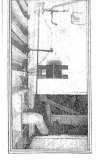

Four Horse Power Gasoline Engine Which Fills the Storage Batteries in Seven Hours.

The Edison 20th Century Electric Suburban Residence at Llewellyn Park, N. J.

Electric Vacuum Cleaner.

Numerous Comfort Devices.

independent of the nearness or farness of the big electrical companies. He can buy a farm in the Middle West or New England and be as free of worries over lighting and heating as if he were a householder on Forty-second Street. He can erect a tent in the desert, if he is so minded, and still read himself to sleep a night under a convenient electrical chandelier, and shave himself the next morning with water heated on an electrical stove.[19]

This laudatory reception encouraged the quest for independence at the lowest cost. This "electrical wonder" was ostensibly equipped with every household gadget and appliance, from the washing machine to the phonograph, as well as video projectors and an electric coffee grinder. Each room had an air-conditioning and heating system. The mechanical equipment functioned via batteries, continuously charged by a small very compact electric generator designed to be installed in a garden, hangar or basement. Edison estimated the cost of this equipment at only $500. He planned, to underline independence, to connect the oil generators to small residential wind turbines. With this project, Edison responded to a genuine demand. In urban centers, connection only concerned the most privileged inhabitants, and "autonomous" or "basement" electricity production was the prerogative of a few large companies that had the means to manage such a system. For the small tradesman or "simple" city or rural inhabitant, access to this service would only come much later. Involved in mass urban connection with Edison General Electric, this new "autonomous" home system was first directed at farmers or rural or peri-urban inhabitants. It was designed for sectors that were not served by the network. Edison's twentieth-century suburban residence "would provide cheap, independent power to any suburban abode with a lot or the needed building space as well as the rural home beyond the lines of city power plants."[20]

If his architectural concerns and built projects were little known, his investment in the car industry was more renowned. In 1913, Edison collaborated with Henry Ford to develop an electric car whose objectives (as for the house) were to be as practical and inexpensive as the Ford Model T. Several articles were devoted to this project, raising the possibility of recharging the batteries at the foot of a domestic wind turbine or in stations. But at the height of its success in 1913, the electric car was still expensive, and with its low autonomy and the drop in the price of gasoline it was doomed to disappear.[21] In 1922, Edison worked with Henry Ford to propose a "self-sufficient industrial Arcadia," along the Muscle Shoals river, in Alabama. They planned a hydroelectric dam that would ensure the community's electricity self-sufficiency. Composed of houses, workshops, factories, farmland and cultural centers, The Muscle Shoals Project was rejected by Congress in 1924.[22] The same fate was in store for the electrically autonomous house; despite a handful of successes with the press and professionals, it sank into total oblivion and the hypothesis of its mass production was never brought up. Whereas alternating current was developing nationally on a large scale, for economic and monopoly reasons, the small domestic electric plant was an invention without a future. For Edison, autonomy exclusively concerned electricity, and his timid political stances on governance remained those of a cautious businessman. Frank Lloyd Wright's commitment to energy decentralization from a political and economic viewpoint would be more direct.

Frank Lloyd Wright: the quest for self-sufficiency or the "minimal" connection

Self-sufficiency runs throughout Frank Lloyd Wright's work and thinking. It was a founding element of the American pioneer spirit, that of his Welsh ancestors who conquered the Wisconsin River valley, a heritage to which Wright would consistently lay claim. In 1897, at the request of his schoolteacher aunts, Wright built a windmill in this valley called Romeo and Juliet to pump the water required for the Hillside Home School, which had been designed a few years earlier. This technical equipment demonstrated his striking geometric and structural ability, and the windmill became a landmark of the surrounding countryside (see Figure 33).

In 1910, Wright began the construction of the Taliesin, which was both a home, a studio, a garden and a farm.[23] Located 60 km from the city of Madison, Taliesin was the archetype of the self-sufficient colony where community life and land, worked by the strength and intelligence of people and the machines that modernity had designed to serve them, offered everything needed for life. This 80-hectare "place was to be self-sustaining if not self-sufficient […]. It had to be its own light-plant, fuel yard, transportation and water system." With a spring, a pond and a stream, Taliesin had its own water distribution network.

> The water below the falls thus made was sent by hydraulic ram up to a big stone reservoir built into the higher hill, just behind and above the hilltop garden, to come down again into the fountains and go on down to the vegetable gardens on the slopes below the house.[24]

Moreover, Wright specified the building's eight large stone chimneys were designed to create an atmosphere, rather than meet heating needs; he pointed out that "the whole place is heated by steam and lighted by our own hydro-electric plant" located on the site (see Figure 34).[25]

Despite two successive fires that destroyed many of the buildings, Wright constructed and experimented throughout his life with his convictions on the use of local resources and cooperation. Subsequent to the 1929 financial crisis, he founded the

Figure 33 Frank Lloyd Wright, Romeo and Juliet Windmill (1897)

Taliesin School of Architecture to welcome and train young architectures. Learning and community life were linked: each resident apprentice had a room, set hours for work and study and meals taken with the other students. The young people were manually involved in the construction of new spaces at the college (galleries and workshops), in restoring certain buildings on the site, but also in daily tasks on the farm and in the garden. In Arizona, Taliesin West would be built on the same principles in the late 1930s, as a winter residence and a new structure for the college. Convinced

Figure 34 Frank Lloyd Wright, The Taliesin Small Hydroelectric Power Station (1910)

of the relevance and smooth functioning of the community, Wright wrote: "we could have filled the valley with hopeful young workers and might have started Broadacre City right then and there, ourselves."[26]

In 1932, Wright explained this new lifestyle on the scale of a territorial utopia. Broadacre City proposed the reorganization of the local small industries, farms, schools and leisure activities based on a system of multidirectional communication and energy micro-networks. Technology played a positive role in Broadacre. Wright brought the advances from the cities of New England to it. The telephone, the radio, the car and electricity were the "new slaves" of people and the American master made the decentralization and relocation of resources the foundation of his project. Fully aware of the development and circulation of electricity, he called for local production and ardently defended the decentralization and creation of micro-networks instead of large power plants and complex interconnections.[27] The multiplication of energy points over the landscape contributed to the dissolution of the city: "it is in the nature of universal electrification that the city is nowhere and everywhere."[28] Wright formulated a clear criticism of the scale of the industrial city's infrastructures, in both their spatial and centralizing dimensions. Decentralization was an essential element of his territorial, economic and political strategy. Wright defended the diversification of energy sources (hydraulic, fossil and wind) and the construction of dams and wells on a small scale, like the communities that operated them. The ownership and management of these electricity production units was given over to the citizens; governance modalities, however, were not spelled out.

Wright planned for a limited connection to such a degree that architecture, through the control of thermal effects like passive solar energy, ventilation systems and natural lighting, would strengthen their independence vis-à-vis the networks: "connections will be minimal and very economical."[29] In addition to the economic dimension and the comfort requirement, the network and its infrastructures were an aesthetic challenge: reducing needs and therefore the utility system would be an advantage for the Broadacre landscape, whose beauty would benefit from the "developments in wireless telegraphy which will make poles, trestles and wires a memory of the disappearing city."[30] Broadacre's author compared the pervasiveness of the industrial city's electricity, telephone and telegraph networks to scars left by clumsy scaffolding on a remarkable building. Wright announced that the technical maturity of our civilization would soon make "this violence against the landscape" disappear and that electricity as well as the other cabled systems would rapidly find "avenues of distribution in more conservative and economical channels ."[31] There was a dual ambition in this: reduce dependence, while making the necessary connection as logistically and economically efficient as possible. Wright's concern about utilities was present in most of his projects, but it was at Taliesin and Broadacre that his commitment to self-sufficiency in food, energy and materials was most direct.[32] His personal quest for autonomy was part of this perspective of a democratic ideal; his vision was more territorial than architectural. In the context of the economic instability of the 1920s and 1930s, energy and food resources were a major concern. It was more precisely this question of subsistence that Leberecht Migge would tackle, proposing to reform, according to this vital need, the modern garden.

Leberecht Migge's call: "Everybody Self-sufficient!"

The architect, landscape designer and urban planner Leberecht Migge raised the question of self-subsistence in an astonishingly clear manner in 1918. His position and his writings gave him a very specific place in the history of urbanism and gardens.[33] His works must be understood in the context of Weimar Germany, where the theme of decentralization and the *Heimstätte* ideal were shared by building companies like Gagfah and Gehag, despite the fact that these organisations did not think as much in ecological or "green" terms as Migge. For the launch of the large-scale production of single-home garden cities in 1917, Gagfah distributed brochures presenting "models" of houses for workers and employees. These were:

> [l]inked to the gas, water and electricity distribution system, as well as to the sewer system. The adjoining garden was planted and provided with fruit trees by the contracting authority, which also installed a henhouse of 4 m².[34]

Migge would stress the role of the food-producing garden as a fundamental element of social and economic reform. In his new city-country, nature and technology combined so that housing and gardens would form a coherent and ecological whole, offering the inhabitants total food self-sufficiency. If everyone could be self-sufficient, "then one could be freed from the domination of the capitalist system." This was the idea he presented and developed, in 1918, in the brochure *Jedermann Selbstversorger!* ("Everybody Self-sufficient!"). In another text, with more direct political content, "Der Soziale Garten: Das Grüne Manifest," ("The Social Garden. The Green Manifesto"), published in 1919, under the pseudonym of "Green Spartacus," the author called on Germany to become a federation of small food-growing gardens.[35] According to David Haney, Migge was the first to use the word "green" as a political term. For Migge, this word symbolized abundance, biological cycles and the economic and social health of a new form of human settlement. Without rejecting the historic city, he envisaged an agro-urban fabric in which technological innovations would be within reach of each individual to improve home self-sufficiency. This green policy would be a "third way" – a sort of alternative to capitalism and communism.

Influenced by the English garden city movement, Migge's leanings would be more radical than those of Ebenezer Howard or Raymond Unwin. In *Die Gartenstadt* ("The Garden City") (1910), Migge criticized the garden cities he had seen in England, reproaching them for treating the garden more as a decorative element of a rediscovered nature rather than a springboard for economic and political change. Like many German reformers, Migge had read Peter Kropotkin's *Fields, Factories, and Workshops* (1899), which had demonstrated with a number of figures on production, consumption, export and import, the need to associate agriculture and industry by decentralizing production as much as possible to obtain a relative economic independence. Migge planned this program in his self-sufficient house-gardens.

> In the future: the new family properties will be directly connected with the land. [...] In the future: there will be new residences equipped with pure water wells and dry toilets. [...] In the future: there will be new *Siedlungen* with self-sufficient gardens – in which all the household waste will be reused. [...] In the future: the new *Siedlungen* will be the receptacles of a new and natural lifestyle, on, with and by the land.[36]

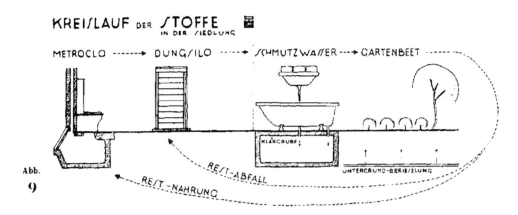

Figure 35 Leberecht Migge, diagram of the recycling system in Ziegbigk-Dessau (1926)

Migge asserted the "regreening" of systems available to everyone, such as the rototiller, the irrigation pump, rainwater collection and dry toilets using compost and fertilizers. In the second edition of *Jedermann Selbstversorger!*, he provided further detail on the ideal garden city. The houses would all be of different sizes and forms, and the possibilities of associations and cooperatives between neighbors were also highlighted. All of the streets and plots would be bordered by fruit trees (see Figure 35).

Migge presented schematic plans of the collective facilities for the group of autonomous houses. In a chapter titled "Heat, wind and water," he discussed the virtues of natural air conditioning, and sunlight and wind for greenhouses. With the right gardening techniques, he anticipated, fertility and climate are created.[37] Migge developed outdoor kitchens and solar bathtubs (see Figure 36). The wastewater from kitchens was collected and filtered like organic waste, which after treatment, could be used to fertilize the gardens. His later diagram, "Tree of Waste" (1923) explained how these systems functioned (see Figure 37).

The natural cycle, from the house to the toilet, can be seen in this diagram. Migge believed that the domestic confines had to be rethought from a biological viewpoint, which had too often been ignored in architectural schemes. The first operating concept of the man who was nicknamed the architect-horticulturalist was the decentralization and increase in autonomy of housing units. The project was highly political: "For the smallest form of government – according to the people's will – the new lifestyle is self-administration."[38] In order to undermine the domination of the centralized capitalist production system, Migge studied the question of land distribution and proposed giving the individual back their role as producer. The architect considered that the relationship of buildings to natural energy systems had become

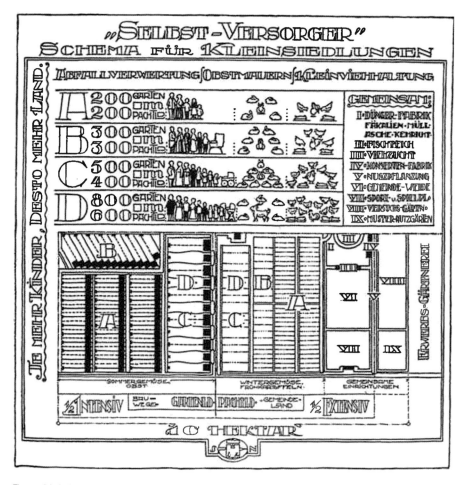

Figure 36 Leberecht Migge, garden plan and nutritional needs (1919)

necrotized. Squeezed into tighter and tighter frames, it became increasingly difficult for the house to produce its own resources and still less treat its waste. If a few of his architect colleagues remained skeptical about his proposals, many modernists such as Adolf Loos, Bruno Taut, Martin Wagner, Hannes Meyer[39] and Ernst May[40] discussed them with interest. Later on, Friedensreich Hundertwasser would lay claim to his legacy.

Migge was associated with the most radical *Siedlungen* projects. His food-producing gardens were planted in Berlin, Frankfurt, Kiel and Breslau. The scale of the garden city was debated with the shift from the *Siedlung* to the *Großsiedlung* (large colony), like the *Großsiedlungen* of Frankfurt for the "new Frankfurt" proposed between 1925 and 1930 under the direction of Ernst May, with Migge's contribution.

Figure 37 Leberecht Migge, "Tree of Waste" (1923)

The kitchen garden, the henhouse and water-collection systems for watering made food self-sufficiency possible, but all these elements were connected to the urban electricity networks and had sewer systems. A compromise emerged between the desire to keep small-scale food self-sufficiency and the desire to rationalize and modernize the home and the city, which would involve the mechanization of construction, the accessibility to housing for everyone and improvements in the circulation and utilities systems.

The optimism of Richard Buckminster Fuller

One of Richard Buckminster Fuller's major focuses in 1928 was disconnection. Driven by an ideal of mobility and buoyed by the criticism of the traditional utilities system, his proposals unquestionably intensified the trajectory of energy autonomy. Fuller's productions and analyses on the subject are a major reference. If his work remained anecdotal for a time, his fame is long established: he is hailed everywhere as an indispensable figure in the history of twentieth-century architecture and technologies.[41] The *Dymaxion House* (1928), the *Mechanical Wing* (1938) and the *Autonomous Living Package* (1948) are essential contributions and doubtlessly the best known in the history of energy autonomy. In *Utopia or Oblivion*, Fuller asserted: "energy distribution networks and industrial infrastructures are infinitely more important than all the politicians in the world."[42] Ever since the autonomous and inexpensive *Dymaxion House* was unveiled in 1928 at the American Institute of Architects as the prototype of the prefabricated house, Fuller continued to question the energy infrastructure (see Figure 38).

Disseminated throughout the United States, Fuller's houses, emblems of the science of universal design, aimed to decentralize the living environment and decongest large metropolises. In 1929, he explained his project:

> My idea was an autonomous house, weighing no more than three tonnes, that could be delivered by air and installed in the most remote places, those that are not connected to highways or that do not have airstrips.[43]

Autonomy was initially associated with mobility and lightness, as in the dirigibles and vessels that fascinated Fuller. In 1927, the largest dirigible ever constructed, the German-built *Graf Zeppelin*, was preparing to cross the Atlantic. In 1969, Sidney Rosen stressed the importance of this event:

> But what was a dirigible? It was really a long floatable house. And like a ship at sea, this floating house was self-sufficient; its power and disposal units were all built-in. Slowly, the plan for a light, movable house began to form in Bucky's mind.[44]

The *Dymaxion House* was described on several occasions by its designer as independent of the utilities network:

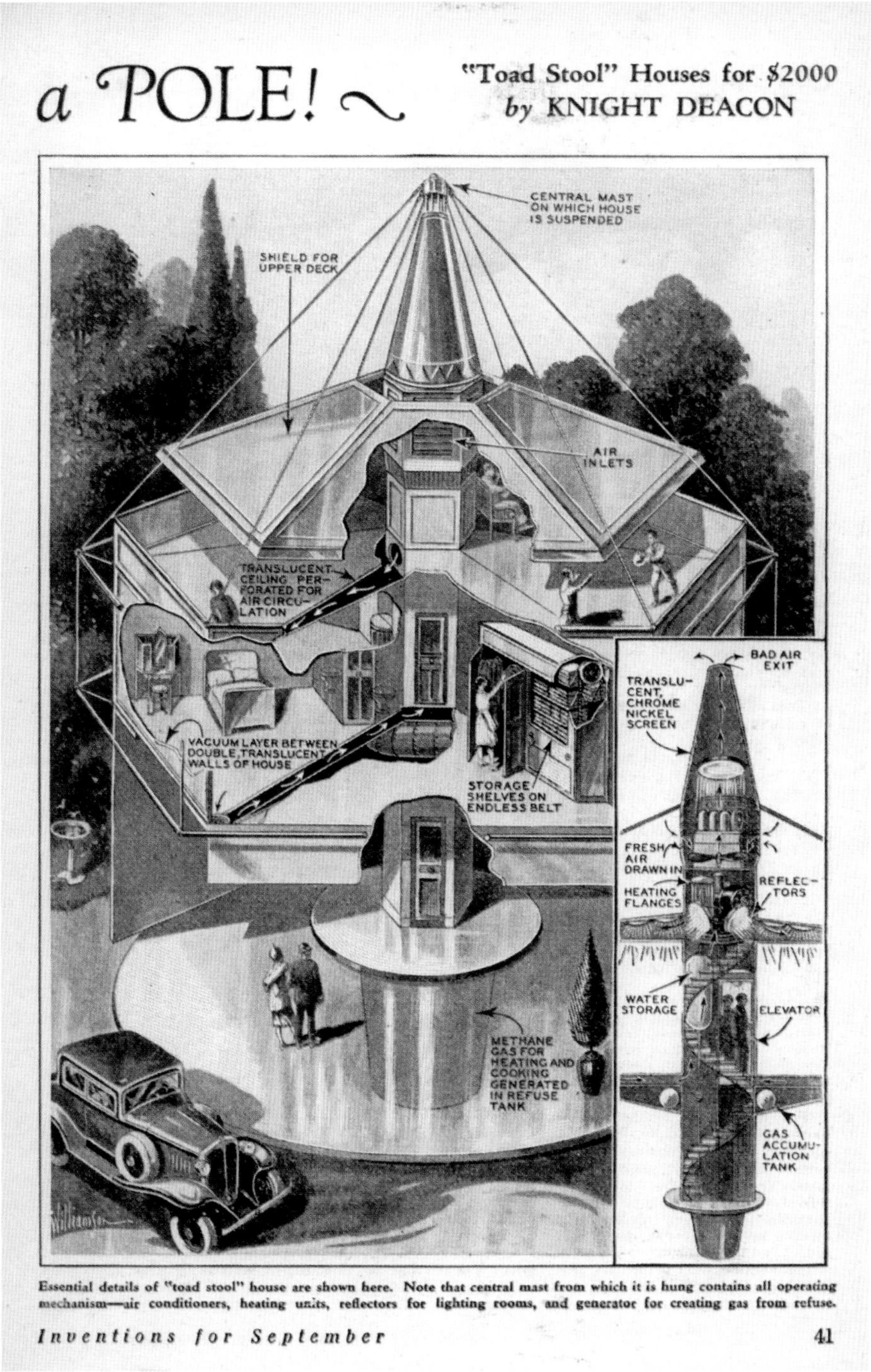

Figure 38 Richard Buckminster Fuller, Dymaxion House (1928)

The techniques used by the navy or the air force – which no longer bother with pipes, cables or roads – why not apply them to land constructions? Like a boat, the house will be almost independent of the hydraulic network.[45]

During a presentation of the *Dymaxion House* in New York in 1929, Fuller detailed the energy system. After the house was delivered, a service assistance group went to the site with its tools and installed a tank with three compartments in the ground: two septic tanks and a fuel tank.[46] The water was filtered, sterilized and recycled, waste was hermetically packed, stored, then sent to the chemical industries, and the toilet functioned without water:

> You press a button, and the air goes out. You press another button, and the air goes in. They pop into air position, just filling their rim like a tire. You will probably use a pho-to-electric system. Instead of pressing a button, perhaps all you will have to do is clap your hands. Mind you, these are full of air, just like the floors, so as to kill sound. That controls, light, sound, heat, etc.[47]

The technical descriptions of the systems that Fuller introduced are incomplete. Apart from the structural and functional aspects, major uncertainties remained as to the energy supply: Fuller lacked clarity. The unit was described as "practically independent" or "semi-autonomous"; his presentations were studded with: "it should be possible," "we imagined," and "probably."[48] The narrative was often told in the future tense. This tentativeness was induced by the limit of the period's technological advances, which made it possible to envisage, but not yet to ensure, the production of a housing unit's total autonomy. Fuller asserted that autonomy was possible and within reach. Later, the war industry and NASA's achievements provided a glimpse of new energy possibilities. However, their architectural applications seemed uncertain: the technologies remained inadequate, and the shift from prospective to industrial production resulted in a certain perplexity within the profession. During his lecture in 1929, the utilities unit aroused doubt and questions remained:

> Mr. Walker: I didn't gather from what you said Mr. Fuller, whether you made your own juice in this house or not?
>
> Mr. Fuller: That was apparently left out. I have one utility unit which has air cross-sections, a water-softener and air-generator all in one unit, which is hung up in that bevel. It is hung sprung from the mast so that the vibration won't go through the house.
>
> Mr. Walker: Is it fully accessible?
>
> Mr. Fuller: Yes. You do generate your own juice. There is much that I have left out as far as the philosophy of the design is concerned, because it is so terribly hot today and it is pretty hard for people to stay here. I could keep on talking for hours on this thing.

[…]

Mr. Walker: I am wondering whether they would dare to go into the production of that house.[49]

Mr Walker was one of those unbelievers who considered these proposals as revolutionary as they were premature. Fuller continued his research in *Mechanical Wing* (1938), abandoning the inhabitable structure to focus on the mechanical core. He built it around a frame that could be attached to and supply any type of structure to make it viable. Reyner Banham praised the daring of this mechanical reduction.[50] The idea of the utilities box was continued with the *Autonomous Living Package* (1948), which opened and unfolded. In 1952, during a lecture on mass production at the Massachusetts Institute of Technology, three *Autonomous Living Package* prototypes were presented by students working under Fuller's direction.[51] Houses 1 and 2 displayed a mechanical core in the center of the dome, around which spaces developed that were rather traditional for Fuller. Inversely, the plan of House 3 showed a version of the *Dymaxion World Map*: here, the cartographic view of the world proposed an inhabitable elevation based on its exploded plan (see Figure 39).

In this last proposal, domestic utilities displayed an idealistic anticipation: the utilities block had disappeared and energy seemed dematerialized. The dome became the energy interface.

It seems that a place which has an annual rainfall or five inches would have a water source which would provide five gallons of water per person per day. So, the dome would be a water shed, deflecting the water to the perimeter where it would be collected for treatment and for storage under pressure. There would be no pipes because it is a pipeless facility. We are merely using a hose, possibly of plastic, which could even be used for watering the yard. The hose could be brought into the kitchen, and it is designed with a facility for heating the water at the point of use. For bathing of detergent and water and washing we would have an atomized pressure spray. It would require only a very small amount of water. When one of these was designed at Chicago, it was found that a whole bath might be taken without leaving a drop of water on the floor. You could just stand in the middle of the bedroom and have a bath. This house is the projected prototype of 20 years hence. It is hard to describe because you almost require a new language. The water source is rainfall. We had information which led us to believe that this might be possible.[52]

Fuller evidently had no fear of anticipation, venturing into issues that went beyond both him and his period. Though autonomy was suggested, it was never totally asserted or technically detailed. In Fuller's presence, the students pointed out that

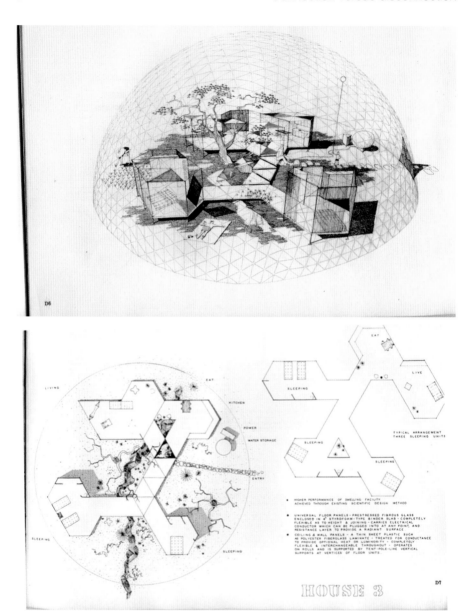

Figure 39 Richard Buckminster Fuller, Autonomous Living Package, House 3 (1952)

if the first project was feasible with the period's technological and industrial means, the other two required a few advances: "they could be expected in the coming years." Fuller proposed more functional uses than what was, at the time, generally considered necessary or simply possible. Despite his enthusiasm and imagination, Fuller therefore had to confront the limits of technology and the pitfalls of the production system.

Notwithstanding the prospective success of most of his proposals, a large part of his work remained theoretical, conceptual and prototypical. With Richard Buckminster Fuller, autonomy would become more precise both architecturally and technically. The *Dymaxion House* nonetheless remained the first model of the autonomous house in the twentieth century.

In 1965, Alexander Pike, who directed a research program on energy autonomy in the United Kingdom from 1971 to 1979, returned to Fuller's contributions and difficulties in an article he wrote on prefabricating the mechanical core:

> In spite of twelve prototypes and the considerable interest shown by the Phelps-Dodge Corporation, this extremely advanced concept exerted a negligible immediate influence – for reasons that have never been adequately ascribed. The project, requiring large and expensive matching dies, was designed essentially for mass-production, and in consequence must have been one of the first building elements of its kind to encounter the vicious cycle of production. Low volume of production means high unit cost; high unit cost means a small market; a small market means a low volume of production. This factor has bedeviled all attempts at prefabrication and mass production up to the present day, and if not the prime reason for the failure of the *Dymaxion Bathroom*, it must have been a strong contribution. Nevertheless, even in this failure it carried the concept of mass production of a Service Unit several stages further.[53]

Pike identified the difficulties of adapting to industry and, inversely, having industry agree to produce buildings that were both experimental (from the energy viewpoint), nascent (from the technical viewpoint) and risky (economically). He believed that the solution was prefabrication: not only because it assumed dismountable and interchangeable components, but because it implied reconciling manufacturers and architects. Pike considered Fuller's most daring projects purely technical exercises, without any explicit development of the application of disconnection. If these proposals were perceived as constituting a technological utopia, Fuller was resistant to being confined in this sole register. Fuller's contribution in *World Design Science Decade* to the study of the economy of scale by way of analyzing resources and their moderate use, his geometric research, and his questioning of governmental energy infrastructures would influence generations of architects and engineers. Fascinated by cutting-edge technologies, Fuller very much updated reflection on the network. An architect of disconnection for the autonomous energy systems that he anticipated, Fuller reformed, in the same dynamic, not only the image of the network, but its accessibility. With the *Dymaxion Air-Ocean World Map* (1954), a world energy and information transmission grid, Fuller imagined the possibility of a connection everywhere on the globe, prefiguring the network in its most contemporary meaning.

Which energy program for the house of the future?

Though futuristic home environments received a great deal of attention shortly after the Second World War, energy innovations that aimed to disconnect from the network were rare. In *Communitas: Means of Livelihood and Ways of Life* (1947), Percival and Paul Goodman formulated a critical querying concerning the technologies that composed the "modern city": "What form of technology and living standards are desirable? [...] What kind of city do you want to live in and what do you want in a postwar house?"[54] The war had modified the production system: technical progress had guaranteed a new efficiency and a better output, and various types of materials had also appeared, enabling experimentation in form and layout for bathroom and kitchen units. The post-Reconstruction house of the future would absorb the period's consumer and futuristic imagination and appear as a housing unit that incorporated all of the new technologies. In the same way as cars, there were dream kitchens, dream bathrooms. But was there dream home equipment, an ideal energy infrastructure?

The most celebrated postwar houses of the future, such as the *House of the Future* by the Smithsons (1956) or the *Monsanto House* (1954–57), offered a few answers. They were heightened by the fear and hopes of the birth of civil nuclear power, whose rapid development occurred in the 1970s. In 1954, the perspective of electronuclear power fostered the hope of energy autonomy in a few countries, but this remained within the sphere of connection: no one talked about a home nuclear micro-reactor yet.

The Suez Crisis of 1956 can be considered the "first" oil crisis, heralding that of 1973. The prospect of the development of electronuclear power opened a new utopian field to architecture and urban planning. Planners were excited about this new source of unlimited energy.

The *House of the Future* by Peter and Alison Smithson bore witness to this search, and revealed a certain program that was independent of the exterior (see Figure 40).[55]

> The food is stored and preserved for a long stay and the rainwater is collected from the roof, allowing inhabitants to eventually cut themselves off [...] All the food is bombarded with gamma rays – an atomic byproduct to kill all bacteria.[56]

Beatriz Colomina demonstrated that each detail could be perceived as a defensive system against exterior threats: noise, pollution, dust, cold, the view, microbes and visitors. It seemed possible to survive for several days using stored food and water. The first plan of the exhibition, ultimately abandoned, envisaged a gigantic artificial

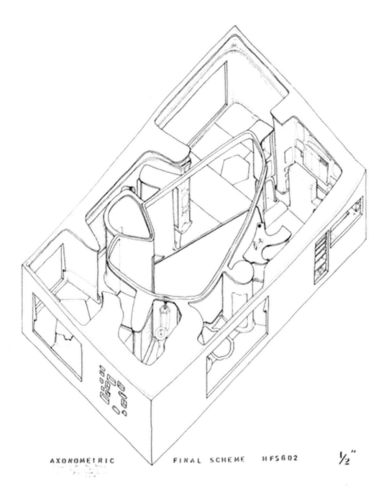

AXONOMETRIC   FINAL SCHEME   HFS602   ½"

Figure 40 Peter and Alison Smithson, The House of the Future (1956)

sun and a cloud hanging above the patio. The only opening seemed to be this patio, which collected water and brought in light. The space was air-conditioned and aseptic; the bathroom was "a room in its own right … and its continuously spinning self-digesting unit needs no flushing mechanism"; the bathtub and the windows were self-cleaning.[57] Energy autonomy was in no way set out as a principle, but the maximum control of the environment, the omnipresence of technology, the formal disconnection with the exterior, the multiplication of automatisms and the host of survival elements like food stores, rainwater collection, sun and light tubes, were major features of the proposal. This desire for regulation was conveyed by a gradual transfer of military technologies to the home setting, markedly transforming the private sphere. However, if the form, size, materials, layout and relationship to the exterior were questioned, the domestic core remained largely unchanged and dependent on the energy infrastructure. In the description of the Smithsons' project, it was pointed out that an atomic power station built nearby would produce all the energy needed for a comfortable life.

The same energy system is hinted at in the *Monsanto House*, designed by the architects of the laboratory of the Massachusetts Institute of Technology. Built on the Disneyland site in California, this house demonstrated the potential of the plastic and futuristic qualities of an environment in which the automatons and mobile equipment of the "atomic kitchen" could be seen. The flyer that accompanied it describes the project:

> Visit the Atomic Kitchen with its revolutionary microwave oven and ultrasonic dishwasher. Go through the two children's bedrooms, one for the boy of the future, and the other for the girl of the future, with their shared bathroom, to access the master bedroom and its bathroom. Finish your visit in the elegant lounge, with its giant TV wall screens.[58]

This was how Disneyland presented its attraction Tomorrowland, open to the public in 1957, highlighting nuclear energy in the line of its publication *Our Friend the Atom*.[59]

The enthusiastic reception of the Smithsons' *House of the Future*, the *Monsanto House* or even Ionel Schein's "all-plastic" house revealed a fascination with new materials, unconventional industrial aesthetics, flexibility, technical efficiency and the power of the atom. If the intuitions of a few early autonomy advocates on solar or wind potential were announced, nuclear power was anticipated as the domestic energy source of the future: "electricity should be regarded as the source of power and heat to link up with the development of atomic power stations."[60] Alexander Pike would first predict in 1956, continuing in the 1970s, that "the autonomous housing project requires a rigorous analysis of the network and a consistent development of its specific technologies. The autonomous house – it takes at least forty years to see it land in the history of architecture! It is too early. No one is ready today to support such an adventure."[61]

Most architects and engineers in the 1950s were pro-connection. Autonomy was a technological narrative with blurry contours. Initially, the house was autonomous in terms of energy – without any link to a distribution network – and this principle historically comprised the dominant form of all human housing throughout the world. However, through a slow germination of ideas, challenges and means, this principle became a project in the period's specificities and precise spatial-temporal coordinates played an important role. This concept gained ground when urban energy infrastructures became the widespread supply point in the urban territories of the northern hemisphere. In other words, it was in contrast to a dwelling that was linked to and

Figure 41 Heinz Haber, *Our Friend the Atom* (1956)

dependent on the network that the autonomy project began to assert itself. It was
a project of our modern and contemporary societies, as was shown by the desire to
adapt the technologies used by the navy and aviation to architecture. Architects often
encourage their profession to take hold of new tools to solve the problems of their
time. At the end of the Second World War, it was industrial production and forms,
new materials and the aesthetics of the engineer that enabled housing to be renewed
and the *mass-produced house* to be envisaged. But if the autonomous building seemed
to be a creation of the machine age, it was in opposition to the technological renewal
project: modifying its relationship to energy and inventing a mechanical core that
used local energies, in order to create a new type of house that could autonomously
provide essential necessities. This twofold movement revealed the complexity of the
resolutely new program.

Etzler, Edison and Fuller's projects were not entirely successful, but they did comprise a sort of energy "avant-garde" warning against dependency on fossil energies and
calling for the development of other systems. Despite their number and potential, no
alternative was encouraged by the public administration.[62] The technical development
of energy systems that would enable a house or a community to be autonomous did
not seem ready, and research on the subject was not encouraged for several reasons.
Firstly, efforts were focused on optimizing a symbolically, technically and economically promising structure – that of the network – which was henceforth a priority.
Concerns were concentrated on universalizing a model whose efficiency had already
been proved. The network represented incommensurable progress for civilization.
Moreover, the abundance of fossil energy resources enabled large-scale development
without any misgivings. The national desire to centralize and unify industrial and
domestic consumption on the large scale therefore overshadowed research on other
energy sources. The dazzling success of the world fairs were a symbol of the advent
of a technological society full of promise. The technical enthusiasm inspired by the
potential of ever more powerful electric power plants activated the inebriation of
the Western world for the accumulation and concentration of the power of energy.
Immediately after the Second World War, consumerism and the productivist boom
generated an acceleration of confidence; urban sprawl, the deployment and reinforcement of the existing networks and an overconsumption of energy were a sign of the
times, much more than a questioning of the latter through energy savings.

Notes

1   Panos Mantziaras, "Autogouvernement, patriotisme citadin et planification urbaine," in
    Panos Mantziaras, *La Ville-paysage: Rudolf Schwarz et la dissolution des villes* (Geneva:
    MétisPresses, 2008).

2 Alain Milhou, "Sufficientia (les notions d'autosuffisance et de dépendance dans la pensée politique espagnole au XVIᵉ siècle: de la Castille des *comuneros* au Pérou colonial)," *Mélanges de la Casa de Velazquez*, vol. 17, no. 1 (1981), pp. 105–145.

3 Henri Laufenburger, "L'autarchie allemande et les tendances du deuxième plan quadriennal," *Politique étrangère*, vol. 1, no. 6 (1936), pp. 72–79.

4 Catherine Maumi, *Usonia ou le mythe de la ville-nature américaine* (Paris: Editions de la Villette, 2009), p. 33.

5 *Ibid.*, p. 49.

6 Letter addressed to James Jay in 1809. Cf. John P. Foley, *The Jeffersonian Cyclopedia: A Comprehensive Collection of the Views of Thomas Jefferson* (New York: Russell & Russell, [1967] 1990), p. 24.

7 Pierre-Joseph Proudhon, *Théorie de la propriété* (Paris: L'Harmattan, [1866] 1997). However, even though he supported land ownership (including the right to inherit), he militated for property to be distributed in a more equalitarian manner and that it be limited in size in order to be really used by individuals, families and workers associations.

8 Peter Kropotkin, *La Conquête du pain* (Paris: Sextant, [1892] 2006), p. 79.

9 *Ibid.*

10 Panos Mantziaras, in his work *La Ville-paysage*, returns historically to dispersion as a project approach and spatial strategy questioning its ideological foundations.

11 John Adolphus Etzler, *The Paradise Within the Reach of All Men, Without Labor, by Powers of Nature and Machinery* (New York: Kessinger Publishing, [1833] 2007).

12 *Ibid.*

13 Cf. Rouillard, "Utopie."

14 Henry David Thoreau, "Paradise to be (re)gained," *The United States Magazine and Democratic Review*, November 1843.

15 John Adolphus Etzler, *The New World; or Mechanical System to Perform the Labours of Man and Beast by Inanimate Powers, That Cost Nothing, for Producing and Preparing the Substances of Life* (Philadelphia, PA: C. F. Stollmeyer, 1841), p. 27.

16 *Ibid.*, p. 56.

17 Thoreau, "Paradise to be (re)gained."

18 Theodore Waters, "Many electrical problems now solved by Edison's discovery," *The Atlanta Constitution*, 25 August 1901, p. 5. Cf. also "Edison's new battery," *The Atlanta Constitution*, 27 May 1901, p. 4.

19 "Edison's latest marvel the electric country house," *New York Times*, 15 September 1912, p. 9.

20 *Ibid.*

21 Edwin Black, *Internal Combustion: How Corporations and Governments Addicted the World to Oil and Derailed the Alternatives* (New York: St Martin's Press, 2006).

22 Reynold M. Wik, *Henry Ford and Grass-Roots America* (Ann Arbor, MI: University of Michigan Press, 1972).

23 Frank Lloyd Wright, *An Autobiography* (New York: Duell, Sloan and Pearce, 1932), p. 155.

24 *Ibid.*

25 *Ibid.*, p. 526.

26 *Ibid.*, p. 575.

27 Frank Lloyd Wright, *The Disappearing City* (New York: William Farquhar Payson, 1932). Republished in Bruce Brooks Pfeiffer (ed.), *The Essential Frank Lloyd Wright: Critical Writings on Architecture* (Princeton, NJ: Princeton University Press, 2008). See the chapter "Power Units," p. 257.

28 *Ibid.*

29 *Ibid.*, p. 246.

30 *Ibid.*, p. 52.

31 31 *Ibid.*

32 Let us cite, in particular, the Imperial Hotel of Tokyo in 1923, in which the water conduits and electricity cables were placed in independent trenches and not built into the hotel. The basin and its water collection system also played a major role. Let us also mention the commissioning of the San Marcos tourist resort in the Arizona desert in 1926, which raised the question of resources in the desert. In view of the study of the San Marcos construction site, Wright and his team set up their work camp on the site: Ocatillo, which became a full-fledged project. It was a light wood and canvas structure that had several individual cabins and a very large workshop space. Wright vaunted this retreat and its self-sufficiency in the heart of the desert with a generator and gasoline lamps. The 1929 crisis would lead to the suspension of the San Marcos project.

33 Cf. David H. Haney, "Leberecht Migge (1881–1935) and the modern garden in Germany," (PhD thesis, University of Pennsylvania, 2005) and *When Modern Was Green: Life and Work of Landscape Architect Leberecht Migge* (Abingdon: Routledge, 2010).

34 Christine Mengin, *Guerre du toit et modernité architecturale: Loger l'employé sous la République de Weimar* (Paris: Publications de la Sorbonne, 2007), p. 246.

35 Leberecht Migge, *Jedermann Selbstversorger!* (Jena: Diederichs, 1918) and "Der soziale Garten: Das grüne Manifest," republished in *Die Tat* (Berlin: Gebr. Mann Verlag, [1919] 2000), p. 56.

36 Migge, "Der soziale Garten," p. 67.

37 Migge, *Jedermann Selbstversorger!*, p. 20.

38 *Ibid.*, p. 19.

39 Hannes Meyer, an actor in the agrarian and urban reform movement and a great admirer of Migge, stressed the introduction of the vital processes idea for home economics. He would constantly uphold his commitments. He would return to the idea of function, in such a way that the "machine à habiter" was paired with a "biological system meeting

material and spiritual needs," and stated: "Building means organizing the vital processes in a well-reasoned manner. Building, as a technical process, is therefore only a partial process." Hannes Meyer, "Construire," *Bauhaus*, no. 4 (1928), translated in Ulrich Conrads, *Programmes et manifestes de l'architecture du XXe siècle* (Paris: Editions de la Villette, 1996), p. 144.

40 After his involvement in the establishment of the new Frankfurt in the 1930s, Ernst May went to Russia with his team to work on the new cities program. He then flew to Africa, to Tanganyika (today Tanzania) and Kenya, where he established a self-sufficient farming colony. See Kai K. Gutschow, "'Das Neue Afrika': Ernst May's 1947 Kampala Plan as cultural program," in Fassil Demissie (ed.), *Colonial Architecture and Urbanism in Africa: Intertwined and Contested Histories* (London: Ashgate, 2009).

41 Cf. the exhibition "Buckminster Fuller: Starting with the universe" at the Whitney Museum, New York, 26 June to 21 September 2008; Federico Neder, *Buckminster Fuller* (Gollion: Infolio, 2008); Federico Neder, *Les Maisons de Fuller: La Dymaxion House de R. Buckminster Fuller et autres machines à habiter* (Gollion: Infolio, 2009).

42 Richard Buckminster Fuller, *Utopia or Oblivion: The Prospects for Humanity* (Toronto: Bantam Books, 1969), p. 5.

43 Robert Snyder (ed.), *Richard Buckminster Fuller: An Autobiographical Monologue/Scenario* (New York: St Martin's Press, 1980), p. 83.

44 Sidney Rosen, *Wizard of the Dome: R. Buckminster Fuller, Designer for the Future* (New York: Little, Brown & Company, 1969), p. 53.

45 Snyder, *Richard Buckminster Fuller*, p. 71.

46 Richard Buckminster Fuller, "Dymaxion House. Meeting, Architectural League, New York, Thursday, July 9, 1929," in Joachim Krausse and Claude Lichtenstein (eds), *Richard Buckminster Fuller: Your Private Sky, Discourse* (Baden: Lars Müller Publishers, 1999), p. 94.

47 *Ibid.*, p. 93.

48 On the use of the term "semi-autonomous," cf. Richard Buckminster Fuller, "International Symposium on Architecture. Mexico, October 10, 1963," in Krausse and Lichtenstein, *Richard Buckminster Fuller*, p. 271.

49 Buckminster Fuller, "Dymaxion House. Meeting," p. 100.

50 Reyner Banham, "A clip-on architecture," *Design Quarterly*, vol. 35, no. 63 (1965), in Alain Guiheux (ed.), *Archigram* exhibition catalogue (Paris: Centre Pompidou), pp. 197–200.

51 The primary objective of this encounter was, as Carl Koch (architect at Arcon) underlined in his introductory speech, to weave a link between the world of architecture and that of construction ("Housing: Mass Produced," lecture given on 14 January 1952, published by the Massachusetts Institute of Technology, the Albert Farwell Bemis Foundation and the School of Architecture).

52   Richard Buckminster Fuller and John Rauma, speech presenting House 3 during the lecture "Housing: Mass Produced."

53   Alexander Pike, "Product analysis 5: Heart units," *Architectural Design*, vol. 36, no. 4 (1966), pp. 206–211.

54   Percival Goodman and Paul Goodman, *Communitas: Means of Livelihood and Ways of Life* (Chicago, IL: University of Chicago Press, 1947).

55   Beatriz Colomina, "Unbreathed air," in Dirk van den Heuvel and Max Risselada (eds), *Peter and Alison Smithson: From the House of the Future to a House of Today* (Rotterdam: 010 Publishers, 2004).

56   Peter Smithson and Alison Smithson, "The House of the Future," in *Daily Mail Ideal Home Exhibition* (London: Olympia, 1956), p. 99.

57   Colomina, "Unbreathed air," p. 68.

58   Monsanto, "Plastic home of the future," flyer accompanying the attraction, 1957.

59   Heinz Haber, *Our Friend The Atom* (Walt Disney Productions, Buryn Books, 1956).

60   Alexander Pike, "Better homes, space utilisation and mass-production" (1956), graduation paper, London County Council School of Building, p. 98, AAP.

61   Nona Pike and Peter Cavanagh, interview with Fanny Lopez in Cambridge in February 2007.

62   Cf. Lewis Mumford, *Technics and Civilization* (New York: Harcourt, Brace & Company, 1934); Debeir, Deléage and Hémery, *Les Servitudes de la puissance*; Black, *Internal Combustion*.

3 Toward energy emancipation

In the early 1950s, the "externalization" of pipes and conduits became widespread, making it difficult to distinguish between what was mechanical and what was structural. The exaggeration of mechanical visibilities became a deliberate choice, a decorative or obvious element. What the Modern movement had generally removed from view would appear in the foreground and explode in a spectacular manner. And it was the megastructure projects in the 1960s that would take this technical rhetoric to its summit. The city was to be apprehended in terms of networks, energy or information connections. In *Megastructure: Urban Features of the Recent Past* (1976), Reyner Banham explained the resonance of the city-machine analogy, stressing that:

> As against the International Style's classicizing view of technology and machinery as neat smooth regular solids of anonymous aspect, the younger megastructuralists clearly saw technology as a visually wild richness of piping and wiring and struts and cat-walks and bristling radar antennae and supplementary foul tanks and landing-pads all carried in exposed lattice frames, NASA-style.[1]

A certain number of megastructuralists played on the register of a rapidly evolving postindustrial architecture, the leaders being the members of Archigram, whose machinist extrapolations would influence several generations. Though many megastructures were built, for Banham, the Centre Pompidou remained the ultimate example of the decade that saw the birth of this concept. The optical manifestations and the interplay of energy circulation signage marked a significant turning point. Despite this formal fragmentation, the urban energy network had very few detractors. From a technological viewpoint, the megastructure would mostly develop along the lines of the acclaim for progress and connection in the twentieth century.

In the late 1960s, a wave of nihilism and dystopia triggered a mutation in this progress. In the context of this widespread crisis, the idea of nomadism emerged. Mobility would challenge the possibilities of a change in the habitat on the vertical, horizontal or territorial energy grid. A first deterritorialization occurred – it was the famous "twilight of the sedentaries."[2] But this disappearance of architecture to the benefit of the network would make the question of the dependence on and illusion of disconnection rise to the surface. A few years before the 1973 oil crisis, its apprehension would lead to the disfavor of postwar technological optimism, promoting an unprecedented boom in so-called alternative and renewable energies and bringing about a second deterritorialization: total energy autonomy.

Mobility and connection

In the second half of the 1960s, an experimental shift from infrastructure-architecture to territory-infrastructure and vice versa could be seen: the "magical territory" on which the radicals, Archigram, then Archizoom and Superstudio, would push architecture as far as its disintegration.[3] The desire for nomadism in the 1960s would reveal certain constraints regarding the energy supply network. From its predominance to its disappearance, Reyner Banham, Yona Friedman, Archigram, Archizoom and Superstudio questioned the functionality as much as the visibility of the infrastructure, playing on the possibility of it erupting from the underground to create an architectural structure or, on the contrary, on its concealment in the thickness of the nomadic territory. The connection question was raised in each case, and when energy autonomy was raised, it was first envisaged as a solution to accentuate mobility.

In the late 1950s, Yona Friedman's analyses of the network and his preliminary research on the ideal infrastructure-architecture underscored this issue. In *L'Architecture mobile: Vers une cité conçue par ses habitants*, Friedman introduced the subject with the definition of infrastructure. It was the technical elements of a city needed for its inhabitants' daily life: distribution and evacuation networks, circulation networks and bearing structures. The inhabitants only used "equipment *connected* to these networks, that is: electrical appliances, bathroom fixtures, etc. The application of the mobility principle envisaged for the rigidity of the infrastructure (neutral elements) and the detachability of the equipment connected to it."[4] The consideration of the technical dimension of the city and the connection as a perquisite to the architecture was unusual. Friedman detailed his spatial infrastructure: a three-dimensional grid, on piles, above the ground surface. The project was renowned: housing, offices and other buildings were inserted into this structure's voids, in the raised zone (see Figures 42a–42c).

"Heavy uses," like traffic circulation and industry, occupied the ground surface under the grid. The spread out piles contained the circulations and the vertical connections such as pipes, elevators and staircases. The structure of the spatial city was the infrastructure. What these considerations implied for Friedman was that the architects' task was nothing other than the construction of infrastructures, including

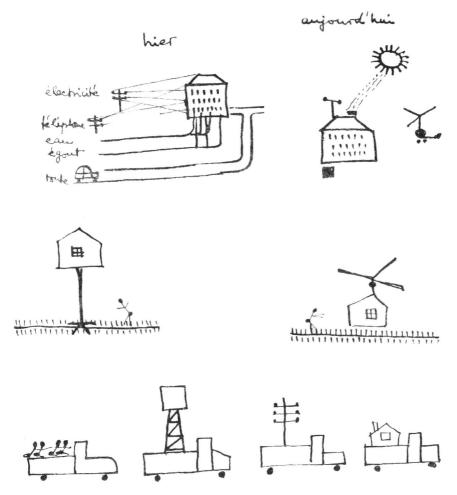

Figure 42 Yona Friedman, "Ville Spatiale" (1959)

the energy network. The choice of the infrastructure met criteria that corresponded to the possible variations in how the space was filled and the admissible number of breakdowns. In this indeterminate urbanism, the inhabitants created the architecture and the city; the architects and urban planning consultants have had to build the ideal infrastructure. The spatial city was organized according to its distributions and the major architectural task seemed to be the orchestration of the network. Its pre-eminence in Friedman was quite original. Moreover, it was this importance given to the network that triggered the need for its re-evaluation, leading thirty years later to the autarkic city-states of the modernized peasant civilization.

The spatial city called for a reorganization of certain urban planning methods and techniques. In 1957, Friedman described how new technical processes could provide flexibility and the construction of temporary urban areas, while avoiding the demolitions caused by their periodic fragmentation. He notably envisaged techniques that could move the water and energy supply networks, the sewers and circulation, without degrading the land and without causing the losses incurred by demolition. If the "heavy" networks freeze the structure of the city, let us note that Friedman imagined disconnection in 1958.

> Only the new techniques in physics and chemistry will meet the requirements of dispersion: autonomous house with photoelectric cells eliminating the need for conduits; overhead circulation or circulation on an air cushion eliminating the problem of roads, etc. [...] The problem that is raised is that of managing to find a technical solution that will free the home from these networks, so that it remains in a certain way free of any obstacle blocking its transformation. [...] The application of this attempt will have absolutely unpredictable repercussions on the future of cities. The inhabitants, no longer being dependent on supply (and circulation) networks that force them to group together, can be dispersed.[5]

Interacting with its environment, the house is freed from its dependencies and seems to float as lightly as a helicopter. The ground is spared by a perched or suspended architecture. The autonomous house is easily dismountable, transformable, movable, which is impossible with the "traditional" utilities system.

Friedman considered immobility, fixity, the weight and cumbersomeness of utilities as obstacles to the transformation of cities and architecture. By minimizing the occupation of the land, the inhabitants could consequently be dispersed and/or grouped together without leaving any trace. These new "supply techniques" would be ideal for straddled structures and would encourage the construction of temporary urban areas. Friedman wanted to free the home from its networks, and in his first theses autonomy was envisaged as a solution for dispersion. The question of technologies in general, and the evocation of energy autonomy, were a decisive point for mobile urbanism. Disconnection would facilitate both nomadism, adaptability and the temporary nature of constructions, since less surface space would be taken on the ground. Autonomy, in Friedman, would take a more radical turn a few years later, becoming a vehicle for economic, social and political upheavals. In *L'Architecture mobile*, it remained secondary to his theses on democratization, participation, spontaneous urbanism and mobility. The conceptual importance of his infrastructure-architecture would be unanimously acknowledged. It was part of this primordial shift from the cell to the capsule, stressed by Reyner Banham in his article "Stocktaking" (1960), in which he introduced the idea of the "clip-on".

From the "clip-on" to the "plug-in"

For Banham, Ionel Schein's mobile hotel cabin in 1956 crystallized this shift. It was so well equipped that it "became almost an independent living capsule that could have been put into orbit."[6] In succeeding the cell, the capsule would raise new assembly problems, questioning the layout of utilities and the connection to the network.[7]

> In larger structures room-units might be carried in an independent frame, but in either case the result should be that service-rooms, which needs to be connected to the public mains, might be treated as expendable clip-on components, thus obviating some of the difficulties of the Appliance House Project, which runs the risk of degenerating into a series of display-niches for an ever-changing array of domestic machinery.[8]

Though it was specified that Schein's hotel rooms were to be attached to an energy structure, no details were provided. It was Banham who raised the question of these units' energy supply. He would develop the "clip-on" idea, which he contrasted to that of the "plug-in" in his article, "A clip-on architecture" (1963):

> The Smithson and the Schein Coulon motel unit are more in the nature of a clip-together architecture, but as soon as they begin to be clipped together they raise a problem which neatly turns the clip-on concept inside out.[9]

Banham compared the clip-on to an outboard motor. It was a small mechanical package that transformed an undifferentiated structure into something with a function or purpose, "any old shack or hole in the ground into a habitable dwelling." This clip-on was none other than Fuller's *Mechanical Wing* or the *Transportable Standard-of-Living Package* that Banham developed a few years later: a mechanical unit that could be clipped onto an inflatable structure, a dome or a shell. This ontological decomposition (a mechanical core and a structure) clearly appeared in his celebrated article "A home is not a house" (1965), illustrated by a series of drawings by François Dallegret (see Figure 43).

Anatomy of a Dwelling could be compared to the complexity of the intestinal system:

> When your house contains such a complex of piping, flues, ducts, wires, lights, inlets, outlets, ovens, sinks, refuse disposers, hi-fi reverberators, antennae, conduits, freezers, heaters – when it contains so many services that the hardware could stand up by itself without any assistance from the house, why have a house to hold it up? When the cost of all

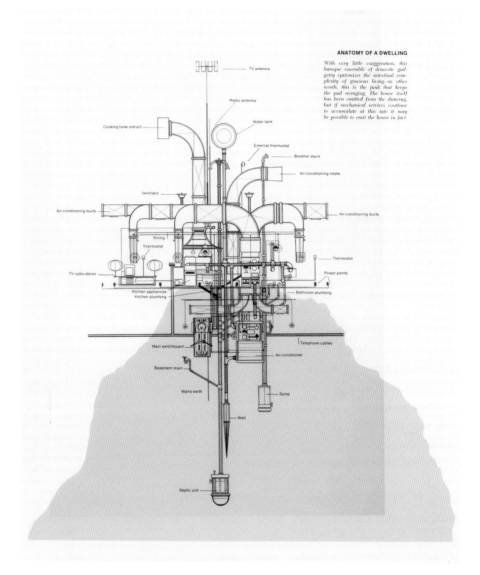

ANATOMY OF A DWELLING

With very little exaggeration, this baroque ensemble of domestic gadgetry epitomizes the intestinal complexity of gracious living—in other words, this is the junk that keeps the pad swinging. The house itself has been omitted from the drawing, but if mechanical services continue to accumulate at this rate it may be possible to omit the house in fact.

Figure 43 François Dallegret, "Anatomy of Dwelling" (1965)

this tackle is half of the total outlay (or more, as it often is) what is the house doing except concealing your mechanical pudenda from the stares of folks on the sidewalks?[10]

The "weight" of home economics was a major preoccupation. Following Fuller, Banham reduced architecture to its utilities, baring the mechanical core; he thus conveyed the victory of technologies over both architecture, nature and the climate.[11] With this lightened home equipment, architecture was secondary. But if the living space and mechanical package units were accumulated, individual pieces of equipment were stacked.

This capsule concept and the proliferation of small units would deeply modify the relationship to infrastructures. If the clip-on illustrated equipment that could be hung – an autonomous energy baggage – the idea of the plug-in put forward the opposite proposal that inhabitable units were charged and connected to a supply structure-system: "Too late and unresolved, Europe had reinvented the American mobile home,"[12] Banham asserted as to this possibility of inverted connection. Though Friedman's spatial city heralded this concept, *Plug-in City*, developed between 1962 and 1964, would become the image par excellence of this urban area-connection. Warren Chalk, Michael Webb, Dennis Crompton, Ron Herron, Peter Cook and David Greene reinvented a network architecture by redeploying the underground system above ground. All sorts of energy sources that supplied the secondary units circulated within this structure (see Figure 44).

A crane at the top supplied a tube system with open "maws," which redistributed the energy needed for the networked city in various reservoirs. Energy was no longer transmitted between an infrastructure and the building because, in Friedman, it was a building-infrastructure. The structure-connection concept continued with the *Plug-in Dwelling* (1965) and the *Free Time Node Trailer Cage* (1967). In the former, bathrooms, kitchens, bedrooms and different types of facade elements were attached and connected to a vertical energy grid; in the latter, trailers were recharged at the connection points. Archigram pursued the interpretation of the city as an energy and media link. In *Computer City* (1964) as in *Instant City* (1968), the networks were predominant (see Figure 45).

The units were unhooked whereas the conduits of the large frames infiltrated the ground, beginning a new conquest of the land and reinventing connection. The technological optimism of the 1960s offered the narrative of a ground-nourishing fabric, a continuum of utility points, energy and information hubs where new architectural vehicles strolled. But if these objects guaranteed a breakaway, autonomy here went hand in hand with structural mobility. Energy independence had not yet laid claim to a position as such in terms of its environmental and/or economic perspectives. The path from the cell to the capsule had, however, brought about a radical change in the relationship between edifice and infrastructures. The mobility and supply question took on a great deal of importance.

The electric Eldorado

Fascinated by mass production, technology and science fiction, the experiments conducted in the early 1960s in England playfully asserted architectural negation

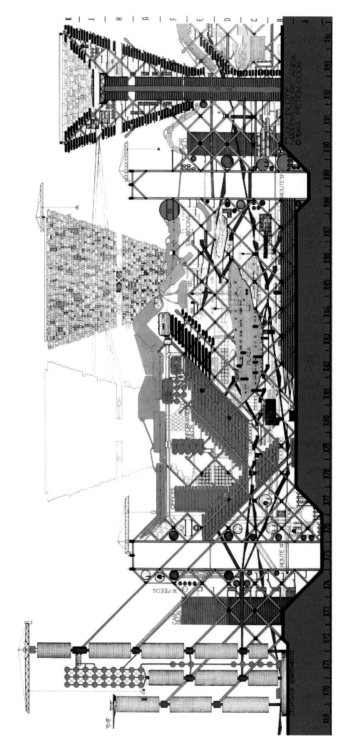

Figure 44 Plug-In City, section, Max Pressure Area, Peter Cook (1964)

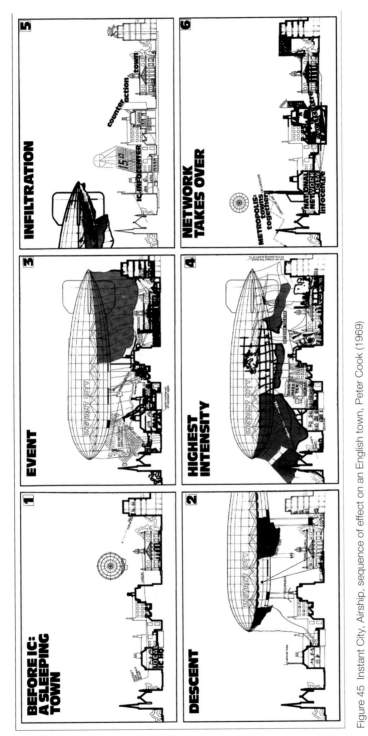

Figure 45 Instant City, Airship, sequence of effect on an English town, Peter Cook (1969)

and total mobility: "With apologies to the master, the house is an appliance for carrying with you, the city is a machine for plugging into.[13] In a utopian tradition, Archigram projected architecture in a liberating technological narrative, taking the network question to its apogee. In "Territoire magique," Dominique Rouillard provides an account of the transformation and metamorphosis process in Archigram, shifting from the *Plug-in* to the *Living Pod*, from the *Rokplug-Logplug* to the *LAWUN* (Locally Available World Unseen Networks): "Only the technological networks that a number of architects, first among them Archigram, wished to integrate or conceal, in a rediscovered, reinvented or reflected nature, will subsist."[14] There was a total deterritorialization of thinking regarding the inhabitable structure: home equipment was carried on a person's back. *Living Pod* (1965), *Cushicle* (1966) and *Suitaloon* (1968) could be regularly recharged on the innervated surface. Mobility was radicalized. The territory became the place for the proliferation of industrialized modules. The excitement that these mobile units aroused was illustrated, among others, by the publication of *Clip-Kit: Studies in Environmental Design* (1966)[15] With *Rokplug-Logplug* (1968), David Greene enhanced the connection; the infrastructures were invisible and integrated into the natural environment, taking the form of a tree trunk or a rock (see Figure 46).

These charging points offered direct and alternating current, a cold water inlet, as well as an international information network: all that was needed was to place

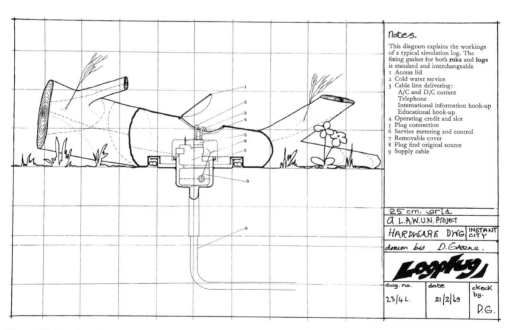

Figure 46 Logplug, diagram explaining the workings of a typical simulation log, David Greene (1968)

one's order and insert a credit card to activate the connection. The idea of the territory-oasis was magnified with LAWUN. The energy was available and the electrical connections came out of the ground. "Life is no longer linked to a place but to what you can do there: all you need is to be able to plug in."[16] This project recalled the principle of Fuller's *Dymaxion Air-Ocean World Map*, which presented a global information and energy transmission network that enabled the simultaneous connection to the four corners of the earth, reviving Tesla's dream of free energy. With Archigram, the territory contained and became the infrastructure at every point. This is what Crompton called the "Piped Environment":

> It seems to have all started with Bell, Baird, Faraday, and the rest, although I doubt if they thought of it in this way. What they did was to discover the facilities which have led to the Piped Environment. The immediacy of electrical response gave independence from the sun for light and heat and freed up many other situations in which the time-lag of reaction had become an embarrassing restriction.[17]

In a carefree shared energy scenario, the network became the mediator of every spatial reality: the multiplication of circulations and its branches, a mobility accelerator. As Georges-Hubert de Radkowski defined it in 1967, it was the "twilight of sedentaries." The anthropologist observed the appearance of a continuous network space that was replacing the former space centered on sedentaries:

> Our reality is inserted in this network space, whose links are constituted by all the communication paths – land, sea, air, roads as well as electric or telephone cables, even Hertzian waves – transporting people, goods (among them energy) and information. It no longer represents an autonomous unit, a center inserted into the surrounding countryside, but a specific condensation zone around intersecting points: 'interchanges' – of the said communication paths. 'Inhabiting' no longer designates here residing but – virtually or in reality – communicating (whose best-known aspect is circulating). The city-dweller-resident is a 'subscriber' to these nodal points of the network space, his residence a connection to this network.[18]

By definition, the space of the large network makes local autonomies difficult: the connection became a lifestyle. This analysis also sheds light on and explains the accentuation of the nomadic condition. Furthermore, it marked a change in direction from Rouge's text "L'organisation de l'espace et les réseaux." Radkowski diagnosed a civilization crisis linked to the demographic explosion, territorial mutations, the disappearance of nearby farmlands and the enormous development of the network space. For the author, the nomadic era clearly heralded the "end of the architecture" that Fuller and Archigram had addressed. To explain the twilight of sedentaries, he argued that the city is agriculture's daughter, the center of the agricultural space on which the existence of city-dwellers is dependent. Today, rural zones no longer produce food and the urban milieu compensates for this loss through the substitution of an international food-processing and distribution industry. This has led to the radical inversion of the independence relationship:

> [T]he primitive city entirely depended, for its subsistence, on its environment, without the latter depending on it; today, it is the countryside that entirely depends on factors whose the original milieu is the urban space.[19]

Radkowski determined the replacement of the spatial contiguity and balance between the city and the countryside by the space of the network. The fragmentation of the rural sector and its subsistence economy encouraged mobility. First, the acceleration of the installation of networks, in particular the road network, opened up the area to the circulation of merchandise and goods. Next came the detachment of city-dwellers from farmland and the transfer of a local food-producing space to a limitless, totally unrestricted consumption space that promoted nomadism: wherever one goes, there will always be an energy or food supply point. The countryside became the "terminus" of the urbanized space, an area for relaxation and amenities, while the city became the transforming force of the agricultural space that it used and synthesized. It was the capture of resources and the reinvention of a synthetic nature with and by the network. Urban civilization, after having been freed from the hold of the surrounding milieu, was in the process of "smothering it between its links," wrote Radkowski, who predicted the end of architecture, the city, and perhaps even nature.[20] Nature was in fact mistreated by technological turbulences, notably by the radicals. At Archigram, nature was artificial or recreated – the result of this mutant nature can be seen in issue 9 of their eponymous magazine (see Figure 47).

The disappearance of the natural was even more visible in the artificial environment of the Italians. But if the modern nomad could do without architecture and nature, they needed "utility points" more than ever. For Archigram, technology was progress; it was politically neutral.

The illusion of a disconnection

Though deterritorialization seemed to have been reached by absolute geographic liberty, energy dependence persisted. The nomad still needed connection to inherited infrastructures. David Greene warned: "A motorized environment is a collection of service points [...]. The forests of the world are your suburb – so long as there's a gas

Figure 47 *Archigram 9, Outgrowth*, cover by Tony Rickaby (1970)

station somewhere." He added: "when no hardware is plugged in, the village ceases to exist."[21] At Archigram, the illusion of autonomy dominated and the network was omnipresent. *Rokplug* was attached to the energy grid by cables. The supply problem was raised as a basic prerequisite to mobility:

> Until an effective device is developed, short-term energy sources such as batteries and gas cylinders will be used. For one-time stops, it will be necessary to connect to the main network by means of a plug. This need will be met by *Rokplug* and *Logplug*. [...] They serve to conceal service outlets for semi or non-autonomous mobile living containers.[22]

The network was disguised. The illusion of this simplified access to energy and seeming abundance stemmed from an ultra-positive vision of technology. Mobility introduced awareness of energy dependence, but was energy really deterritorialized?

It was, insofar as it became a series of new proposals for mobility. However, if one attempts to decipher the energy system that encoded these territories, dependent relationships remained: one still had to recharge. Since energy autonomy was partial, nomadism was limited. Moreover, as in Friedman's early work, autonomy was a synonym of dispersion. The energy production method remained unchanged; rather it was its distribution and accessibility that were modified. Peter Cook thought that the later research on energy disconnection and decentralization was fascinating, but he believed that dependence on the network had never been envisaged as a threat or a condition to be avoided:

> I believe that autonomy is implicit in some of our projects, particularly those that allowed the individual to build his own environment and be mobile. [...] I think that technology has now solved most of these problems and there is a greater potential for dispersion. But to some extent, we will always be dependent on networks and it is ridiculous to pretend otherwise. Nomadism is always limited; we would like to reach the farthest part of the galaxy, but we would always be dependent on the Earth![23]

In the vocabulary of the architect, nomadism is often confused with autonomy. Yet autonomy of movement is subordinate to energy dependence. Subject to the "innervation" of the territory, emancipation is reduced: the slightest dysfunction in the network makes all these proposals obsolete. Archigram reflected on access to the network, but it did not rethink either its foundations or energy: "The social aspect of utopia – the architectural project will save humanity – is replaced by a utopia of surface, technological and emancipating, immediate but without any promise or prowess, but sensual."[24] The network system is a prerequisite whose legitimacy is not challenged.

A connection dystopia

Besides the technical dimension of the network, some people were not unaware of the political aspect of the system. For Archizoom, the ultra-technological dimension made it possible to theoretically question the form and foundations of the capitalist city. In their representations, they transposed the technocratic power of capitalism into its simplest form: connection. Archizoom and Superstudio would push the critical utopia to a point of non-return. Nomadism was envisaged as a permanent condition, ensured by an infinite energy and information network. Running counter to the British group, which imagined an individual freed by technology, the radical Italians toppled this all-powerful technological confidence. More than a warning, it was a nightmarish protest, annihilating any idea of the city and any architectural reference. In *Mouvement continu* (1969) by Superstudio, individuals are neutralized on a uniform grid:

> All you have to do is stop and connect a plug: the desired microclimate is immediately created (temperature, humidity, etc.), you plug in to the network of information, you switch on the food and water blenders[25]

In 1972, on the occasion of the celebrated exhibition Italy: The New Domestic Landscape at the Museum of Modern Art (MoMA) in New York, Superstudio created a 35-minute animated film.[26] It traced the principles of the creation of the energy and information grid-network, which was similar to a "universal plug for primary needs" (see Figures 48a and 48b).

This exhibition also presented the works of Gianantonio Mari, Mario Bellini, Joe Colombo and Ignazia Favata, Alberto Rosselli and Isao Hosoe, Ettore Sottsass and Ula Saloara, Gruppo Strum and Archizoom. The title of the exhibition, The New Domestic Landscape, described how these radical design projects took part in the bursting apart of the domestic sphere, which was reduced to symbolic domestic objects moving in a landscape. This idea was used in *No-Stop City* (1969) by Archizoom, in which rented equipment and mobile furniture for temporary housing circulated on an endless plateau. The utilities appeared in the foreground and the grid is strewn with toilets. Architecture is reduced to one of its objective prerequisites: the basic infrastructure.

In *La distruzione degli oggetti: parcheggio neutro* [Parking neutral] (1971), Archizoom presented a paradoxical universe; the primitive appearance of the naked, hairy and crouching characters contrasts with the frozen machines in the center of the room (see Figure 49). The city is designed as an endless space in which all the living functions are pushed to their technological development extremes. For Archizoom, the dissolution of the city was the result of the historical development of capitalism.

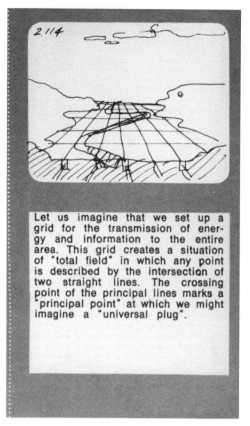

Let us imagine that we set up a grid for the transmission of energy and information to the entire area. This grid creates a situation of "total field" in which any point is described by the intersection of two straight lines. The crossing point of the principal lines marks a "principal point" at which we might imagine a "universal plug".

We may imagine an invisible grid with only a few points just visible in the grass, but immediately traceable, which constitute the universal plugs. In the model, these plugs are visualized as a magic box (black box) to which various sophisticated and miniaturized devices can be attached. Through these devices (the dream of electric appliances), everyone can synthesize the elements necessary to his existence. A universal plug for primary needs.

Figure 48 Superstudio, The Universal Plug (1972)

Pier Vittorio Aureli, in *The Project of Autonomy*, examined the group's theoretical positioning.[27] He looked at how the political discourse of autonomy, which crossed the Italian Left in the late 1950s, influenced the theory of architecture. According to the Italian group, "the birth of the modern capitalist city does not allow the current city to have an autonomous political growth, but simply to acquire characteristics that, once the ideological mystifications are set aside, permits the debate to be scientifically developed."[28] It was a poetic and political project in which the connection, the symbol of modernity, was pushed to its extreme.

In these technological narratives, architecture is reduced to a piece of equipment: the city or the territory, to a network of totalizing flows. The utility core endures, resists and reigns as an ultimate survivor of this vast deconstructive undertaking. At the risk of electrocution, energy remains the "thing" around which a residue of architecture would be constantly objectivized. The only freedom becomes the autonomy of movement: mobility and flight.

Figure 49 Archizoom, Parking Neutral (1971)

The positivity of nomadism and deterritorialization

In the late 1960s, nomadism was established as a concept to which a great positive distinction value was given. It was used as a vehicle of flight, representing the possibility of
emancipation and resistance in the face of the fixity of the systems that created subdivi-
sions and hierarchy. Christian Girard formulated the hypotheses according to which the
nomad concepts did not provide a reading grid for architecture. On the contrary: "The
nomad concept is the promise of not being locked into a dogmatism and its presence is
the symptom of a resistance to dogmatism rather than the inability of a discourse to be
theoretically solidified."[29] Nomadism made multiplicity, proliferation and juxtaposition
possible. We must look to Gilles Deleuze and Félix Guattari, since it was with their
"geophilosophy" that nomadism was instituted as a concept in the early 1970s.

Guattari's ideas of smooth and striated space, the nomad machine, territorialization, deterritorialization and reterritorialization ran throughout *Mille plateaux*,
and more specifically the "Traité de nomadologie: la machine de guerre ["Treatise of
nomadology: the war machine"]."[30] The authors formulated a "science of nomadism"
that resonated with the projects mentioned above. Though no architect previously
cited used the term 'deterritorialization,' it nonetheless has a stimulating evocative
power for the analysis that concerns us here. This link is justified by the historical
period itself: in the late 1960s, which generated the idea that space is where the
question of power is raised, in philosophy as in architecture. The concepts of this

period – nomadism, sedentary lifestyle and flows – were used in both the fields of architecture and philosophy. Other than common vocabulary, the strategies and stakes of
power and counter-power, which the coding and decoding of flows expressed, relate
to our introductory analyses on the idea of the network. Faced with this question of
power-alienation that territorializes and freezes, deterritorialization was instituted as
a major idea that found an effectiveness and materiality in architecture as in many
other areas. The reigning power imposes functioning and organization codes: this is
territorialization. Being deterritorialized, the authors tell us, is escaping alienation.
The "Treatise of nomadology" raised the questions: how is the state apparatus formed,
and how is this formation averted? One answer is nomadism. Nomadism and deterritorialization are concepts that make it possible to leave the territory of constraint.
Being deterritorializing is cutting a link, it is abandoning a territory to create another
one, real or imaginary, on which one's little war machine is installed. The war machine
is nomadic and "outside the state apparatus."[31]

This observation expresses a politicization of the nomadic condition. It is opposed
to the system and is described in detail by the authors, who offer historical, geographic
and philosophical analysis of nomadism:

> [The nomad] is a deterritorialization vehicle. He adds the desert to the desert, the steppe
> to the steppe through a series of local operations whose orientation and direction con-
> stantly vary. The sand desert does not only include oases, which are like fixed points, but
> rhizomatic, temporary and mobile vegetation depending on local rain, and that determine
> changes in the itineraries' orientation.[32]

Let us note the importance given to the flow of materials and energy points. Mobility
is generally subject to supply and the trajectory is strewn with stops. Nomadism
reveals the dependence on utilities. It is a detachment forced to return to the essential
resource (water point, oasis, campfire), it is exactly what the "magical territory" idea
evoked in radical architects. The nomadic war machine is the mobile occupant:

> [T]he furniture in the smooth space, as opposed to the geometry of the building in the
> striated space. The nomadic digital unit is the traveling fire, not the tent, still too much like
> real estate: 'The fire prevails over the yurt.'[33]

The citation is absolutely architectural. In an interplay of correspondence, an echo
is created between the smooth space, the autonomous piece of furniture, the mobile
occupant and the neutral space in Archizoom's *No-Stop City* or Superstudio's
Mouvement continu. In this extract, which presents a radical nomadism, the liquidation of architecture is continued. Though fire – representing primitivism and

the absolute reduction of inhabitability – appears as the only sedentary moment, nomadism is relativized:

> But there is no pure nomad, there is always and already a camp where things, no matter how few, are stored, where one belongs to a group and leaves again, gets married and eats [...]. There have to be stocks for there to be flows that can be tapped.[34]

Nomadism is as much characterized by freedom of circulation as it is limited by the dependence on supply points. However, its detachment and disconnection power, even periodically, makes nomadology a science that contrasts with state-sanctioned science. To protect itself, the latter uses hydraulic science and military metrics that "limit, control and localize" nomad science, thus prohibiting it from being used in the social field. What interests us in this "Treatise of nomadology" is the evocation of flows (notably energy flows) as a coding, a territorialization system; it is also the idea of nomadism as a deterritorialization vehicle and revealer of energy flows. Let us point out that though there is no link between these philosophers and the architects mentioned above, inversely, Deleuze and Guattari wove links with architecture and urban planning, citing in turn Lewis Mumford, Paul Virilio and Vauban.

The concepts of territorialization and deterritorialization resonate with those of connection and disconnection, as well as the image of the territory that captures energy through the network. Since deterritorialization corresponds to the diverting of an object or a thought from its initial state, use or function to make it potentially freer, when faced with energy domination, disconnection is a deterritorialization process.

To optimize its freedom and emancipate itself from this hierarchic grid, nomadism sought new inspirations that would permit the architect's world to refine its energy project. If the technological enthusiasm of the 1960s was greatly marked by space conquest, it behooves us to examine the transposition of these systems to architecture.

Space technologies in architectural prospective

Highly efficient autonomous energy equipment was first developed by the military and space industry. Exerting a genuine fascination, space technologies offered new energy possibilities. Seeking new solutions to supply its satellites, the combined knowledge of NASA (National Aeronautics and Space Administration), the Russian space agency then the ESA (European Space Agency) gave rise to extremely sophisticated units, ranging from spaceships, stations and colonies to temporary shelters and anti-nuclear bunkers, as well as survival kits. In the United States, the General Electric

Company[35] began the construction of its Appliance Park in 1951, experimenting with the application of a few energy systems derived from the aerospace industry, including the fuel cell, on its site. But it was not until the development of NASA in the late 1950s that a genuine transposition was launched.[36] In an almost prophetic speech in 1963, Fuller had provided an account of the potential and hope conveyed by the success of these technologies:

> We will no longer have to have water pipes and sewer systems, mankind will suddenly start mass reproducing the space-house prototype's pipe less, wireless, trackless ability to deploy man around the Earth's surface as well as in space. [...] I know that what I am saying to you, as architects, may at first make you uncomfortable, but I want you to realize that this is what is happening. I am trying to make it clear to you that for the first time in the history of man on Earth, we are actually applying the highest scientific capability to that extraterrestrial space dwelling, underwritten, inadvertently and exclusively, by weaponry supremacy ambitions for celestial control of world fire power. This celestial supremacy involves, however, an unprecedented weaponry system requirement – that of making man a successfully, semi-autonomous, biological intelligence system, remote from Earth, where he will be unable to survive normally by himself, as detached.[37]

The idea spread rapidly. Between 1965 and 1970, architectural reviews gave increasing attention to the question of prospective and technological innovations. First fascinated by form, design and the new materials, architecture would go on to take hold of these energy systems. The February 1967 issue of *Architectural Design*, titled "2000+," presented an astronaut's helmet on its cover (see Figure 50). John McHale, the guest editor in chief, reviewed the performances of the aerospace industry. The popularity of space programs – from the Skylab to inhabited colonies – greatly inspired architectures, as shown by the proliferation of autonomous modules and vehicles (by John Frazer and Ant Farm), autonomous houses (by Clarence G. Golueke and William J. Oswald and the Grumman company) and megastructures in orbit (like *Asteromo* and *Torus* by Paolo Soleri).

Space stations in orbit became a recurring theme in architectural design in the mid-1960s. The production phases and technologies of Skylab and the Lunar Module were broadly disseminated by the architectural press. Under construction since 1963, Skylab was the first manned American space station (see Figure 51). At the end of 1966, an agreement was reached on the layout and the interior design was entrusted to Raymond Loewy. Skylab contained an observatory and its energy was supplied by large solar panels.[38] Initially scheduled for 1968, it was launched in 1973 and orbited until it disintegrated in 1979. The Lunar Module was a technical adventure that was just as memorable: in July 1962, a dozen firms were invited to submit proposals for

Figure 50 *Architectural Design 2000+* (1967)

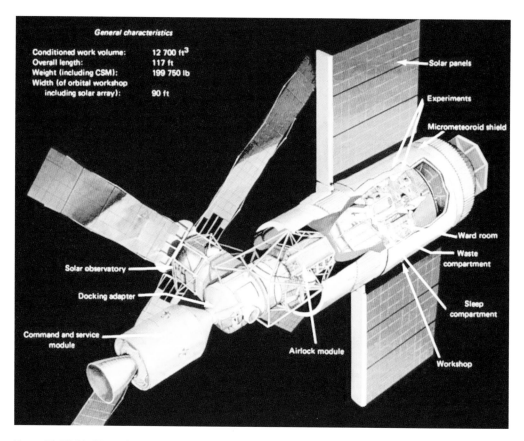

Figure 51 NASA, Skylab (1977)

Apollo's Lunar Module to NASA. The Grumman Aircraft Engineering Corporation won the contract. Many proposals and models were presented and led to a first flight in January 1968. The Lunar Module would be used during the Apollo 11 to 17 missions from 1969 to 1972. An integral part of the Apollo ship, the Lunar Module was composed of a first module containing the fuel tanks and the engine for the descent, and a second module that housed the team, oxygen and water reserves, electrical systems and the engine for the ascent.

These technologies rapidly found terrestrial applications. Arousing a great deal of interest due to energy concerns in the early 1970s, technologies offering energy autonomy were increasingly discussed. A certain number of architects experimented on small-scale combinations of mobility and autonomy. In 1969, John Frazer, a fifth-year student at the Architectural Association School of Architecture, proposed caravan models with autonomous energy: the *Mobile Autonomous Dwelling Facility.*

This represented autonomy on a micro-scale for those who want to wander freely. An autonomous servicing system was proposed to enable the caravan to tour away from the restriction of caravan sites.[39]

The influence of aerospace technologies can clearly be seen on the utilities panel. A generator, a fuel cell, solar collectors and batteries provided the appliances' electricity. Water was collected, filtered and distilled. Frazer's ambition was to conquer the vacation home market through the concept of a "model which was highly mobile and independent of caravan sites, but was highly serviced, spacious when unfolded, and free of the problems of overlap of functions encountered with traditional designs."[40] He presented two examples of units that were opened around an energy core. Easily towable, the caravan or trailer could be used in its compact form on the road and unfolded during stops (see Figures 52a and 52b).

In the first model, the sides were lowered and canopies inflated into two bubbles on either side of the structure. Beds could be disconnected and the kitchen-bathroom unit was reversible in order to have a full kitchen or bathroom space. The second model functions on a tensegrity system: the sides of the caravan unfolded to create a plateau in the center of which a mast rose, with four telescopic legs that strengthened the structure. The utility core was located in the center. These caravans had an oven, a refrigerator and a chemical toilet. In line with Fuller's technological tradition, Frazer proposed foldable and energy-autonomous mobile homes. No prototype was produced, but each model presented a series of plans, sections and construction details.

Independently of infrastructures, household equipment became a sophisticated unit that produced its own energy. The autonomous vehicle would also be envisaged by Ant Farm as a militant nomadism object (see Figure 53). Designed in 1971, the *Media Van*, by Curtis Schreier and Doug Michels, was a sophisticated documentation tool on alternative architecture. It had a computer unit, cameras, film projectors, slides and recorders, but also included a *Life Support Module* composed of solar collectors, batteries, a generator, an inflatable shower and a mobile kitchen. At each halt on its Truckstop Tour in 1970–71, the *Media Van* demonstrated the principles of energy autonomy and the inflatable object that one of its structures deployed: *ICE 9*. Ant Farm proposed a network of nomadic relays: the *Truckstop Network Placemat* (1971).

Bus communes would determine route, duration of excursion and may even develop their own systems of economics, social interaction, laws, in short become self-sufficient user-controlled mini-cultures with the bus station an alternate urban form.[41]

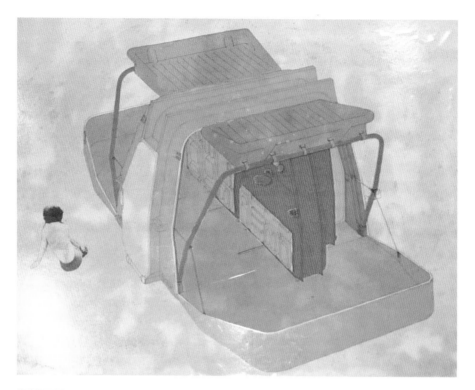

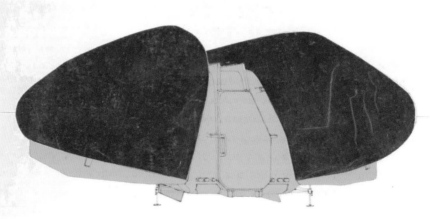

Figure 52 John Frazer, Mobile Autonomous Dwelling, Model 1 (1969)

The architects mapped alternative sites that a host of autonomous units could cross: Pacific Domes, Media Access Center, Arcosanti, Zomeworks, Earth People's Park and Videofreex. Fifty or so Media Vans could thus travel between New York and San Francisco, creating an economic and social micro-organization.

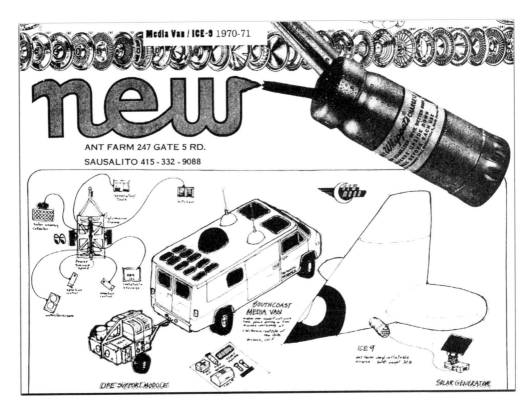

Figure 53 Ant Farm Media Van (1971)

Manfred Schiedhelm's *Mobile House* project, created in Japan in 1969 and published in the spring of 1971 in *L'Architecture d'aujourd'hui*, is an example technically
similar to those by Frazer and Ant Farm. With different possibilities for combining
volumes, this module was totally independent of any connections thanks to hydraulic
generators, batteries, an air-conditioning system, a water filter and an incinerator for
household waste. In the same way as John Frazer's caravans, the exterior walls could
be lowered to form a platform. A pneumatic-structure bathroom could be deployed,
as could the other inflatable structures.

Autonomy for stationary homes

Whereas the technologies developed by the aerospace industry initially reinforced and
improved nomadism, autonomy would gradually be envisaged for more stationary
structures. The energy transposition had begun. Alexander Pike presented the fuel
cell, under the name of *Total Energy Package* (1968) in *Architectural Design* (see
Figure 54).

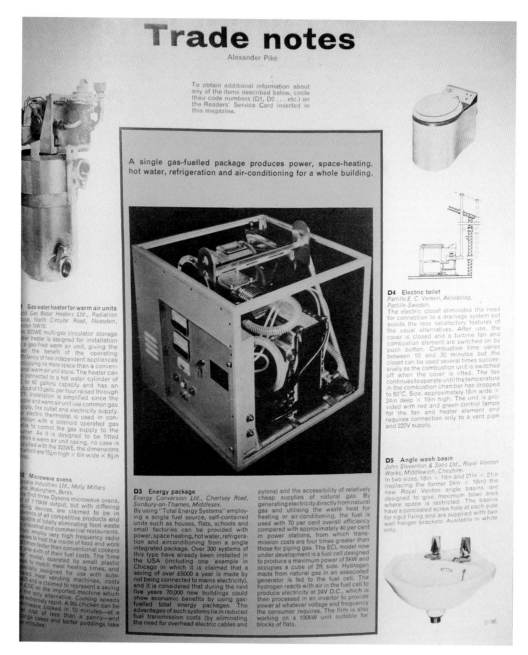

Figure 54 Alexander Pike, "Trade Notes" (1968)

This same image would be used by Charles Jencks in his work *Architecture 2000* (1971). Jencks stressed the liberating and revolutionary potential of this future "autonomous energy box."[42] The operating principle of fuel cells was discovered in 1839 by William Grove, but lay forgotten until their use in the space programs of the 1960s, before diversifying their application in the early 1970s. Providing the energy supply and heat or cold generation, this system was envisaged as an autonomous unit that could produce all of the energy needed for stationary or mobile applications like buildings, hotels and islands.

> More than 300 such systems have already been installed in the United States for public or private buildings, including one in Chicago, saving £5,000 per year compared to the traditional system of connections to urban energy infrastructure.[43]

For Alexander Pike, the reduction of distribution costs (if one considers the elimination of overhead electric cables and pylons) and the possibility of decentralized energy production would be the principal advantages of such systems.[44]

Alternative energies began to be called for in architectural projects. Much more explicit on this question, the Grumman Aerospace Corporation, which built the Apollo Lunar Module, clearly defended the transposition of space technologies to the home. In 1972, the group imagined an autonomous integrated system, which offered the recycling and maximum reuse of materials, flows and energies, such as the purification of gray water (see Figure 55).[45]

Similarly, in 1970, the scientists Clarence G. Golueke and William J. Oswald of the Sanitary Engineering Research Laboratory at the University of California, Berkeley, collaborators in NASA research programs and pioneers in waste treatment and water purification using algae, developed an autonomous house for four people, a cow and thirty hens (see Figures 56a and 56b).

Particularly well adapted to tropical regions, in this closed system the waste produced was used to feed the algae and produce methane and electricity was provided through solar energy. Designed in concentric tanks, the algae cultivation had a purification and feeding function for the animals, while also providing additional heat through the anaerobic digester placed in the center. A sedimentation chamber and a solar still completed the system. Golueke and Oswald stressed the necessity of giving each family the responsibility for the functioning of household utilities. Despite their desire to launch the creation of a prefabricated prototype, the model would remain in the design stage.

Autonomous vehicles and houses proliferated. The deconstruction of NASA's complex energy machines and the difficulty in readapting them for terrestrial housing initially seemed to suit small-scale experiments. But large-scale utopian urban projections also called on energy autonomy, such as Paolo Soleri's environmental

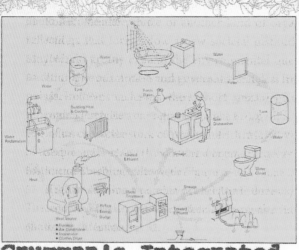

Grumman's Integrated Household System

The Grumman Corporation's biotechnology group was established to develop life support systems for astronauts. When the space business slumped some of its energies were redirected to finding terrestial commercial applications for the techniques and hardware they had developed. The principal result of these efforts has been the development of an Integrated Household System. The system is intended primarily 'to reduce civil water requirements, air and water pollution and refuse disposal'. It is seen as being applicable to new housing only and then only in communities where a large percentage of the dwellings can be fitted with the system. It is further assumed that the households will continue to use standard inefficient consumer devices such as dish-washers and that they will be too conservative to use recycled water for drinking, cooking or dishwashing.

The individual pieces of equipment involved in the Integrated Household System are mostly unremarkable and the processes which led to their selection are disappointing but the ways in which they are integrated are quite interesting. The reduction in input of water and output of pollutants is achieved by carefully balancing component design and the flow patterns of matter and energy (e.g. water and heat) within the system, by assigning multiple functions to individual components (as happens in living systems) and by reusing matter and energy as much as possible. All these approaches were initially used in the design of life support systems for spacecraft.

The water sub-system is principally interesting for the air evaporation unit which it contains. This unit was developed for lengthy space missions (to Mars and beyond) and could be used to produce drinking water from urine and other waste water. The Grumman researchers felt this would be psychologically unacceptable to consumers and therefore restrict the output to the air conditioning system. The evaporation unit also acts as a heat transfer — taking in the waste heat from household systems to bring about evaporation and releasing it on condensation. Mains supply water is used in the lavatory, the kitchen sink and dishwasher. Used water from these sources passes through a biological waste treatment unit and then mixes with mains supply to be re-used in a clothes washer and shower/bathtub. Storage tanks are used to balance the internal flows of water and waste water.

Despite the application of this equipment a four person household would

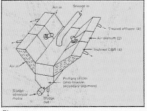

Bio-reactor

still be expected to require a daily input of 181 gallons of mains water during the summer and of 62 gallons during the winter. This is a considerable volume of water and could easily be further reduced to under ten gallons per day if the water closet were redesigned and the cleaning equipment was replaced by atomised water units.

The most interesting component of the sewage system is the oxygenating bioreactor for secondary treatment of sewage. The unit, like the air evaporation unit, was developed for spacecraft and is one-fifteenth the size of commercially available units. In the household system it would probably occupy almost as much room as a septic tank as it would require a surge tank to cope with variations in household water use. The unit consists essentially of a V-shaped array of 0.006 external diameter tubing which provides a large surface area for the activities of the bacteria which break down the sewage. The bacteria are aided in their task by oxygen (from the air) which diffuses through the walls of the tubes. The treated effluent is discarded together with the treated water which is not to be recycled. Grumman claim that this effluent could be piped straight into a flowing stream without doing any harm. This is none too good an idea for a variety of reasons. A better suggestion of theirs is that it could be used during the summer for landscape irrigation. They also suggest that it might be possible to use it in the production of aquatic food (crustacea and fish).

Wastes other than sewage are fed into two-stage incinerators which are claimed to cause little air pollution and seem to be marginally justifiable on the grounds that they reduce the problems of traditional waste disposal and provide some excess heat to feed the air evaporator unit. The wholesale oxidation of wastes seems an unnecessarily drastic measure. If paper, board, wood, aluminium and other metal wastes were baled, shredded or compacted there would be little need for two-stage incineration. The project director even expresses doubt about whether it will be psychologically possible to replace brick chimney-stacks with the small diameter heavily insulated pipes necessary for waste heat reclamation on an effective scale.

The Integrated Household System is largely centred around the two space components it contains: the air evaporator unit and the bioreactor secondary sewage treatment plant. In order to create a market for these two devices and to bolster the market for dishwashers and incinerators, an apparently sophisticated system has been made counterproductive and its potential has been largely curtailed. Grumman see attempts to create a completely closed loop system independent of municipal servicing (electrical power, fuel, water, sewage and refuse disposal), as 'a long range idea that might well take several decades to achieve.'

423 AD/7/72

Figure 55 "Grumman's Integrated Household System" (1972)

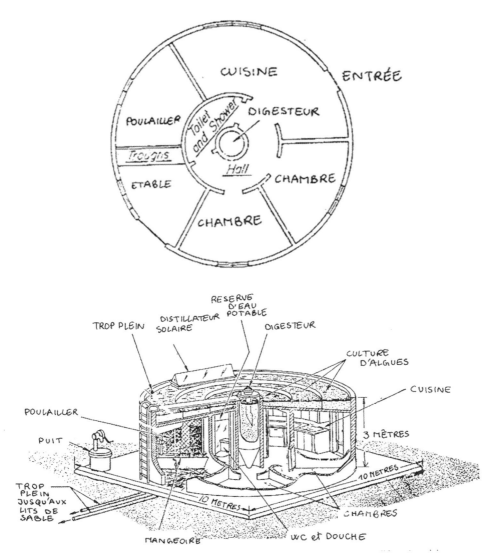

Figure 56 Clarence G. Golueke and William J. Oswald, plan of the autonomous house and axonometry section (1979)

megastructures. In April 1966, the Italian architect imagined *Asteromo*, an orbiting solar city in a total self-sufficient system, called "artificial ecology" or *Arcology* (see Figures 57a and 57b).

No fewer than 70,000 people could live on this asteroid in a frightening density. In *Arcology: The City in the Image of Man* (1969), Soleri presented thirty or so dense and miniaturized metropolitan structures. These "arcologies" were structures in which life, work, education, culture, leisure activities, health and agriculture were measured

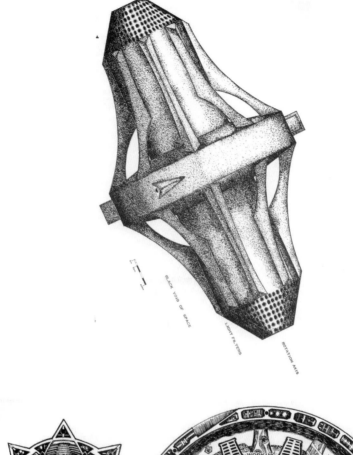

Figure 57 Paolo Soleri, "Asteromo" (1969)

on the pedestrian scale. Like an ocean liner, these mega-machines interacting with the environment were envisaged as an alternative to the ecological tribulations caused by spatial dilution. In a futurist and machinist perspective, infrastructure and energy were highlighted. Soleri embarked on a rapid critique of the network and the existing energy infrastructures. He compared them to an "organism trying to survive with thousands of weak hearts, frantically pumping tired blood, through sclerosed and inadequate veins, with thousands of livers, thyroids, lungs."[46] Apart from the obsolescence of the equipment, the architect raised the land, energy and material waste of urban sprawl:

> The saddest aspect of energy waste is that, no matter how much we produce and install horsepower, kilowatt-hours, gas pipes, fuel tanks, coaxial cables, their connections are inevitably far too weak for a truly complex and invigorating society. Real life can't be spread so finely.[47]

For Soleri, urban compactness and the reinvention of an infrastructure system on the scale of these megastructures made it possible to densify and ecologically maximize space. He defined arcology as a "well-balanced service system that addresses the waste of time and space." As permeable as they could appear externally, their principle was a complex interrelationship with the environment, aiming at maximum self-sufficiency. In the maritime arcology *Novanoah I*:

> Arcology, like a huge digestive system, would ingest the mass of water, extract the elements designated by the function of the various plants, and eliminate the water used in an uninterrupted cycle. The various materials – plants and animals, chemicals and minerals – once fixed would be processed and/or stored, then partly consumed and exported as food, fertilizer, or used as a material for food production in agricultural areas.[48]

This 20-km-long metropolitan strip connected vertical and horizontal circulations and several layers of services, including production, warehousing, storage, transportation and depollution. In his metabolistic and biological analogies, Soleri imagined a group of synergies in a spatial quest that was almost ontological. City and infrastructure were envisaged as a single piece: *Arcanyon* was an aqueduct city in which water was superimposed on three levels, generating an urban river and canals creating a transport, distribution and irrigation network; *Arcvillage* proposed an urban life in a rural arcology based on seasonal cycles. *Arcodiga* was built in a dam, thus meeting water and energy needs; *Infrababel I* and *Arcoindian II* could be built on a cliff or in the desert, creating, like the preceding cities, the conditions of twenty-first-century urban life through technological processes using natural resources. In these macro-structures, hydraulic and solar energy, air-conditioning systems, the connection of agricultural, industrial and cultural spaces were used. However, as regards his self-sufficiency research, the functioning of these ideal cities was not limited to the use of natural resources. In *Novanoah II*, "the power plant could be operated with atomic energy or on-site fuel such as gas, oil or tidal cycle hydropower."[49] The details of each arcology were relatively succinct and technical feasibility was not really the major concern of Soleri, whose objective was to reinvent, in the same utopian spirit, architecture and infrastructure. As fictional as these proposals were, they would generate *Arcosanti*; initially planned as a self-sufficient town of 5,000 people in the Arizona desert, the construction that began in 1972 would finally be on the scale of a small community.

Soleri focused on the environmental question in the late 1950s, but if a few technical applications were gradually used in *Arcosanti*, energy and food self-sufficiency would never be attained. Even if the built projects did not live up to the proposals, the aerospace industry's energy research had strong repercussions on architectural and urban prospective. In return, architectural programs dealing with the conquest of space and how they took autonomy into account had to be questioned.

Self-sufficiency in artificial environments

Working alongside architects and engineers, NASA and the American Society for Engineering Education launched the first major study on the feasibility of inhabited space colonies in 1975. This program was conducted under the direction of a leading figure in the conquest of space: the physicist Gerard K. O'Neill. The report on this study, *Space Settlements: A Design Study* (1977), was a great success and helped popularize his research (see Figure 58).[50]

Among the group of models proposed, this work presented an artificial life scenario based on an inhabitable megastructure, *Torus*, imagined by students at Stanford University and inspired by *Island One*, by Gerard K. O'Neill. It was a cylindrical tube, 130 m in diameter and 5.6 km long, forming an enormous ring, 1.8 km in diameter, that could house a community of 10,000 inhabitants (see Figure 59). This self-sufficient colony was composed of residential, commercial and public spaces, industrial and agricultural zones, a transportation network and complex energy machinery: production, processing, storage and distribution of electricity, water and air, and total waste recycling). Self-sufficiency was "the big issue of artificial environments."[51] The authors defined the different types:

1. the capacity of a community to survive and develop without any interaction with others
2. the capacity to survive in case of isolation

Figure 58 Gerard K. O'Neill, *Space Settlements: A Design Study* (1977)

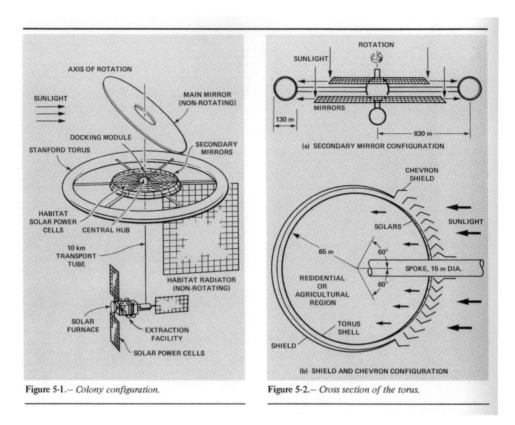

Figure 5-1.– *Colony configuration.*

Figure 5-2.– *Cross section of the torus.*

Figure 59 Technical details of Stanford Torus (1977)

3. the incapacity to survive without interaction with other communities, but in financial autonomy, with an import–export trade balance
4. the capacity to produce for export.

Torus would be in the second category: a colony whose dependence would be limited, but inevitable, on Earth. It is difficult to envisage the existence of space communities without the material support of Earth, in terms of medicine, information technology and electronics. For the *Torus* thinkers, autonomy was limited by "modern" needs, or, in other words, those derived from a complex and energy-consuming production process. Moreover, as scientific research would be conducted from Earth, the programming of this artificial city would have to keep a link with this external observation pole. Autonomy cannot be total, quite simply because space is not "naturally" viable, and the models developed depended on a planning projection. An environment that can support human life has to be recreated. The question of terrestrial control is always raised because this control permits survival. Autonomy in space would therefore be even more complex than on Earth, because the further one goes from our planet the more indispensable autonomy becomes, and it must be infallible.

In this orbiting colony, the water required for the life of the community was extracted from the atmosphere by condensation, similar to a humidification and dehumidification system. All waste (solid, liquid or gaseous) was chemically recycled and restituted in the different milieus of the orbital space in order to recreate the biological and atmospheric balance. Natural sunlight lit the ring, using an inclined mirror above the city's core. An orbiting solar station supplied the energy networks of *Torus* to run a closed ecological system. The energy transmitted by microwave beams was recovered on the surface of the inhabited ring, adapted, then brought into the electricity network. Analogous to the terrestrial energy system, a distribution tunnel was planned around the perimeter of the enclosure for the mechanical installations and networked utilities.[52] One notices that the terrestrial network model and centralism were used; autonomy was solicited, but it concerned the relationship of the colony to Earth. If cutting-edge technologies enabled autonomy to be attained, what would autonomy enable in its turn? For O'Neill, what was at stake in this technological challenge was to ensure the survival of the human race in the event of a natural, ecological or nuclear disaster. The creation of new autonomous territories would also offer a solution to the demographic explosion.

The detractors of space colonization objected to the exorbitant cost, the speculative nature of these technologies and their imperialistic foundation. We will see in the second part of this work that the reappropriation of these cutting-edge technologies and the idea of autonomy will be asserted for purposes that are above all social, economic and environmental; antagonisms and contradictions of the formula clearly emerge. The composition of this artificial orbiting world was worked out on the consumption and growth model of the United States, which a number of protagonists of the energy autonomy movement would challenge. For these advocates, energy autonomy had the virtue of recreating natural biological cycles, favoring farm-to-table distribution, degrowth and the invention of economic alternatives. A point of radical incompatibility between nature and artifice even seemed to appear in the term autonomy itself. The technological evolutions of the industrial and postindustrial era, which for nearly a century have dramatically changed then transformed the life of populations, appear as one of the keys of this insurmountable dualism. On *Torus*, cutting-edge technologies and energy autonomy were supposed to make it possible to recreate the conditions of life on Earth, to prolong them and strengthen them without going beyond a critical point in its established order. The technical means that made autonomy an artificial hermetic system would result in closed communities of variable scales, both libertarian and totalitarian, the possibility of existing side by side without the functioning of one influencing the other. The question was a purely material capacity to survive. The creation of overparametrized artificial bubbles that could control the climate's atmosphere, vegetation and reproduction, like lunar colonies, clearly differed at the time from the more political claims that certain small groups of autonomy advocates would defend. Artificial or controlled autonomy of space colonies prompted reactions from the actors of the energy autonomy architectural movement. The proposals of scientists went too far and frightened architects. These issues would be raised in *Space Colonies: A CoEvolution Book* (1977) (see Figure 60).[53]

The creator of the *Whole Earth Catalog* and the *CoEvolution Quarterly* proposed a debate in this work on the feasibility of and interest in these anticipations. He asked for the opinion of several personalities, such as Lewis Mumford, Ant Farm, E. F. Schumacher and Steve Baer. The confrontation was heated. Arguing that no closed ecological system had yet been built on Earth, the contributors criticized the scientific community for its distraction on the paths of foolhardiness and excess. Refocusing the debate on ethics and emergencies here on Earth, Stewart Brand emphasized the futuristic and demented nature of this research, stressing the major ecological and biological problems, but also those of engineering, that artificial environments raised. If autonomy in space is more complex than on Earth, given its environmental, economic and political potential, he considered that one had to begin by testing on our planet. The techniques developed by the aerospace industry had well-known repercussions in the discourse on technologies, but also in the counterculture's architectural and energy experiments. Responses oscillated between fascination, rejection and diversion. Certain personalities would exorcise the overindulgence of technological society and the technical austerity, often as radical as that of the Shakers, that had governed populations for nearly a century. Other self-builders would see in this self-sufficiency concept the illusion of a return to nature in which biological cycles enabled self-managed and interdependent communities to grow in abundance and in which individual autonomies strengthened collective organization and general emancipation. Despite these criticisms, autonomy did not have a more effective activator than the conquest of space.

From the disposable to the sustainable

The growing environmental issue raised new challenges; it seemed that domestic architecture could no longer anchor itself in the territory in the same way. The disposable theme and the energy optimism of the 1960s gave way to sustainability and moderation, and increasingly asserted questions about the inherited energy order. Reyner Banham grasped these mutations in *The Architecture of the Well-tempered*

Figure 60 Stewart Brand, *Space Colonies: A CoEvolution Book* (London: Penguin, 1977)

Environment (1969), which presented itself as a major historiographical reference and one of the first works calling for the reconciliation of architecture and the environment, toward a global energy reconsideration. Through his disenchanted analysis of the Modern movement,[54] his support for the new generation of postwar architects and his interest in technical invention, Banham was one of the most influential and prolific historians and critics of his generation. Luc Baboulet set out Banham's determination to burst the limits of the architectural discipline "by including in the architecture field what is generally excluded from it." (see Figure 61).[55]

Banham proposed a genealogy of the "well-tempered" home environment and demanded a technology capable of broadening its possibilities. He argued for key works of modern architecture to be evaluated based on their energy performance, rather than their formal newness. Banham attracted our attention to naturally available energy, mentioning Eastern models of bioclimatism and other passive systems that decrease consumption and needs, such as the Trombe wall, thermal buffers, and natural lighting and ventilation. A certain number of examples are cited of buildings that used these systems, including the *Victoria Regia water-lily house* at Chatsworth, designed in 1850 by Sir Joseph Paxton. Banham considered it a pioneer for the ingenuity of its environmental performances, which included glass walls and elaborate heating and ventilation systems. Another exemplary building is *St George's School*, built in England in 1961 by Emslie Morgan, which had an enormous solar wall. In

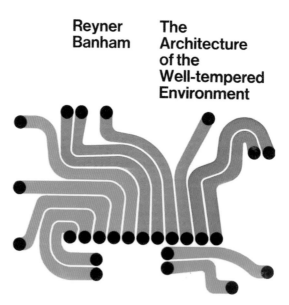

Figure 61 Reyner Banham, *The Architecture of the Well-tempered Environment* (London: The Architectural Press, 1969)

"The well-tempered home," Banham illustrated his discussion using the *Prairie Houses* (1889–1910) by Wright, owing to their adaptation to the milieu and the site (natural light, air circulation and the indoor–outdoor relationship), but did not include anything on *Broadacre City*. Banham focused on technologies in the history of the habitat, highlighting environmental control as a prerequisite to a viable home space. However, the historian helped to establish the network as an element of structural planning and the connection as a phenomenon.

The first edition of the work, in 1969, was not a success; it was the second, in 1984, that made the author renowned. Banham updated it to include the major changes that had occurred right after the energy crisis. He added a few examples, and this second edition was more a work on the history of architecture than one on the history of technologies. It thus seems that the second edition's additions did not sufficiently stress the phenomena of the major technological renewals that followed the 1973 crisis. This book certainly revealed the importance of the environmental question, but it is curious to observe that the energy autonomy issue was never brought up in this revised and corrected work. Notwithstanding the last pages, dedicated to the rapidly developing alternative technologies, Banham devoted little space to the energy experiments of the 1965–1980 period. "Reyner Banham stopped where the nightmares of technology began," Martin Pawley would rightly observe.[56] The counterculture phenomenon had been quickly discussed in the first edition with the example of Steve Baer's *Zome House*, for its erring technological ways and weak performances. In the second edition, however, Banham lingered on Richard Rogers's practice with the rise in what he called the "high-tech wave," which he considered more promising.

The architectural premises and first attempts concerning disconnection in the late 1960s represented the technical foundations of the changes to come. The critiques gradually became more radical and the propensities to technological excesses lessened. Despite the optimism of the 1950s and 1960s, the abundance of new materials in the postwar period that constituted the reign of the disposable and the illusion of an unlimited access to energy was coming to an end. Consumerist impermanence and frenzied and energy-consuming nomadism were replaced by a return of architecture and the question of its sustainability. In 1974, Alexander Pike formulated a critique of all of Archigram's small ephemeral units:

> We are familiar with the glut of 'plug-in' tools which decrease our labor and increase our environment control. The excesses of this mobility lies in the disposable aspect of these objects – like Mike Webb's Suitaloon – which makes environmental pollution more acute. [...] Uncontrolled growth and the proliferation of these small units would make the environment even more rigid and polluted.[57]

Constant, reliable energy, moderation and the economical would replace the perishable, energy dilapidation and the ephemeral. Disposable and connected architecture would give way to a sustainable and disconnected architecture. Abandoning futuristic anticipations, some would put technological innovations to the test in a new form of housing, notably using renewable energies and seeking the "utopia of the social." In a 1976 lecture, Alexander Pike examined the shift that occurred in the late 1960s and the architect's dilemma faced with technology:

> So the architect finds himself in a dilemma. Fifteen years ago it seemed that technology had reached the point where it could provide all our needs, cheaply and with so little effort that one of the emerging problems seemed to be how people would fill their leisure time. We were considering, without realizing the implication, high-energy buildings, factory-manufactured structures for mass production, 'throw-away' architecture with a built-in obsolescence factor, 'all plastic house' – adopting what we now call a hard technology in general. Now we must investigate the design of low-intensive building, utilizing renewable resources, demanding minimum inputs of energy during manufacture, construction and occupation – built to give an extremely long life expectancy, but providing sufficient flexibility of choice for a range of different lifestyles. We are reassessing the standard economic theories, and the possibilities for growth and expansion, formerly taken for granted, are being seriously questioned by economists such as E. F. Schumacher and Ezra J. Mishan.[58]

Unlike Banham, Pike grasped here the paradigm shift in architectural practice, which henceforth had to simultaneously consider the environment and technology, the economic and the social, in a critical perspective of the traditional utility system.

A critique of modern technical orthodoxy

The counterculture would bring together all the intuitions that had been emerging up to that point, triggering a major break in the history of architecture and regional development. A crisis phenomenon corresponding to the end of the dizzying postwar growth cycle of Western societies, the counterculture movement was born in the United States in the early 1960s and spread to Europe during that decade.[59] Long underestimated, its effects on the world of architecture have made history today. The political and economic context of the period in the United States and Europe gave rise to disillusionment and challenged the dominant ideology. This questioning of the foundations of the established order originated in the late 1950s. It was in this global context that the autonomy project would spread. Initially, the counterculture totally rejected the objects of the consumer society, establishing pleasure, disobedience and

fun at the center of a new order. But in the late 1960s, in response to international economic and political events, the phenomenon radicalized into a social movement that
was critical of every aspect of modern capitalism. Protest gave way to a determination
to eschew society and a desire for decentralization in terms of politics, the economy
and energy.

The rejection of authority was joined by the proposal to 'do-it-yourself,' and
an attraction for nature and the rural milieu that offered the hope of a different life.
Despite the sharp decline of postwar technological optimism and the criticism of
industrialization, the counterculture was not anti-technological, but rather ambivalent to its advances. Its protagonists moved between technophobia and technophilia:
the rejection of specialization was combined with the reappropriation of so-called
cutting-edge technologies, the nature cult and communitarian utopianism. If the
community movement had always been very active in the United States, the phenomenon was amplified as of 1965. The crisis of ideals was accompanied by a technological
crisis kindled by the intensification of environmental concerns. The growing interest
in technologies in the movements in the late 1960s would be encouraged by the work
of European and American intellectuals.

While the industrial city was becoming more and more dense, questions on
the urban choices and infrastructure models that formed the future were raised. A
revamping of thinking on urbanism was underway; works queried "the future" of
the city. In *City Sense* (1965), Theo Crosby depicted the urban accelerations and
questioned its technical foundations:

> There is, of course, an optimum size for everything, and the great cities of the world are
> now too big to function efficiently, because their original infrastructure of roads and
> services is obsolete.[60]

Historians, philosophers and theoreticians contributed to the critical re-evaluation of
the basic principles of modern technical orthodoxy. Lewis Mumford, Paul Goodman
as well as Herbert Marcuse, Theodore Roszak and Jacques Ellul – starting from different viewpoints – would bring the reflection on the modern technological society and
the technical mindset to the forefront of social criticism.

Mumford, in *The City in History*, titles a chapter "Paleotechnic paradise: coketown." He described the dark aspects of the nineteenth-century industrial city, its
principal mutations and the arrival of the underground city a an extension of the
"coketown."[61] He described the underground city, and its galleries of water and gas
utilities and underground machinery, as an extension of the mining milieu. He added
that the influence of the coketown:

grips even tighter, and the final effects are even more inimical to life. This is in the knitting together of necessary underground utilities to produce a wholly gratuitous result: the underground city, conceived as an ideal.

In an analogy with the trenches and shelters of warfare, the underground city reproduced, in its anarchic clutter and the palpitations of its depths, the archetypes and structures of the nineteenth-century city. With the persistence of mining substructures, it was as if the city of the Industrial Age had infiltrated and extended its darkness and its surface pollution in the contemporary subsoils, as if the carboniferous technological infrastructures of the Industrial Age were continuing to disseminate their evils. Among these infrastructures were those of energy. Mumford did not focus on them but queried their durability, pointing out that the price of the cables and the underground network: "the relative cost of these underground pipes and wires and conduits has increased; while with every extension of the city, as with every increase of internal congestion, the cost of the whole system disproportionately increases, too."[62] Networked installations were discussed in these works on the city, architecture and the history of technology. We must also remember that Mumford was a member of the Regional Planning Association of America, founded in the mid-1920s, and that the link between ecology, planning and large infrastructures like dams was an important issue, as the forester and planner Benton Mackaye described in 1940.[63]

However, Mumford was one of the louder critics of the large technical system. In *The Myth of the Machine: the Pentagon of Power* (1970), Mumford painted a damning picture of technological civilization, describing how the hopes of modern technology had been demolished by an authoritarian and destructive technology. Jacques Ellul, in *La Technique ou l'Enjeu du siècle* (1954), had already proposed an extreme hypothesis of the same kind, stating that economic, political and symbolic life in the twentieth century had fallen under the domination of technology. In "Authoritarian and democratic technics," Mumford proposed that:

> [F]rom late Neolithic times in the Near East, right down to our own day, two technologies have recurrently existed side by side: one authoritarian, the other democratic, the first system-centered, immensely powerful, but inherently unstable, the other man-centered, relatively weak, but resourceful and durable.[64]

The apprehensions of another energy possibility emerged. In *One-Dimensional Man* (1964), Marcuse described capitalist as well as socialist societies as composing a vast repressive technological civilization, controlling every aspect of people's lives. Marcuse offered a more positive vision in *An Essay on Liberation* (1969), calling on science and technology to become agents of liberation:

For freedom indeed depends largely on technical progress, on the advancement of science. But this fact easily obscures the essential precondition: in order to become vehicles of freedom, science and technology would have to change their present direction and goals; they would have to be reconstructed in accord with a new sensibility – the demands of the life instincts. Then one could speak of a technology of liberation, product of a scientific imagination free to project and design the forms of a human universe without exploitation and toil.[65]

What then should this technology of an emancipated society resemble? How can one imagine this technological renewal?

If these questions offer a critical look at technology in general, they also raise the issue of the conflictual relationship between energy equipment, the city and architecture. These analyses comprised a theoretical base that gave impetus to a new imaginary idea of infrastructure. Concurrently with these diatribes and indictments, the so-called soft, experimental, intermediate, radical, alternative technologies spread, as so many remedies giving free reign to an overflowing imagination. Opening a new experimentation territory for architecture and urban planning, they quickly fascinated those from every horizon: amateurs, the curious, professionals and institutions optimistically and confidently leapt into the race, with variable stakes and means. The use of these technologies – based on the founding advances in solar, wind and geothermal energy from the interwar years – would give rise to a huge range of experiments. The process accelerated in the late 1960s; the counterculture, with its changes in technological paradigm, conducted a host of experiments and imagined multiple hypotheses giving autonomy unprecedented momentum. The control to be avoided was the governmental energy machine, which created fixity both in terms of energy concentration and poor resource management. On a backdrop of the energy crisis, the autonomous house became an icon, turning itself into a disconnection ideal as a vehicle of new possibilities of life, consumption and planning in the rural, peri-urban and urban milieus. By popularizing a technological program whose key feature was independence, these experiments heralded an unprecedented questioning of the energy foundations of the Industrial Age and called for a total toppling of traditional power systems.

Notes

1 Reyner Banham, *Megastructure: Urban Futures of the Recent Past* (New York: Harper & Row, 1976), p. 17.

2 Georges-Hubert de Radkowski, "Le crépuscule des sédentaires," *Janus*, "L'homme et la ville," no. 13, January (1967), pp. 43–50. Republished in G.-H. de Radkowski, *Anthropologie de l'habiter: Vers le nomadisme* (Paris: PUF, 2002), pp. 139–148.

3 Dominique Rouillard, "Territoire magique," in Dominique Rouillard, *Superarchitecture: Le futur de l'architecture 1950–1970* (Paris: Editions de la Villette, 2004), pp. 377–414.

4 Yona Friedman, *L'Architecture mobile* (Paris: Anpassungsfähiges Bauen, 1958). Published by the author in 300 copies in 1959, republished in 1970 by Casterman in Paris, p. 9.

5 *Ibid.*, pp. 13–16. To illustrate this citation, in the first French edition of *L'Architecture mobile*, in 1959, a few drawings explaining this shift to autonomy were presented that the 1970 Casterman edition did not include.

6 Reyner Banham, "Stocktaking," *The Architectural Review*, vol. 127, no. 756 (1960), p. 99.

7 The "Capsule declaration" by Kisho Kurokawa appeared in *Space Design* in March 1969.

8 Banham, "Stocktaking," p. 99.

9 Reyner Banham, "A clip-on architecture," *Design Quarterly*, vol 35, no. 63 (1965), p. 198.

10 Reyner Banham, "A home is not a house," published for the first time in *Art in America*, vol. 53, no. 2 (1965), then republished in *Architectural Design*, vol. 39, no, 1 (1969), pp. 45–48.

11 Dominique Rouillard, "Le climat contre l'architecture," in Thierry Mandoul et al. (eds), *Climats: Les conférences de Malaquais* (Gollion: Infolio, 2012).

12 Banham, "A clip-on architecture," (1963), p. 32.

13 David Greene, "Living Pod," *Archigram 7*, 1966.

14 Dominique Rouillard, "Territoire magique," in Claude Prelorenzo (ed.), *Infrastructures, villes et territoires* (Paris: L'Harmattan, 2000), pp. 23–28.

15 Penny Gardiner, Peter Murray and Geoffrey Smyth (eds), *Clip-Kit: Studies in Environmental Design* (self-published magazine, 1966). The IDEA ("International dialogue of experimental architecture") meeting, which took place in 1966 in Folkestone, was fairly representative of this research.

16 Rouillard, *Superarchitecture*, p. 381.

17 Dennis Crompton, "The piped environment," *Archigram 8* (1968).

18 De Radkowski, "Le crépuscule des sédentaires," p. 48.

19 *Ibid.*, p. 49.

20 *Ibid.*, p. 50.

21 David Greene, "Rokplug, Logplug," *Architectural Design*, vol. 39, no. 5 (1969), p. 274.

22 David Greene, "Rokplug, Logplug," *Archigram 9* (1969).

23 Peter Cook, interview with Fanny Lopez, held on 15 January 2010.

24 Rouillard, "Territoire magique," in Prelorenzo, p. 26.

25 Emilio Ambasz, *Italy: The New Domestic Landscape: Achievements and Problems of Italian Design* (New York: Museum of Modern Art, 1972).

26 Superstudio, "Vita, educazione, cerimonia, amore, morte. Cinque storie del Superstudio, 1," *Casabella*, no. 367, July (1972), pp. 15–27.

27 Pier Vittorio Aureli, "Archizoom: the autonomy of theory versus the ideology of the Metropolis," in P. V. Aureli, *The Project of Autonomy: Politics and Architecture Within and Against Capitalism* (New York: Princeton Architectural Press, 2008), pp. 69–79.

28 Archizoom, "Città catena di montaggio del sociale. Ideologia e teoria della metropoli," *Casabella*, no. 350–351, July–August (1970), pp. 22–34.

29 Christian Girard, *Architecture et concepts nomades* (Liège: Mardaga, 1986), p. 183.

30 Deleuze and Guattari, *Mille plateaux*, pp. 434–527.

31 *Ibid.*, p. 434.

32 *Ibid.*, p. 471.

33 *Ibid.*, p. 485.

34 Gilles Deleuze and Félix Guattari, *L'Anti-Œdipe: Capitalisme et schizophrénie* (Paris: Minuit, 1972), p. 174.

35 Founded in 1892 through the merger of the Edison General Electric Company and the Thomson-Houston Company.

36 In 1954, three American researchers, Chapin, Pearson and Prince, developed a highly efficient photovoltaic cell. The first satellites supplied by solar cells could be sent into space.

37 Buckminster Fuller, "International Symposium on Architecture," p. 271.

38 W. David Compton and Charles D. Benson, *Living and Working in Space: A History of Skylab* (Washington, DC: National Aeronautics and Space Administration, 1983), p. 11.

39 John Frazer and Peter Colomb, "Mobile autonomous dwelling facility," in *Architectural Association School 125th Anniversary Exhibition* (London: AA School, 1969), p. 82.

40 John Frazer pointed out that in 1965, 250,000 people in the United Kingdom lived year-round in caravans, that 500,000 used them for holidays and the industry produced 45,000 of them a year. Original drawings, photographs, diagrams and texts on the *Mobile Autonomous Dwelling Facility*: John Frazer's archives, consulted at his home on 3, 4 and 5 February 2005.

41 Ant Farm, "Greyhound: in the flow with mobile hardware," n.p., n.d., Ant Farm's archives, cited in Felicity D. Scott, *Living Archives 7: Ant Farm* (Barcelona: Actar, 2007), p. 94.

42 Charles Jencks, *Architecture 2000: Predictions and Methods* (London: Studio Vista, 1971).

43 Alexander Pike, "Trade note, energy package," *Architectural Design*, vol. 48, no. 2 (1978), p. 95.

44 Fuel cells have aroused strong interest since the 1990s, which has particularly increased since 2005 (notably with the possibility of envisaging their functioning with sources other than fossil energy, such as hydrogen). In the 1970s, International Fuel Cells built and produced a certain number of them.

45 "Grumman's Integrated Household System," *Architectural Design*, vol. 43, no. 7 (1972), p. 423.

46 Paolo Soleri, *Arcology: The City in the Image of Man* (Cambridge, MA: MIT Press, 1969). Translated as *Arcologie: La ville à l'image de l'homme* (Marseille: Parenthèses, 1980), p. 16.

47 *Ibid.*

48 *Ibid.*, p. 37.

49 *Ibid.*, p. 38.

50 Gerard K. O'Neill, *Space Settlements: A Design Study* (Washington, DC: National Aeronautics and Space Administration, 1977).

51 *Ibid.*, p. 31.

52 *Ibid.*, p. 33.

53 Stewart Brand (ed.), *Space Colonies: A CoEvolution Book* (London: Penguin, 1977).

54 Reyner Banham, *Theory and Design in the First Machine Age* (London: Architectural Press, 1960).

55 Luc Baboulet, "Du bâtiment à l'environnement par la technique. Une lecture du livre de Reyner Banham, *The Architecture of the Well-tempered Environment*," *Les Cahiers de la recherche architecturale*, no. 42–43 (1997), p. 174.

56 Martin Pawley, *Theory and Design in the Second Machine Age* (Oxford: Blackwell, 1990).

57 Keith Lapthorne and Graeme Aylward, *Designing for Stability in Designing for Change*, working paper no. 3 (Cambridge: Cambridge University Press, 1974).

58 Alexander Pike, notes for a lecture given at the Architectural Association School of Architecture (3 February 1976), AAP.

59 The term appeared in 1960 in an article by J. Milton Yinger, "Contraculture and subculture," *American Sociological Review*, vol. 25, no. 5 (1960). Theodore Roszak would use it a few years later in *The Making of a Counter Culture: Reflections on the Technocratic Society and its Youthful Opposition* (New York: Anchor Books, 1969).

60 Theo Crosby, *Architecture: City Sense* (New York: Reinhold Publishing Corporation, 1965), p. 13.

61 Lewis Mumford, *The City in History* (New York: Harcourt, Brace & World, 1961). Translated as *La Cité à travers l'histoire* (Paris: Seuil, 1964), p. 603.

62 *Ibid.*, p. 601.

63 Benton Mackaye, "Regional planning and ecology," *Ecological Monographs*, vol. 10, no. 3 (1940), pp. 349–353.

64 Lewis Mumford, "Authoritarian and democratic technics," *Technology and Culture*, vol. 5, no. 1 (1964), pp. 1–8, p. 2.

65 Herbert Marcuse, *An Essay on Liberation* (Boston, MA: Beacon Press, 1969). Translated as *Vers la libération* (Paris: Minuit, 1969), p. 32.

Part II: The energy autonomy movement, 1970–80

4 Counterculture radicalism

Faced with intense energy concerns, the myth of abundance would be overtaken by a focus on autonomy. A self-sufficiency imaginary dimension corresponded to this reassuring space: a new technological system ensured vital necessities and their restocking from local resources. The energy autonomy movement offered several approaches that fragmented an architectural unity of principle and intent. The various ambitions concerned self-building techniques and archetypes as well as industrialization processes and space technologies. Energy autonomy, however, gave rise to two major orientations: a first wave, which was derived from the American counterculture's self-building movement, radical and eminently political, and a second more institutional and technical approach in line with a scientific and architectural tradition.

Following the wave of the oil crisis, this energy approach would become widespread in the mid-1970s. The multiplication of projects and an evolution in programs and scales established an institutionalization of the subject of energy autonomy. If most of the research initially concerned the inhabitable unit, these energy anticipations then spread to the city and the wider landscape. Though architectural questions were never at the forefront of the counterculture ideology, self-building became the principal tool of a reconquest of space, with a view to establishing peer-based and libertarian communities. The exhibition at the Museum of Modern Art in New York and the publication of Bernard Rudofsky's *Architecture Without Architects* (1964) would make "architecture without architects" the self-builders' slogan.[1] Encouraged by the ideological enthusiasm of do-it-yourself, a host of collectives became involved in construction experiments and alternative energies. The interior space of the autonomous home illustrated, for self-builders, a dual relationship of intent: a break with the network and all its symbols of dependence, but also the effects of a more efficient management of home economics than this system offered, allowing the inhabitant to self-guarantee his or her vital necessities. In the late 1960s, American counterculture creations spread. Caroline Maniaque traced the dissemination of this phenomenon from the United States to France, through the figures of architects who both traveled and participated.[2] Maniaque demonstrates how the counterculture became a mass movement accompanied by a host of publications such as *Inflatocookbook, Undercurrents, Shelter, The Whole Earth Catalog* and *The Mother Earth News*.

The counterculture generally designates a period from the 1960s to 1975, during which the counterculture movement triumphed; however, it was following the 1973 energy crisis that the autonomy project became more refined and expanded beyond this period. The oil crisis marked a turning point: a radicalization and an accentuation of the subject of energy autonomy. Moreover, it must be emphasized that the claim of energy autonomy was not unanimous in the counterculture's building experiments. Autonomy was raised only sporadically: it would never be treated as a full-fledged phenomenon. There were many uses of so-called alternative technologies, but there were many fewer architectural and urban planning proposals that called on these technologies to develop a new energy system, in a critical vision of the network.[3] The energy autonomy project was a separate history in this wave of innovations.

A few countercultural figures asserted independence vis-à-vis traditional utilities, but very few would achieve it between 1965 and 1970. Prior to the energy crisis, *Drop City* (1965) by Steve Baer, the *Prototype I* by the Integrated Life-Support Systems (ILS) Laboratories in the United States, and the *Ecol House* (1971) in Canada, can be considered the most representative examples.

Early steps: rudimentary and rebellious ships

In 1965, the *Drop City* community in southern Colorado was one of the first to experiment with the self-building of zomes, domes and autonomous energy systems, in collaboration with Steve Baer, an expert in thermal physics and the founder of the Zomeworks Corporation. Baer built a house in New Mexico in 1971 that would have a resounding echo. Its instant fame meant that it would be widely disseminated and acquire iconic status (see Figure 62).[4]

From the late 1960s, in the United States, as in Canada, a large budget was allocated to the development of new energies, a large part of which was earmarked for the construction of experimental habitats on university campuses. This was the case for the *Ecol House*, which acquired its name from Buckminster Fuller when he visited the McGill University campus in Montreal (see Figure 63).

Led by the Minimum Cost Housing Group, construction started in 1972. The aim of this group of students and architects was to build a low-cost model of an autonomous house for developing countries.[5] The unit was mostly composed of recycled materials, water recycling was established and the distillation system and waste treatment was carried out in the bathroom. The construction of the house, the electrical materials and bathroom fixtures was estimated at $1,900, though this figure did not include the cost of the 400-watt wind turbine built by the Brace Research

Figure 62 Steve Baer House, Corrales, New Mexico (1971)

Figure 63 *Ecol House*, Minimum Cost Housing Group (1972)

Institute. When it was built, the *Ecol House* looked more like a survival shelter than a durable inhabitable unit. Let us once again cite ILS Laboratories, founded in 1971 by Robert and Eileen Reines and Malcolm Shannon, Jr. in Tijeras, New Mexico, whose *Prototype I* was 10 meters in diameter and completely independent of any auxiliary system.

The architectural press widely disseminated these experiments and this quest for autonomy spread considerably beyond the United States. In London, the Street Farmers' proposals were typical of these first attempts. Bruce Haggart, Peter Crump and Graham Caine, fifth-year students at the Architectural Association School of Architecture (AA) (brought together under the name of Street Farmers), reacted to the technological and futuristic supremacy of Archigram. They published two fanzines, *Street Farmer 1* (1971) and *Street Farmer 2* (1972), illustrated with provocative collages: urban guerillas regreening the city and working the streets, and cows nibbling buildings, thus creating room for vegetation and agriculture (see Figures 64 and 65).[6]

Graham Caine's fifth-year graduation project was a self-sufficient house made of recycled wood and plastic. Built in 1972 in a southern suburb of London with the financial support of the AA, Caine would live there with his family for two years. Estimated at £1,000, the unit was equipped with a solar water heater, wind turbine, water collection and purification system, a digester to produce methane and a tropical greenhouse in which bananas and tobacco grew. In the event of drought, the house could connect to the city's water network. The aim was to prove that a house that was independent of the centralized energy network and the food distribution system could be inexpensively built by someone without any particular skills. It was a strong argument for Caine's approach:

> As someone who knows my carpentry skill, or lack of, said: *if you can build it, anyone can.* I consider the project not to contain a romantic attitude but a revolutionary one in that it indicates both a possible means to revolution, and the stimuli, in that it exhibits a realistic alternative to the exploitational vision of the environment.[7]

Lacking an occupancy permit from the municipality, the building would be dismantled in 1975 before having reached the level of autonomy its designers had set.

The experimental house by the Dutch group De Kleine Aarde, led by the architect Jaap 't Hooft, took a similar approach (see Figure 66). A 75 m^3 geodesic dome was built on farmland in the Boxtel commune. Its lattice-covered frame was sheathed in a cork and cement shell. Using all of the natural resources needed to function in a closed circuit, this inexpensively built and rather small unit was quickly abandoned.

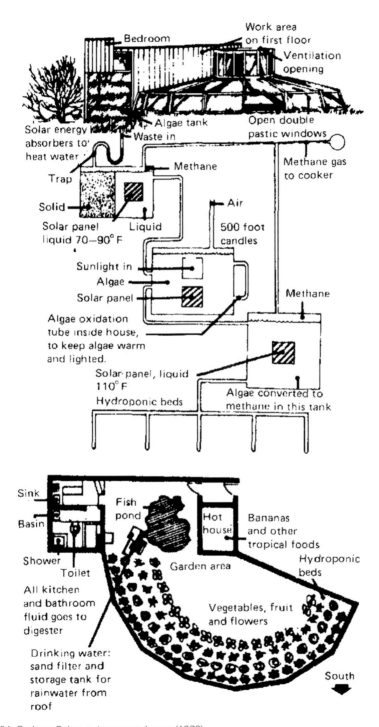

Figure 64 Graham Caine, autonomous house (1973)

Figure 65 Street Farmers, Farmage (1976)

These projects envisaged autonomy on the scale of a family or small community. The reduction in production costs and self-building led to a considerable drop in living standards, since they were designed and built in a short period of time and were modest in scope. There was no dominant typology, and many were based on the model of a shelter or cabin. They were mostly small domestic modules, rarely with more than one level. There was no ambition to create an autonomous architectural model and few urban planning concerns. Before 1973, energy autonomy remained a fragile undertaking; however, Alexander Pike's *Autonomous Housing Project (AHP)*, which will be detailed further on, is a notable exception. Earlier creations, built with precarious, unadapted means, would not capture the imagination. Regarding the first attempts at alternative technologies, autonomy was often attained at the cost of comfort, which was deemed elementary and hard to "popularize" by others. A change in orientation in the counterculture can, however, be noted in the early 1970s. In his chapter, "Epilogue, the fall of Drop," Alastair Gordon described the loss of impetus and the degeneration of the first experiments. Though the review *Shelter* continued to promote other ways of inhabiting, part of the movement attempted to analyze the problems encountered, from relational crises to the impoverishment of daily life, including the drug problem. In 1973, Lloyd Kahn, editor in chief of *Shelter*, published photos of the abandoned and dilapidated domes of *Pacific Height* and *Drop City*.[8] Peter Rabbit, one of the founding members of the Colorado community, wrote on this double page: "There are ghosts behind every

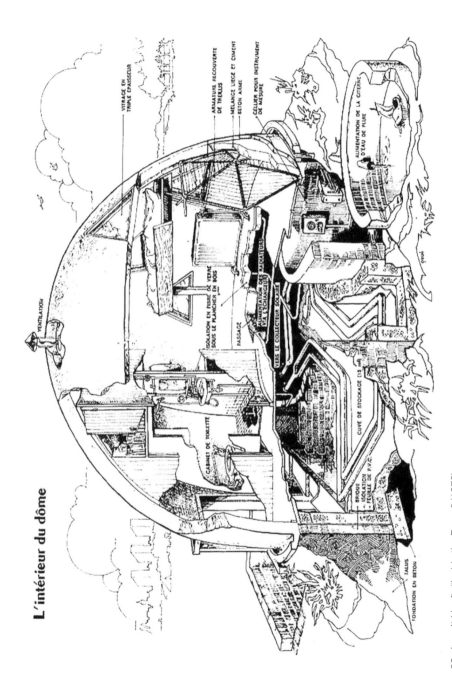

L'intérieur du dôme

VENTILATION

VITRAGE EN
TRIPLE ÉPAISSEUR

ARMATURE RECOUVERTE
DE TREILLIS

MÉLANGE LIÈGE ET CIMENT
BÉTON ARMÉ

CELLUR POUR INSTRUMENT
DE MESURE

ALIMENTATION DE LA CITERNE
D'EAU DE PLUIE

ISOLATION EN FIBRE DE VERRE
SOUS LE PLANCHER EN BOIS

ALIMENTATION DES RADIATEURS
VIA L'ÉCHANGEUR

PASSAGE

VERS LE COLLECTEUR SOLAIRE

CUVE DE STOCKAGE (12 m³)

CABINET DE TOILETTE

BRIQUE
ISOLATION
FEUILLE DE P.V.C.

TALUS

FONDATION EN BÉTON

Figure 66 Jaap 't Hooft, "Inside the Dome" (1972)

broken window. In less than ten years, Drop City has become a ghost town."[9] Most of the architectural and community experiments that had flourished in the mid-1960s would be as fleeting as they were spontaneous. Led by peer groups, autonomy first concerned the individual and semi-collective habitat. It nourished the communitarian utopia founded on reduced ties and the illusion (by the control of one's consumption and energy and food production) of the reinvention of a better world. The counterculture's first attempts were a relatively homogeneous constellation; however, with the implementation of a high-performance autonomy, these projects contributed to the movement's genesis. The second wave of experiments, triggered by the energy crisis, would be more interesting.

The 1973 crisis: acceleration

As the oil-producing countries suspended their supply to the American and European markets in 1973, the autonomy project became concrete. This event brought energy servitude to the fore and revealed its economic stakes. The *New York Times* examined the national objective newly proclaimed by President Nixon: "the 'independence project,' which formulated the hypothesis of a America that was self-sufficient in energy by 1980, if the Arab countries continued to refuse to sell oil."[10] The oil crisis dramatically revealed energy dependence and encouraged an acceleration of research and publications on alternative energy on every level of society. John and Sally Seymour's *Self-Sufficiency* (1973) and *Farming for Self-Sufficiency* (1973) focused on farming, while Carol Hupping Stoner's *Producing Your Own Power* (1974) and David Ernest Robinson's *The Complete Homesteading Book* promoted energy produced at home by inhabitants (see Figures 67a–67d). In the vast majority of cases, these titles provided an account of self-building techniques to make dry toilets or solar water heaters; they were often accompanied by texts with an ideological bent on wasting resources and the energy lobbies.

Many public and private institutions and research units invested in the study and application of these technologies in the United States and elsewhere in the world. The Solar Energy Society created its section in the United Kingdom in 1973–74. The Centre for Alternative Technology was founded by Gerard Morgan-Grenville in 1974 in Wales.[11] In France, *La Gueule ouverte*, the first magazine to claim that it was "ecologist," was founded in 1972, and the experiments on solar energy in Odeillo were in full swing. In this favorable context, energy autonomy became more credible. First experimented on in rural zones or on university campuses, it began to be introduced into the urban fabric.

The exhibition "1973: sorry, out of gas. Architectural innovation in response to the oil crisis," held by the Canadian Centre for Architecture in 2007, gave an account

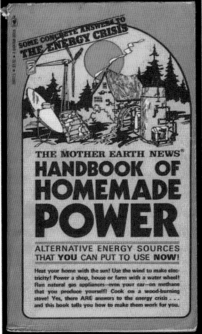

Figure 67 Selected covers of publications on the subject of energy or food self-sufficiency in the home

of the historical moment of the crisis and its repercussions through a presentation of projects catalogued according to their dominant energy: "Sun," "Earth," "Wind," "Integrated Systems."[12] The latter presented the Ecol Operation and the Integrated Life-Support Systems mentioned above, as well as the New Alchemy Institute (NAI), *Ouroboros South* and *Ouroboros East* and the Farallones Institute. These last three projects showed a strengthening of energy autonomy, an improvement in its technologies and a territorial deployment. The New Alchemy Institute, created in 1969 by the biologists John Todd and William McLarney with the writer Nancy Jack Todd, worked primarily in the rural zone for total self-sufficiency. They described their work in *The Journal of the New Alchemists*, seven issues of which were published between 1973 and 1981. The *Dimetrodon Corporation* in Warren, Vermont should also be mentioned. This co-owned structure, launched in 1973, was a rather typical example of the rural project. In 1974, the architects James Sanford, Richard Travers and Bill Maclay planned ten autonomous houses on the Warren site. In 1977, three units and all their common services, including laundry and a workshop, were completed. There were various energy production methods: electricity was provided via a wind turbine, solar cells were placed on roofs with a sixty degree incline, water was purified for drinking, radical recycling was practiced and all the organic waste was treated by a Phyto-purification system. Five of the ten units were finally built. Despite fragile energy systems, the site was extremely dynamic and active until the 1990s.

Autonomy was a recurring subject in architecture schools in the late 1960s. In 1973, at the University of Minnesota, students supervised by the architect Dennis R. Holloway built the *Ouroboros* project. It concerned the construction of two experimental houses: *Ouroboros South* (1973), in the rural environment surrounding the university's Rosemount Research Center, and *Ouroboros East* (1974–75), a rehabilitation of a building on Laurel Avenue in Minneapolis. The NAI and *Ouroboros* marked an evolution in the autonomy project and a new degree of efficiency was reached. Similarly, in 1973, students at the University of Sydney began the construction of an autonomous unit under the supervision of Colin James. In Australia, the architects John Baird, John Cuthbert and Colin Mitchell, associated with the Royal Melbourne Institute of Technology (RMIT) and the architecture school, built a few *Self-Sufficient Dwellings* in the rural zone, composed of lightweight structures and recycled materials. Here too, the objectives were clearly focused on autonomy:

> The aim of the owners is to ultimately achieve complete self-sufficiency. They currently produce their own electricity from the wind, hot water and heating from the sun, collect rainwater for all domestic needs, grow a large proportion of their total vegetable requirement and hopefully produce methane gas for cooking.[13]

Autonomous houses were now legion in the United States, as elsewhere in the world. Where many opted for the reconquest of rural regions, some saw major reconversion possibilities in the urban fabric.

A new urbanity

In 1972, the architect Sim Van der Ryn founded the iconic Farallones Institute in Berkeley, California. Devoted to the study of inexpensive and energy-autonomous building methods, the institute tackled the urban application of "appropriate technologies." The observation of the team at the Farallones Institute is similar to those of other groups:

> What will you do when a transit strike closes your local grocery store, when there is no more gasoline at the local service station, no natural gas in the pipes to the furnace or heater, and so on? What are you doing as food, gasoline, electricity, and natural gas prices rise and water becomes scarce?[14]

The search for other energy possibilities in the urban zone was a strategic choice for those who wanted to undertake an ecological renovation of buildings. The house's structure itself and its internal systems were the key to a reversal of consumption mode. In the work devoted to this adventure, *The Integral Urban House*, the authors wrote that the house "is none other than a space from which I obtain the vital necessities." The ambition of the program, launched in 1973, was to rehabilitate a Victorian house in Berkeley to one independent of traditional infrastructures. The group moved its offices into it in 1974. In a dynamic of reconquering the territory, the transformation of the habitat in the existing urban frame seemed more appropriate and convincing to them than the development of new constructions in the rural zone. They preferred the term "integral" to "self-sufficient":

> [W]e choose this term because we were striving for an integration of ideas about structure both as habitat and life-support system. There is a need for a new synthesis of biological and architectural ideas.[15]

Urban requalification was described here in terms of rehabilitating isolated objects without any global reflection on urban planning. The reorganization of production, consumption and recycling cycles was carried out at the level of the home, which was deemed the most "controllable" and one that could be transformed the most efficiently. But the Farallones Institute expressed its doubts on total autonomy:

We do not think the solution to environmental crisis is self-sufficiency, because such a condition is not possible even if it were desirable. If self-sufficient human communities exist at all, they are extremely rare.[16]

Recognizing the extent of the technical difficulties, the group established a maximum autonomy (use of solar energy, water collection and recycling, kitchen garden and aquaculture), but the house remained connected to the electricity infrastructure for its energy complement and, above all, as they pointed out, to avoid too great a tension with the municipality. Conflicts were systematic: Graham Caine, like Jaap 't Hooft and Sim Van der Ryn, had tough discussions with city administrations. They all mentioned the weight of energy standards (see Figure 68).

In this regard, the polemics set off by the Energy Task Force (ETF) in New York in the 1970s illustrates this urban situation of energy conflict. Taking the initiative of renovating energy, the owners of a building on the Lower East Side founded a cooperative whose primary objective was energy autonomy. The press took hold of this subject, championing the inhabitants:

> The inhabitants of the urban homesteading project at 519 East 11th Street in New York have carried their aim of self-sufficiency beyond the physical rehabilitation of buildings to the production of their own energy supplies. Their latest development is a windmill which generates electricity and feeds its surplus back into the city power lines, reversing the meter and reducing the homesteaders monthly bills. New York City's power company, Consolidated Edison (ConEd), is now threatening to disconnect the supply of electricity, and is taking them to court. Ramsay Clark, one-time Attorney General of the United States and a proponent of civil rights legislation, is defending the community on the Lower East Side.[17]

The cooperative installed thirty solar panels that could supply 85 percent of the building's heating needs, as well as a wind turbine that generated two kilowatts. The polemics that this partial autonomy resulted in shows the reticence of the energy market. This project was initially funded by a $40,000 subsidy from the Public Services Administration in Washington, but the electricity company immediately protested, claiming that this system interfered with the smooth running of its network by creating technical disturbances. Alternative energy advocates took up this trial of strength with activist ends:

> In the grid, that it will distort transformers and computerized equipment, and that it could even create a hazard for repair crew working in the same part of the grid! Nevertheless, ETF and independent engineers are confident that there will be no negative effects. The

Figure 68 Solar panels installed on the roof of 519 East 11th Street, New York City (1976)

court case, if won by the people of the Lower East Side, may become an important legal precedent for a pluralistic structure of power production.[18]

The ETF continued its energy offensive by attempting to equip three other buildings on 11th Street and a larger one in the South Bronx. The city's housing and urban planning department allocated $30,000 to them to install 12,000 m² of solar collectors for twenty-eight apartments. Despite pressure from the electricity company, these funds made it possible to promote the renewable energy market and increase competition between the utilities. At the end of the 1970s, faced with pressure, the 11th Street building was reconnected to the dominant utilities. "Electricity companies do not intend to let energy production slip through their fingers,"[19] one of their resigned supporters would comment.

This example reveals some of the contradictions and hesitations of the energy market: on one hand, state support; on the other, the protest of monopolies. If total autonomy was an ambition, it clearly appears that its achievement remained as complex as it was rare. The counterculture gave birth to a host of projects. Their heterogeneity resulted from the constraints inherent in the sites, the unequal means, the actors' variable endurance and their diverse intentions. Producing a contamination effect, the projects multiplied in a very short period of time with very limited means but an invincible determination. The adventures embarked on were often as short-lived as they were radical, and many projects left nothing to posterity – this was also a specific trait of this historical period.

The handful of cases brought up in this chapter have made it possible to relate the climate of multiplicity and enthusiasm that spread from the United States to Europe. It may be observed that all the projects mentioned were marked by battles. The blocking of municipalities and regional administrations, demanding compliance with technical standards, often accelerated the decline of these experiments. It would seem that withdrawing into the countryside permitted greater freedom arising from the initial absence of infrastructures and the distance from neighbors. However, most of these projects dwindled both socially and technically. In the city, the regulatory connection obligations and disputes with those close by were the principle cause of the project's failure. As the city was considered mostly conquered by the public powers (energy, real estate, etc.), the actors of autonomy invested in the domestic small scale, laying claim to a fragmented, dispersed coherence, without any prior urban planning intention. Often characterized by political radicalism, a desire for decentralization, protest against the established territorial order, and even an anti-urban positioning, the counterculture seized upon renewable energies but seems to have taken part as much in their dissemination as their marginalization. This is at least what the movement was criticized for:

In rejecting the values (technique) of the dominant society, the counter-culture – as documented in this underground press – did not progress very far towards developing a clear perception of the alternatives, despite an ever-increasing awareness of the necessity for doing so. Clearly, a 'new sensibility', as Herbert Marcuse termed it, was being evolved by the counter-culturalists. But overall there was a failure to create alternative structures or to positively define the ways and means of achieving the (ill-defined) alternative society, and this, along with hostility and co-option by the dominant society destroyed the chance of achieving what may, in any case, have been an impossible dream.[20]

The improvisation that accompanied these projects was deemed incapable by its detractors of captivating ambition beyond its movement. The critics were harsh. In an article about the fragility of their communities, the journalist Gerry Foley deplored in 1976:

[P]rosperous middle-class eco-freaks assuming a mantle of poverty and primitiveness but scampering back to the bank as soon as the going gets tough. Their "Arcadianism" and alternative technologies were unleashed … To the impossible realization of their projects is added this dubious social ethic of autonomous housing or energy autonomy; they missed the reality.[21]

Nonetheless, energy autonomy and the communitarian lifestyle had a great deal to do with applying the asserted ideals to daily life. If the crisis clearly caused a radicalization of the architecture of the counterculture – providing genuine momentum to the autonomy project – it was not the subject of any notable conceptualization before the mid-1970s (with the exception of Alexander Pike). A critical approach to centralism and the dominant technology connects these practices, but very few texts were able to comprise an "anthology of energy autonomy": technical popularization prevailed. Between 1965 and 1975, the theoretical link was relatively weak. In this vast ensemble, however, certain figures standout for the iconic nature of their works, the originality of their positions and the longevity of their practices: Michael Jantzen and Michael Reynolds in the United States and Michel Rosell in France. The commitments of these three architects between 1975 and 1980 marked this post-crisis evolution in which disconnection became a genuine project. The heirs and critics of the "first" counterculture, they displayed notable technical progress, both strategically and theoretically, in their analyses and productions. They built experimental sites and inspired still active architectural practices that prolonged, in the 2000s, the energy dream of the 1970s.

The experimental territory of Michael Jantzen

Michael Jantzen believed that the 1973 crisis was a decisive element that would strengthen his architect's profile and guide his practice toward the technical and prospective dimension of energy autonomy. He stated that he had begun to explore these alternative technologies "because of the effects of the oil crisis and because it was a fascinating architectural challenge."[22] If Jantzen's approach to self-sufficiency was above all aesthetic and mechanized, in line with Fuller's ideas, the political component of autonomy was a driving force for him:

> The idea of not being connected to the government for my vital energy needs is important to me. I am also seduced by the possibility of living far from the city and its network services, of being energy independent.[23]

In 1973, he designed an experimental group of autonomous structures on his property in Carlyle, Illinois. Influenced by aeronautical and space design, his modules presented a maximum number of functions in a minimum amount of space; the house became a micro-center of energy production. The *Vacation House* (1974) was composed of recycled agricultural construction materials, with the silos' roofs covering the structure (see Figures 69a and 69b). The house had an upper floor, a ground floor and a terrace. Heating was provided by a passive solar system, electricity by photovoltaic panels and a wind turbine. A few years later, Jantzen built his Carlyle house on the same principles (see Figures 70a–70d).

A reduction in production costs did not mean banal and modest architecture: by combining recycled elements and prefabricated pieces, Jantzen emphasized the stylistic aspect, countering the aesthetic triviality often associated with self-building. Staging the various elements, the interior view of his housing unit showed a computer workstation in the foreground. In 1979, with the engineer Ted Bakewell, Jantzen created an "earthling" capsule that would be featured in numerous publications.[24] One example in the press described the project:

> The dream of a habitation fulfilling the requirements of the future has now been realized: autonomous in energy provision, ecologically and economically competitive and just as comfortable as a house. This experimental project is the home today of Ted Bakewell, who solved all the problems of an autonomous mobile vehicle. [...] Totally independent of public energy networks, it can go anywhere, on the highway, or on water, towed by a boat or a helicopter.[25]

Figure 69 Michael Jantzen, *Vacation House*, Carlyle, Illinois (1974)

Figure 70 Michael Jantzen, autonomous house, Carlyle, Illinois (1978)

This 42 m^2 space was designed for mass production. It had all the equipment needed for a comfortable domestic life. Rainwater was collected and purified in a tank, gray water recycled and waste burned in a micro-incinerator that heated the water for the shower. Complementary energy was provided by a heat pump and passive solar principles. Photovoltaic panels (Arco) supplied the electricity and were stored in cells that also held the kinetic energy from the capsule's towing (see Figures 71a–71d).

Jantzen's approach was thus more architectural and technical, while his formal approach distinguished it from that of earlier experiments. Jantzen described his approach:

> I have always felt that we need to develop a new aesthetic around the technology in order for it to function in most effective way. I feel that conventional aesthetic has often held back the advancement of building technology. Especially when it comes to housing. Of course, my aesthetic preference would be considered futuristic. In response to this idea, I started a non-profit organization called the Human Shelter Innovation Institute. The Mission of the HSII is to design, engineer and prototype alternative human shelters systems, without the constraints of conventional aesthetics and/or conventional thinking.[26]

Michael Jantzen subsequently continued his research, producing a large number of units that could be transformed and adapted to random and evolving forms, such as the *Sun Tower*, the *Wind-Powered Pavilion* and the *Wind Tunnel Footbridge*. The interplay between passengers or inhabitants, natural resources and these automatically and manually modular architectures gradually made the reputation of this architect who, since 1970, has based his entire production on the development of energy autonomy. If all these projects have remained in the prototype stage, Jantzen contributed to the invention of a new typology and a brand new imaginary dimension concerning domestic infrastructure. The very archetype of domesticity was modified by it, the house becoming an inhabitable and evolving production machine.

Michael Reynolds's self-sufficient Earthships

Another representative figure of the autonomy movement is the architect Michael Reynolds. Unlike Michael Jantzen, Michael Reynolds extended self-building, basing it on its vernacular roots and developing a radical discourse on the challenges of autonomy. After graduating with a degree in architecture from the University of Cincinnati in 1969, he proposed the *Earthship* concept in 1970 and created the Earthship Biotecture foundation. His practice was based on the direct use of natural resources supported by a criticism of the network and energy consumption modes

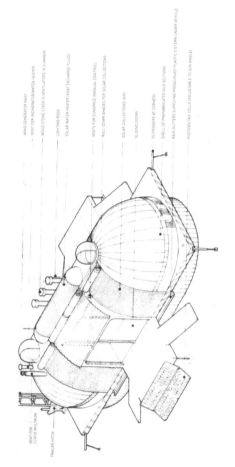

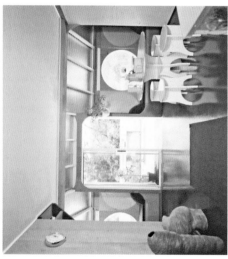

WIND GENERATOR MAST

VENT FOR INCINERATOR/WATER HEATER

WOOD STOVE STACK (3 VENT/LOUVERS IN SUMMER)

LIGHTING RODS

SOLAR WATER HEATER (HEAT EXCHANGE FLUID)

VENTS FOR SUNSPACE (MANUAL CONTROL)

ROLL-DOWN SHADES FOR SOLAR COLLECTIONS

SOLAR COLLECTIONS (AIR)

SLIDING DOORS

OUTRIGGERS AT CORNERS

SHELL OF PREFABRICATED SILO SECTIONS

RAIN GUTTERS SUPPLYING PRESSURISED PLASTIC CISTERN UNDER VEHICLE

PHOTOVOLTAIC CELLS (ADJUSTABLE TO SUN ANGLE)

VENT FOR
CLIVUS MULTRUM

TRAILER HITCH

Figure 71 Michael Jantzen, Earth Capsule, Carlyle, Illinois (1979)

inherited from the nineteenth century. Whereas this position was not explicit in the preceding projects, Reynolds made it a major argument. These architectures were primarily based on the recovery and recycling of materials (tires and beer cans were the basis of his constructions) and aimed at total energy self-sufficiency. Each house had to provide its users with a vital and renewable minimum of energy. In 1971, Reynolds patented his "beer-can brick" technique and used this procedure to build the *Thumb House* in 1972.[27] He created many *Earthships* throughout the 1980s, including the *Spinach House* and the *Turbine House*, built in New Mexico in 1979 and 1982 respectively. Michael Reynolds wrote three works summarizing his practice: *Earthship, Volume I, II* and *III*, published in 1990, 1991 and 1993 (see Figures 72a and 72b).

Though these works were published years later, their content, developed by the author as of the mid-1970s, warrants attention. Reynolds made use of the myth of original independence to state his concept of the *Earthship*:

> Just as Noah needed a life-supporting ship that would float independently without access to land, we are in need of life-supporting ships that will "float" independently without access to various archaic self-destructive systems upon which we have grown dependent. These systems include centralized energy systems which give us acid rain, radioactive waste and power lines lacing the earth like spider webs.[28]

The widespread growth in consumption was a new challenge for construction. According to Reynolds, the building industry no longer offered satisfactory solutions to comfort and energy. These "independent vessels" would be a necessary step in the evolution of the twentieth-century habitat. Michael Reynolds formulated a head-on criticism of the centralized energy system, deploring submission to its vulnerability. He introduced the hypothesis of a natural disaster or simply a breakdown that would be enough to show the irrelevance of this model: "Without these systems, our homes lose all their functionality." He proposed re-evaluating it from the energy viewpoint, not only denouncing dependence, but the illusion of comfort and modernity. Energy systems "give us power in one hand and poison in the other," he proclaimed.

> Centralised water systems always involves electricity in some way, so the water systems are dependent on the electrical systems. This, in addition to questionable purification and treatment processes, leaves many cities with water that is undrinkable and dependent upon the power grid. In rural situations, pumped well water is almost always dependent upon the power grid and in many areas is already undrinkable due to sewage, cattle urine or radioactive waste."[29]

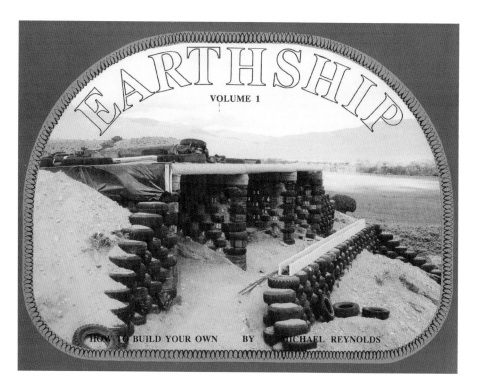

Figure 72 Michael Reynolds, *Earthship Volume I: How to Build Your Own* (1990)

Figure 73 Michael Reynolds, The Sick House, in *Earthship Volume I: How to Build Your Own* (1990)

The rise in the standard of living and energy consumption caused a host of environmental risks. Reynolds believed that the house had fallen ill from its dependencies (see Figure 73).

"A person in vital care in a hospital must always be monitored and "connected" to the various devices that keep them alive. This is our current concept for housing."[30] The metaphor underlines the alarmism of the environmental discourse: the network, which was synonymous with hygiene and social progress, became, in Reynolds's eyes, the image of a pathogenic infrastructure infecting the territory and contributing to an environmental, architectural and urban degeneration (see Figure 74).

As Manichean as these assertions were, Reynolds's call to reconsider the basics of the living environment, shifting to the recreation of a subsistence economy, had a resonance that helped to make him the leader of self-sufficiency. He defended the primacy of the energy function:

[W]e need to evolve self-sufficient living units that are their own systems. These units must energize themselves, heat and cool themselves, grow food and deal with their own waste.

Figure 74 Michael Reynolds, The Sick House, in *Earthship Volume I: How to Build Your Own* (1990)

> The current concept of housing in general, supported by massive centralized systems, is no longer appropriate, safe or reliable. We are now in need of Earthships – independent vessels – to sail on the seas of tomorrow. [...] An Earthship is a vessel to take care of us in the world of tomorrow, when population and global abuse will be reality to reckon with. This tomorrow is coming fast. We will be more concerned with self-sufficient comfort than with style and tradition.[31]

These statements marked a decisive break, generating new priorities for twenty-first-century home architecture. Reynolds stressed, in a critical enumeration of nuclear-generated electricity, water and sewage, gas and food, the failure and danger of network systems that paradoxically made the house "inhabitable." He strongly condemned the utilities' interdependence, the subscription's high cost, the companies' profit, waste and environmental pollution. Reynolds believed that the overconsumption of energy induced a new inhabitability condition. "Energy is now a more important factor in housing than shelter."[32] Since a house without an energy supply amounted to a dwelling without a roof, Reynolds advocated the "battery-house," going beyond the state of dependence instituted by the beliefs and promises of the energy domestication of the nineteenth century. The author detailed the technology of the *Earthship*, fully or partially buried, dealing with the questions of orientation,

heating and material resistance. Energy autonomy was envisaged through the installation of solar and wind energy collection systems and total control of the water cycle
(see Figures 75 and 76).

With a focus as radical as it was idealistic, the architect ardently wished for the
profusion of assembled or isolated *Earthships* to ecologically reconquer the land:
"Today, man must be able to build a self-sufficient and nourishing habitat all over the
world, at the top of a mountain, in the desert or on an island."[33]

Although he had always stressed the experimental nature of his houses, in 1990,
Reynolds was sued by buyers. The State Architects Board of New Mexico stripped him
of his professional credentials, though they were reinstated in 2000. Marginalized by
his peers for his seditious approach, Reynolds subsequently acquired international
renown and his commissions have considerably increased since the 2000s. He initiated three "off-the-grid communities" and there are over 3,000 *Earthships* around
the world. In 2008, he built his first *Earthship* in Normandy, France. The Earthship
Biotecture site is a beehive of activity today, proposing building workshops, rentals
and even sales of *Earthships* in Taos and Phoenix at prices ranging from $300,000 to
$1,500,000.

Eco-queer territories

In the early 1970s, radical political ecology was heavily influenced by eco-feminists
such as Carolyn Merchant and Starhawk, as well as by gay thinkers and activists
like Harry Hay and Arthur Evans. Eco-feminist theorists have shown that sexism,
racism, LGBTQ+ and gender-phobia and climate-sceptic oppression are often intertwined, and that minorities are generally the first victims of crises, whether economic,
social, political, environmental or climate-related. Since the mid-1970s, numerous
publications and journals have testified to the dynamism and commitment of feminists, lesbians, gays, bisexuals and trans people in counterculture on the United States
West Coast, initiatives that were largely ignored in the classical historiography of
counterculture (see Figure 77).[34]

In 1975, the Oregon Women's Land Trust was created with the mission of giving
women access to land in order to regain autonomy and preserve the environment.[35]
The project saw 147 acres of land collectively purchased in Douglas County to create a
place where economically disadvantaged women could stay with other women, without the need for a permanent residence or an invitation. From a separatist perspective,
the return to the land is a way of rebuilding feminist islets of solidarity and struggles.
This is where other ways of approaching the relationship to money and work are
reinvented individually and collectively by setting up systems of energy autonomy
and food self-sufficiency. The French sociologist and feminist Françoise Flamant,

Figure 75 Michael Reynolds, Earthship energy system (1975)

Figure 76 Michael Reynolds, water epuration system (1975)

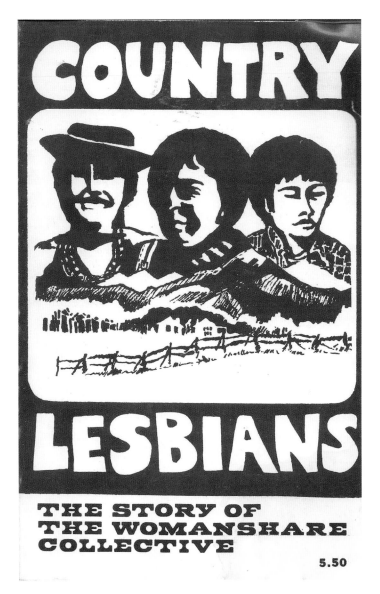

Figure 77 *Country Lesbians: The Story of the WomanShare Collective* (1976)

in a recent book called *Women's Lands* (2015), has retraced the history of those who have lived outside hetero-patriarchal territories from an environmental and also spiritual perspective, including those that borrow from shamanic and/or Amerindian traditions. In all of these rural autonomous communities, the aim was to decon-struct the traditional male-cisgender-hetero-white regimes and technical knowledge systems that maintain a relationship of domination and mercantilization of nature.

The reappropriation of technical skills for empowerment is at the heart of the efforts of many feminist and LGBTQ+ groups and collectives. For instance, in 1978, the Seven Sisters collective was created in California, consisting of women carpenters who were committed to reclaiming the technical know-how of the building industry and fighting against professional discrimination. The Radical Faeries movement, created in 1979 and still alive, focused on creating community and eco-libertarian living spaces (first gay, then more open afterwards). Since 1974, the journal *RFD* (created before the movement) has featured the country-living and alternative lifestyles of the gay community and the Radical Faeries. The movement has since become internationalized. Today, there are Radical Faeries sanctuaries and sites in North America, Europe, Asia and Australia (see Figure 78).

The history of eco-queer movements is now taking shape; it is a diverse and plural constellation whose protagonists define themselves alternately: degrowth activists, neo-rural, close to social justice movements, but the focus of their approach is to be simultaneously ecologist, anti-patriarchal, anti-colonialist and anti-capitalist.[36] Queer identities augment and participate in the implementation of specific activist strategies and practices: to produce other mixed nature-culture worlds; to locally create affinity and solidarity-based militant networks;[37] to fight against the hetero-patriarchal universe and all its normative violence. It is also because sexual and gender minorities have been accused of being "unnatural" that there has been a need to question this concept; these communities thus participate in the deconstruction of essentialist and preconceived ideas of nature. In the projects mentioned here, agricultural work, permaculture, self-organization and self-management, cooperative and collective production methods meet the needs of constituted and small-scale communities. These autonomous approaches, combined with feminist commitments and LGBTQ+ struggles, form the different facets of the same project: building alternatives to capitalism by putting ideas into practice and linking local actions to global political struggles.

Michel Rosell: from the class struggle to the autonomous house

The architecture of the counterculture gathered many "American" cases, but self-building and energy autonomy were in no way limited to the North American continent. In France, the architect and urban planner Michel Rosell was the key figure of this movement. Arriving in Paris at the end of the 1960s, he took part in the ICO (information and worker correspondences). A student in the No. 6 Architecture Pedagogy Unit (UP6 – today the Ecole nationale supérieure d'architecture de Paris–La Villette) in Vincennes, close to Hubert Tonka, Jean Aubert, Jean-Paul Jungmann and Antoine Stinco, he frequented the Utopie group.[38] In the social movement and

Figure 78 *RFD* (Winter, 1975)

internationalist line, Rosell rapidly became familiar with texts and discussions of the American counterculture. Printer at the Ecole des Beaux-Arts, he took part in the creation of the magazine *ZZZ*,[39] whose first two issues he printed at UP6, as he did for *Melp!* and *La Face cachée du soleil* in 1974. Rosell participated in the seminar "Le logis comme plus grand corps" ["The dwelling as a larger body"] given by the architect Jean Cédelle, who was called Laberthonnière.[40] The principles of energy autonomy were compared to biology at the seminar. Laberthonnière condemned the rational organization of the abandonment of the body to the benefit of its requisition in merchandise, and notably experimented with the interplay of form. In 1972, he became concerned about "the turn ecology was taking toward a new hygiene movement and nature as spectacle."[41] He was determined to improve how the ecological niche was recognized in order to define an optimal space. The shell would be both structure, transformer and collector of climatic energy. The concept of the dwelling as a larger body called on the optimization "of energy efficiency directed at usage value." Energy autonomy was subsequently solicited:

> Let us recall that following the example of the shortages of other species, the presence of the physiological shortage being set out as demand is added to the demand for energy merchandise. Its control through the means of distribution, and the latter helping to justify the dependence on the soil that is irrigated by it, raises the problems for us of energy autonomy in the ecological niche. [...] We must be separated from distribution by incorporating flexible components in the shell. But energy autonomy is only one of the forms of a broader autonomy, the one that emerges from cosmo-ecological nesting; outside the purview of meaning, in which the choice of the place is made through the singular and collective knowledge of the space.[42]

Michel Rosell formed part of the framework of the experimental pedagogic practice of UP6. In 1976, he presented his doctoral thesis, "De la lutte des classes à la maison autonome espace du désir" ["From the class struggle to the autonomous house space of desire"] under Laberthonnière's supervision.[43] Verve, rhythm and provocation defined this fiery pamphlet which, in form and content, was more like a scathing Situationist attack than a doctoral dissertation (see Figure 79).

The illustrated cover presented a photograph of Barcelona in July 1936 showing "The proletariat in arms against Franco's putsch"; the second, an arborescent (and sexist) interlacing titled "Wave of grass on the space of desire." It immediately prompted polemics: on 10 December 1975, the Ministry of Culture sent a letter to the director of UP6 asking that the original title be modified, failing which the thesis defense would be cancelled.[44] The wording was toned down and the title was changed to "Search for a house with autonomous energy sources integrated into its

Figure 79 Michel Rosell, "Mémoire de la lutte des classes à la maison autonome espace du désir" (1976)

environment." Rosell reacted with a further provocation: the modified cover was transparent, showing the original on the second page, on which he wrote:

> Concerning a censured title of a thesis: The Ministry asked me to change the title of my thesis (letter sent to the director of UP6 by M. Musy, November 10, 1975) because it is incomprehensible. It is obvious that the poetry is not understood by the public power or the public power understands the explicit poetry too well, which it denies, the poetic title being inspired by two bourgeois taboos: the class struggle and sex. Erogenous architecture has no place at the University. But not having any time to lose with neuropaths at the moment, to enter into a battle at this level with the mass of diverse individualities who do not share the views of the public power at UP6, I allow myself to humorously treat this arbitrary act of 'liberal' power with a transparent cover.[45]

This three-part thesis was composed of collages of texts, tracts and analyses written since 1970.[46] The texts of the first part highlighted the close dependence of architects on the banking and technocratic powers; the radical criticism by the author defended the need for a complete change in perspective, considering architecture as a miniature society and an element of separate power. In the last two parts, two experiments were presented, which Rosell believed showed further possibility: Le Bourdigou, an autonomous vacation village self-built by its inhabitants, which would finally be demolished, and his graduation project: an autonomous house.

After a fierce criticism of the wage and production system in architecture and urban planning, the author analyzed the architecture crisis as a general helplessness, in the face of a growing contradiction between the enormous development of the increasingly oppressive built context (the city) and each individual's aspiration to control his social future to "free himself from the ties of dependence in which his creative ability is alienated."[47] Rosell used the example of the Le Bourdigou fishing village in the Roussillon, near Sainte-Marie-la-Mer to illustrate "an architecture without architects or capitalists." After a first demolition shortly after the war in 1945, the village was rebuilt following the ancient construction tradition of the *barraca*, in reeds and rushes.[48] A hamlet primarily devoted to fishing activities until the nineteenth century, in the late 1960s Le Bourdigou mostly accommodated vacationing families. Rosell emphasized "the extraordinary autonomy and self-organization capacities" of these summer visitors. It was a vacation village "launched without any developer, urban planner, architect or activity organizer; a genuine human community of some 2,000 inhabitants was constituted."[49] Drinking water came from Sainte-Marie-la-Mer, wastewater was discharged into cesspools, there were dry toilets, water extracted from the soil was used for daily life and solar water heater systems were installed. In 1974, there were 450 single-level reed houses, surrounded by kitchen gardens. In 1975, this untouched, free-living leisure community received an eviction order in the framework of the regional tourism development plan for the Mediterranean coast.[50]

For Rosell, Le Bourdigou symbolized the liquidation of "autonomous pockets" and self-building experiments; however, like Jantzen, he considered that an aesthetic and organizational leap had to be pursued in order to create a movement that could support these practices. In this sense, his autonomous house would be "a qualitative and technical leap for a new experimental art that is based on the requirement of the complete creation of daily life as a unique and passionate work of art."[51] Rosell's aesthetic requirement challenged the idea of self-building as it was too often criticized by the profession, even limited to survival. "Self-building is not the construction of destitution, but extends to all of daily life, erases separation and founds the desire for another life."[52] In this respect, Rosell's project was a great deal more than a "house with the sources of autonomous energy integrated into its environment," as the second title described. In "Fondement préliminaire pour une maison autonome" ["Preliminary foundations for an autonomous house"], Rosell writes:

> The period denies the irrational nature of desire, it is fond of technocratic modularity, it sets its sights on the industrialization of the habitat, not on us. The project formalized by planar sketches and models will take its inspiration from the fantastic in which symbolism will resonate with the erogenous zones. It will be extended by the study of various materials and technical implementation. This place will be composed of two complementary forms. One aesthetic, the meeting point of all the poetic and plastic desires, the other a natural energy (solar, wind, etc.) place. The joining of the two will provide an autonomy of what is more than simply a living space. The interest of a project such as this does not only lie in what is built, but also in the adventurous movement that founds it.[53]

In his memoir, *La Grange aux Ardents*, Rosell presented and described an architecture-sculpture of 400 m^2 (see Figure 80).[54]

Inspired by the fantastic architecture and critical heir of the Dadaists and surrealists, Rosell placed this creation at the convergence point of the artistic and psychoanalytic avant-garde.[55] This work was presented by its architect as a psychoanalysis of direct action resulting from an individuation process. He defined this construction as a manifesto against human confinement and the separate arts connecting the following conceptualizations: "space as a larger body," "tracing our desiring relationships in space" and "architecture without architects."[56] From a structural viewpoint, the project was composed of a metal frame made from recycled materials like shopping carts and box springs, while glass bottles were used to insulate the walls, floors and ceilings.

Figure 80 Michel Rosell, La Grange aux Ardents (1976)

The whole was covered with shotcrete reinforced with steel fibers (see Figures 81 and 82).

The surface would be enameled and the differentiation of the layers of walls depended on their function (self-bearing panel, exterior supporting panel). In *La Grange aux Ardents*, the quality of the spaces is thought out according to the following relationships: meeting, isolation, circulation, affectivity, affinity, play. In this part, Rosell described the poetics of the spaces, in which each of the future construction protagonists participated.[57] On the plans, the places are given symbolic names: "Land of the caressing look," "Lavender crescent," "Oc land," "Oïl land." The same was done for the interior space: "Passion hallway," "Terrace of the evening's loop," "Path of the childhood of desires," "Our glances do not have corners," "Meeting room" and "Terrace of the sun's gunfire." The space–poetry relationship is expressed by the continuous interplay of forms and moods, surprises and colors:

> I thought about putting, under the bathroom, a place that would communicate with the pool through the glazed areas. Consequently, while listening to music coming from the Meeting Room and its acoustic point (the form amplifies it, see the aesthetic plan), everyone will be able to contemplate the bathers who cool off, see bodies dance in aquatic weightlessness, through colored screens; what a pleasure to see the woman you love, the beings that you desire, changed into green, purple, orange, garnet. I love to look at sunlight

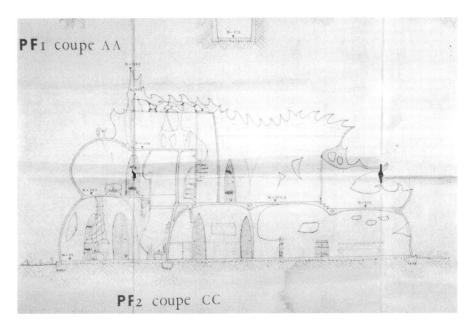

Figure 81 Michel Rosell, study model (1976)

Figure 82 Michel Rosell, La Grange aux Ardents under construction

being diffused underwater. But at night, everything is inverted; if you take a dip at this moment, what a pleasure it is to swim around a buried city that is lit underwater! What a pleasure it is to project, from inside the house, beams of colored light into the pool like a festive lighthouse! And our bodies coiled in the light like drunken fish under the stars! Having red hands on green breasts, delirium of the senses![58]

The central fireplace with its dinosaur feet, the doors in ironwork and the gargoyles, were fashioned as unique pieces. All of the principles of energy autonomy (the biological cycle, Phyto-purification, water collection, solar, wind, biogas) were experimented with, incorporated, and improved over time, through a constant search for energy efficiency. Passive solar systems, including glass-bottle insulation and collector windows, provided heat and hot water. Electricity was produced by photovoltaic panels and a wind turbine, while a second wind turbine pumped water from an underground spring. Rainwater and runoff water were collected and stored. Basins and a self-irrigation system were installed around the house. Rainwater was purified in a tank with natural filters and reverse osmosis.[59] A wastewater basin with antiseptic and filtering plants treated the water.

After obtaining his degree, Michel Rosell left Paris for the south of France, where he began building this project with a group of four people (see Figure 83):

> It is obvious that this work is in progress and we can only deliver, in this report, a part of the study for various time reasons. The complementary studies are intended to be presented as a building permit, as quickly as possible, because our desire to enjoy intensifies our desire to live without any obstacles.[60]

La Grange aux Ardents would be built as described in the memoir. The producer Christian Vincent devoted a short film, *La Part Maudite* (1987), to Rosell, in which the architect describes the project in progress.[61] The uniqueness of his approach was based on several complementary points: first, the scope of the artistic and poetic dimension distinguished the project from a large number of creations during this period, often limited by and prisoners of technical experiments. This construction was part of an architecture-sculpture trend that had some success at the time, with architects such as Jacques Couëlle, Pascal Haüsermann and Antti Lovag. A few purely aesthetic connections could also be drawn with the *Endless House* by the Viennese artist Frederick Kiesler, or the *Jardin des Tarots* by Niki de Saint Phalle in Capalbio, Tuscany, but these projects had little in common with the global approach of the architect of *La Grange aux Ardents*, for whom social, economic, environmental and political issues were inextricably linked to aesthetic, playful and fantasy dimensions. In this sense, Rosell's radical imagination could be compared to the thinking of Cornelius Castoriadis, one

Figure 83 Michel Rosell, La Grange aux Ardents under construction (bottle insulation visible before coating) (1997)

of whose originalities was the creative role of the imagination in the development of praxis. Beyond the explicit desire to free itself from the realm of necessity, Rosell's work showed his desire for a "new global experimental art":

> The separate activities of the plastics arts, literature and kinetics must be gone beyond for a protean understanding of atmosphere, integrated construction and the desire for adventure. It is a battle between use value and the simplistic thinking of the market that wants to make technology serve daily life, knowledge, not only as consumable and quantifiable merchandise but as an experiment for a radical change in lifestyle.[62]

If Rosell had critical affinities with the Situationist International organization, he considered it the last form of representation in that it did not take on praxis. The direct application of energy autonomy, imagined as a creative activity that starts a structural economic upheaval of both reality and culture, would be the key to going beyond it, which was based on self-guaranteeing vital necessities and a self-sufficient economy. With Rosell, autonomy was the focus of a theoretical conceptualization and a radical application:

> Capital's principle is to make people dependent; anything that can emancipate is systematically condemned. These techniques that increase autonomy are of no interest for the market economy; we are systematically marginalized. We must be clear-sighted and move toward total autonomy. Those who are in the antagonistic consensus are not the ones who will build the future. It is always a minority in this case that builds the future, a minority that is outside the principal conflict; it is a minority that changes intentionality.[63]

Through imagination and an active dissidence that aims to create space for economic and social liberation, Rosell proposed going beyond the traditional exploiter–exploited, dominating–dominated struggle for power to initiate a new process of daily life.

The long time it took to build this large-scale project was due to the dearth of material and financial resources (no subsidies, no sponsorship), the decision to conduct peer-based and pedagogic worksites on the free association principle, as well as the multiplication of projects and research carried out simultaneously with the construction of *La Grange aux Ardents*. In the mid-1980s, Michel Rosell's site was baptized *Université d'écologie appliquée et solidaire* (UEAS) (see Figure 84).

Numerous energy experiments and technologies were launched that utilized the biological cycle, including lagoons for wastewater treatment and water purification, starting in the late 1970s, whereby Rosell developed a Phyto-purification system with no discharge. As of 1985, research cycles on biofuels were initiated concurrently with experiments on bioarchitecture and biomaterials, as well as the compressed-air

Figure 84 Michel Rosell, Université d'Ecologie Appliquée et Solidaire (1997)

motor, the water motor and the Stirling motor. The UEAS had a large number of interns and students from all over the world. Many of the creations, working sessions and discussions that emerged from this university were, in France, the driving force of debates on alternative energies, autonomy and degrowth. Teaching at the architecture school of Montpellier in the 1990s, Michel Rosell also led several projects on autonomous individual homes whose prices could not be beaten by the construction market. The technical brochures that accompanied them – "The house at 1,500 francs" (1995), "The free house" (2000), "The rental house" (2006) – were right in line with this political and playful reasoning, whose aim was to challenge the role traditionally assigned to architects and to put the inhabitant back into the heart of the process of building his own space. Today renamed *Espace de recherche sur les arts et l'architecture* (ERAA), *La Grange aux Ardents* is being finalized. This project is the tip of an iceberg of ideas concretizing an itinerary that breaks with the framework of the order of architects.

Many community-based and self-managed sites in the United States and Europe practiced autonomy. The vast majority of these experimental sites were dismantled in the early 1980s, and their protagonists, worn down by dissidence, took other paths. On the other hand, Michel Rosell's ERAA, Michael Reynolds's Earthship Biotecture and Michael Jantzen's HSII are still influential experimentation centers today.

A problematic reception

The criticism of the architecture milieu toward those who laid claim to an architecture without architects was very strong. Iconic avatars of a future technology, certain constructions were accused of technological denial and architectural impoverishment. Academia took little interest in these experiments that it deemed materially weak, technically questionable and ideologically problematic. Indeed, Reyner Banham humorously compared the management systems of these alternative energies to spaceships or satellites, but without their technical efficiency.[64] However, the prototypes of the first creations did not go unnoticed and required a certain amount of maintenance and constant adjustments. The example of Steve Baer's *Zome House* in New Mexico in 1971 was enough for Banham to condemn the technological missteps and poor performance of this type of construction. The technical weightiness and the daily efforts required to close the large insulation panels at night, or open them in the morning, the mobilization of the family – and perhaps, especially women, Banham said – were a return to the past, a restricting domesticity that Catherine Beecher would have looked unfavorably on!

The sometimes "wild" reappropriation of "cutting-edge" technical knowledge gave rise to experiments as avant-garde as they were precarious. For the technology historian Langdon Winner, in avoiding confrontation with the realities of technical, political and social power, "a significant fraction of this movement avoided any in-depth analysis of technologies and the majority of projects that emerged were unsuited to the technical practices they wished to challenge."[65] If the different forms of the counterculture rapidly attracted media coverage, it seems that its impact on construction itself was relatively modest and its architectural heritage weak. Moreover, the latter was very controversial and seemed to raise several problems of an aesthetic, technical and ideological nature; the whole forming a magma that was tackled in many different ways – or concealed, until quite recently, by historians, as its typologies and inventory procedures were very complex. This spontaneous, anti-establishment and directly experienced architecture dissolved with its generation, leaving few manifesto objects, if not a controversial ideology. Many people condemned these productions that gave up the advantages and privileges of modernity for an idyllic and rural setting. Victims of harsh criticism, these creations received few positive distinctions. Spontaneism and technical reliability were systematically challenged by the architectural *doxa*. In France, the scandal set off by the exhibition "Architectures marginales aux USA" in 1975 at the Centre Pompidou, brought to light the visceral reactions of the profession and academics to the world of the counterculture.[66] This skepticism was a major vehicle for discrediting and even marginalizing the movement. In a general wave of unruliness, autonomy operated like a polemic slogan. The English sitcom, *The Good*

Life, broadcast from 1975 to 1978 on BBC 1, played on this register: in a chic London suburb, the Good family decide to transform their house and habits, from one day to the next, to live in total self-sufficiency. Selling vegetables from the kitchen garden, managing goats or installing a wind turbine were adventures that definitively revealed how impossible a self-sufficient life was in the social and economic structures of the twentieth century. Ridiculing as much the Goods' fanaticism as their neighbors' contempt, the series mocked these approaches.

Despite an obsolete heritage, the daring in self-builders of energy autonomy that encouraged them to undertake a process focused on deconstructing energy equipment and complex technologies, to rebuild in an unconventional and non-institutional way, must be noted. They show the appropriation of a fraction of society of a different kind of project, in concrete and situated actions. The counterculture opened an original experimentation field, whether its detractors liked it or not. Starting with the first oil crisis, energy autonomy became a widespread theme in the architectural and urban discourse. Institutions began to take an interest in this movement. Subsidized research emerged, focusing on the improvement in living standards and the production of new, highly developed models, such as the *Autonomous Housing Project*, whose virtue was to attract manufacturers and developers in the building sector. Launched in 1971 by Alexander Pike, this research unquestionably popularized energy autonomy: it remains a major reference for this examination of the recent history of the relation-ship between the infrastructure and habitat.

Notes

1   Bernard Rudofsky, *Architecture Without Architects: A Short Introduction to Non-Pedigreed Architecture* (New York: Museum of Modern Art, 1964).

2   Cf. Caroline Maniaque, "Les architectes français et la contre-culture nord-américaine 1960–1975" (PhD thesis, University of Paris viii Vincennes-Saint-Denis, 2006); Caroline Maniaque-Benton, *French Encounters with the American Counterculture 1960–1980* (Burlington, VT: Ashgate, 2011).

3   These communitarian experiments and self-building processes were detailed recently in the Canadian Centre for Architecture exhibition and catalogue: Giovanna Borasi et al., *Désolé, plus d'essence: L'innovation architecturale en réponse à la crise de 1973* (Montreal/Mantua: Canadian Centre for Architecture/Corraini Edizioni, 2007). See also Alastair Gordon, *Spaced Out: Radical Environments of the Psychedelic Sixties* (New York: Rizzoli, 2008) and Felicity D. Scott, *Architecture or Techno-Utopia: Politics After Modernism* (Cambridge, MA: MIT Press, 2007).

4   Let us recall that the four zomes of the southern side had barrel walls with manual shutters that accumulated coolness or heat depending on the season. Energy was provided by a

wind turbine and solar collectors. Baer noted the operational simplicity and the ease of installation of his system.

5 Alvaro Ortega et al., *The Ecol Operation: Ecology + Building + Common Sense* (Montreal: Minimum Cost Housing Group/School of Architecture/McGill University, 1972).

6 Bruce Haggart and Peter Crump, *Street Farmer 1* (1971) and *Street Farmer 2* (1972).

7 "Street Farmers," *Architectural Design*, vol. 31, no. 3 (1972), p. 140.

8 Lloyd Kahn (ed.), *Shelter* (Bolinas, CA: Shelter Publications, 1973), p. 118.

9 *Ibid.*

10 Patrick Brogan, "President Nixon to replace his energy task today," *New York Times*, 3 December 1973, p. 1.

11 The history of the Centre for Alternative Technology is recounted in *Crazy Idealists? The CAT Story* (Machynlleth: Centre for Alternative Technology, 1995).

12 A selection of projects was included in each; however, their classification appears to be arbitrary: what justifies the place of Michael Reynolds in the "Earth" section, instead of in "Integrated Systems"? Michael Jantzen's position in "Sun" is just as questionable. Except for the projects focused exclusively on energy (such as *Wind Works*, the solar work of the engineer George Löf) or the research on a specific typology (the underground houses by Jay Swayze, for instance), this breakdown is not always convincing.

13 "RMIT *Self-Sufficient Dwelling*," *Architectural Design*, vol. 8, no. 10 (1978), p. 561.

14 Helga Olkowski et al., *The Integral Urban House: Self-Reliant Living in the City* (San Francisco, CA: Sierra Club/Farallones Institute, 1978), p. 4.

15 *Ibid.*

16 *Ibid.*, p. 9.

17 Ariane Van Buren, "Urban homesteading with sun and wind," *Architectural Design*, vol. 47, no. 4 (1977), p. 244.

18 *Ibid.*

19 *Ibid.*

20 Elizabeth Nelson, *The British Counterculture 1966–73: A Study of the Underground Press* (London: Macmillan, 1989), p. 8.

21 Gerry Foley, "Insulated savings," *Architectural Design*, vol. 46, no. 8 (1976), p. 502.

22 Michael Jantzen, interview with Fanny Lopez, 17 January 2008.

23 *Ibid.*

24 John Morris Dixon, "Earthling capsule," *Progressive Architecture*, vol. 62, no. 4 (1981), pp. 146–149.

25 "Autonomia per abitare," *Domus*, no. 610, October (1980), pp. 42–43.

26 Michael Jantzen, interview with Fanny Lopez, 17 January 2008.

27 Michael Reynolds, "Thumb House," *Architectural Records*, vol. 152, no. 4 (1971).

28 Michael Reynolds, *Earthship, Volume I: How to Build Your Own* (Taos, NM: Solar Survival Press, 1990), p. 1.

29 *Ibid.*, p. 4.

30 *Ibid.*

31 *Ibid.*, p. 227.

32 *Ibid.*, p. 11.

33 *Ibid.*, p. 9.

34 See the quarterly journal *WomanSpirit* (1974–84), edited by Ruth and Jean Mountaingrove.

35 Sue Deevy, Nelly Kaufer, et al., *Country Lesbians: The Story of the WomanShare Collective* (Grants Pass, OR: WomanShare Books, 1976); Barbara J. Love, *Feminists Who Changed America, 1963–1975* (Champaign, IL: University of Illinois Press, 2006), pp. 274, 391.

36 Joshua Sbicca, "Eco-queer movement(s): Challenging heteronormative space through (re)imagining nature and food," *European Journal of Ecopsychology*, no. 3 (2012), pp. 33–52.

37 Queers for the Climate, Pink Bloc was present at the Seattle protests in 1999.

38 On the context of France in the 1970s, see Jean-Louis Violeau, *Les Architectes et Mai 68* (Paris: Recherches, 2005).

39 *ZZZ* magazine (ed. Jean-Paul Jungmann), 1 (1973); 2 (1973).

40 Jean Cédelle was one of the creators of the Paris architecture unit UP6. He was close to Roland Castro and Michel Cantal-Dupart in the early days of Banlieues 89.

41 Jean Laberthonnière (ed.) and his team (Jean Duflo, Jean-Pierre Le Dantec, Alex Meranet, François Séguret, Marc Vaye and Sylviane Ricou), "Alternative UP6," "Le logis comme plus grand corps," programs and sub-programs 1–4, pedagogic unit 6, research and seminar project 25 (1972–76), p. 19 (Michel Rosell archives).

42 *Ibid.*

43 Michel Rosell, "Mémoire de la lutte des classes à la maison autonome espace du désir," (PhD thesis, UP6, 1976), p. 76.

44 The diploma jury was composed of Jean Laberthonnière, study director and teacher at UP6, Jean-Paul Jungmann and Daniel Guibert, architects and teachers at UP6, and Jacques Limousin, architect and teacher at the Ecole speciale d'architecture, as well as an exterior figure, Jacques Renou, a heating specialist and plumber.

45 Rosell, "Mémoire," p. 76.

46 Certain of which appeared in the magazine *ZZZ*, 2 (1973).

47 *Ibid.*, p. 15.

48 The architectural constraints of this traditional reed structure gave rise to a study in the framework of an interregional research program on maritime and lagoon heritage: Robert Bataille-Barragué and Christian Jacquelin (eds), *L'habitat en roseau traditionnel: Les barraques de sanills des pêcheurs roussillonnais* (Montpellier: Drac of Languedoc-Roussillon, 1992).

49 Rosell, "Mémoire," p. 31.

50 The history of the demolition of Le Bourdigou is told in the collective work *Bourdigou: le massacre d'un village populaire* (Marcevol: Editions du Chiendent, 1979).

51 Rosell, "Mémoire," p. 6.

52 *Ibid.*, p. 39.

53 *Ibid.*, p. 41.

54 *La Grange aux Ardents* makes reference and pays tribute to Grange-aux-Belles, a historic place of Paris unionism where, on 11 January 1924, anarchist unionists were killed by communist bullets during an electoral meeting.

55 Influenced by the work of Wilhelm Reich, Michel Rosell took part in the founding of the Sexpol and the LOG (Laboratoire d'orgonomie générale) in Paris in 1976.

56 Michel Rosell, interview with Fanny Lopez, 14 June 2009.

57 If this project was initiated by Michel Rosell, three other people were involved in it from the beginning and would participate in its first construction phase.

58 Rosell, "Mémoire," p. 52.

59 Reverse osmosis is a water purification system developed by NASA and marketed in the late 1960s for individuals.

60 Rosell, "Mémoire," p. 56.

61 Christian Vincent, *La Part Maudite* (film, 1987, color, 35 minutes).

62 Rosell, "Mémoire," p. 52.

63 *Ibid.*

64 Reyner Banham, *L'Architecture de l'environnement bien tempéré* (Paris: HYX, 2011).

65 Langdon Winner, *The Whale and the Reactor: A Search for Limits in an Age of High Technology* (Chicago, IL: University of Chicago Press, 1986), pp. 117–119.

66 Maniaque, "Les architectes français," p. 382.

5 Alexander Pike and the *Autonomous Housing Project*, 1971–79

- Darling, tonight's Kilocalary was superb.
- It is because of our high-density energy battery!
- Cooking with digestor gas is so easy.
- Well, you run some grade two water for a bath, and I'll switch the aerogenerator wind rotor into the heat-pump compressor.
- And remember to put the goats out before locking the solar insulation shutters.

I hazard a guess at the film script for the first commercial advertising the Autonomous House, a Science Research Council backed research project being carried out in Cambridge. A revolutionary living unit.[1]

The *Autonomous House Project (AHP)* model was displayed for the first time in 1972 at the annual conference of the Royal Institute of British Architects (RIBA) in London, whose theme was, "Designing for Survival: architects and the environmental crisis." (See Figures 85 and 86.)

This public meeting was a continuation of the celebrated 1972 Stockholm conference on the environment and the Club of Rome publication, *The Limits to Growth* (1972), which introduced the concept of sustainable development.[2] The discussions during the annual RIBA conference focused on the consequences of the environmental crisis on architecture. RIBA's president asked the architectural profession to become involved in these issues. The radical and spectacular response of Alexander Pike and John Frazer was to propose the *Autonomous House Project*:

A typical house can function without any services connections. But the argument is not a return to a 'simple or archaic life.' We defend a very sophisticated self-sufficiency, as implied in the title of our intervention, 'Simple society and complex technologies.' We

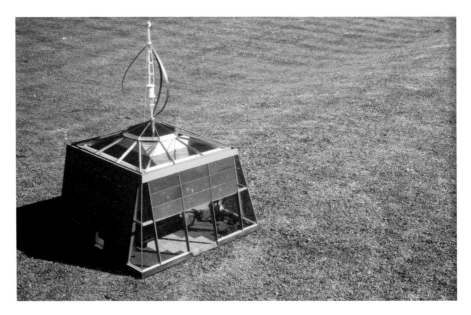

Figure 85 The Autonomous House model (1973)

must use all our technical understanding in order to build efficiency in the use of materials and alternative energies.[3]

The proposal received a resounding ovation that spread to the press and immediately became renowned.

Before the first environmental crisis and the boom in alternative energies, the *AHP* was recognized not only as a precursor – it was the first study on the subject – but also for its institutional and industrial support, its duration and influence, as well as the quantity of documental and technical analyses produced. The *AHP* adventure started in 1971 while Pike, wishing to continue Richard Buckminster Fuller's work on energy autonomy, created a technical research unit in the Architecture Department at the University of Cambridge. His objectives were clear: to create a theoretical and critical base to support the autonomy of energy services; to develop the tools needed to build and test a prototype of the autonomous house, and to promote its marketing. Though this project was influential in the 1970s, the *AHP* remains as little known today as its architect.

But who is Alexander Pike?

Alexander Pike was born in 1924 in London. During the Blitz, his parents' house was totally destroyed in one of the worst air raids that had ever struck the city. In 1941,

Figure 86 Alexander Pike and J. John Frazer (1972)

Figure 87 Alexander Pike, portrait, Cambridge (n.d.)

he entered the London County Council School of Building to take part in recon-struction.[4] Pike joined Arcon, Chartered Architects in 1950, where he was trained in mass-production techniques, including the prefabrication and industrialization of housing, which always remained his major focus (see Figure 87).

In 1956, Pike completed his final-year thesis on the prefabricated house, in which he criticized the construction industry's approach to urbanizing districts on the out-skirts of London.[5] For Pike, taking economic and organizational constraints into account required considering the design, production, transport and construction of housing as a single process. Re-examining the advantages of Arcon's "back-to-back" units (the "utility wall," where the bathroom was located on one side and the kitchen on the other, for instance), the Temporary Housing Programme or Fuller's *Dymaxion House*, Pike called for further experimentation on the prefabrication of the utility core for home use. Concurrently, he stressed the value of renewable energy, which in the end could encourage energy autonomy for buildings. Above all, Pike criticized the interdependence of utilities and the supply network as an intermediate stage, which had to be gotten past. He thus introduced the idea of independent home equipment based on new disposal and heating systems:

It would be more logical to treat waste and sewage at the source rather than at the end as we do with our drainage system, which is extremely complicated and not easy to manage. If the waste liquids and solids can be neutralized and eliminated on site, the house would find itself free of the system of underground pipes, the ground, and the artificial roots so expensive to maintain and which are often the cause of such rigid layouts.

A solution could be to have individual tanks for each house; but the ideal would be to eliminate the waste without burying it in the ground. [...] The heating itself requires reflection and experimentation. It is evident that we have not reached the summit of perfection in the heating system concept for small houses; and the developments to which we are going to assist could well render all current equipment obsolete during the next 20 years. The possibilities of solar heating are far from being exhausted and many other aspects of this could, without doubt, with sufficient research and development, produce very surprising results.[6]

All of the essential elements of his arguments on energy autonomy were already present, arguments that he would continue to develop twenty years later in the context of the *AHP*.

Discounting the *Dymaxion House*, in 1956 it was unusual for architects to think of obsolescence in energy systems. In the early 1970s, the technical developments that would enable autonomy in housing were not fully developed and research on this theme did not have broad support. Thus Pike called for a renewed approach to architecture: "The architect must become a *master industrial-designer*, he is the only one who can confront the coming century."[7] Based on a technical approach to architecture that he would defend throughout his career, this position aimed to shift the boundaries of architectural practice to encompass industrial production and energy innovations. This criticism of the separation between architecture and technology echoed the theories that Reyner Banham developed in *The Architecture of the Well-tempered Environment*. Pike, however, went beyond the analysis of passive systems and focused on the scale of a building to reflect on the network and autonomy from a different angle to Banham.

Pike left Arcon in 1962 to join Taylor Woodrow Construction Ltd, participating in the reconstruction of Euston railway station under the direction of the architect and designer Theo Crosby. In addition to Pike, the team included the young Archigram group – Warren Chalk, Peter Cook, Dennis Crompton, Ron Herron[8] and Michael Webb – as well as Robin Middleton. Nearly the entire team resigned in 1963 when the developers demanded that the program be reduced and redefined. Pike, however, remained close to Crosby, who contributed to the *AHP* through his office, Pentagram Design.

Figure 88 Alexander Pike, The Autonomous House (1971)

Pike became assistant to the architect Colin St John Wilson[9] for the Liverpool Civic and Social Centre project in 1965, and was appointed professor (specializing in the history of prefabrication, standardization and technology) in the Architecture Department at the University of Cambridge in 1969. Pike had a project in mind: creating a research unit to launch a study on the autonomous house (see Figure 88).

Pike joined the Centre for Land Use and Built Form Studies and considered himself an heir both to the work of the architects Leslie Martin and Lionel March,[10] as well as an environmental tradition specific to Cambridge.[11] Since the founding of the Martin Centre, Leslie Martin and Lionel March had examined the connection between land use and the built form. They studied simple forms, found archetypes and created urban models to compare the impact of geometry on density and energy needs for buildings at a time when computer systems were limited. The analysis and comparison of these volumes made it possible to define models and bring to light specific environmental performances, depending on the built forms. The definition of these archetypes and their work became very popular in generic research and were widely adopted. Pike would develop this model idea.

Having recently received his diploma from the Architectural Association under the direction of Peter Cook, Frazer had started teaching Russian anarchist thought and the history of utopias at the Social Sciences Department at Cambridge. His meeting with Pike was decisive: Frazer became fully involved in the *AHP*, and co-directed it with Pike during its early years. In 1972, the architects and engineers James Thring and John Littler joined the team, as well as the chemist and biologist Gerald Smith. Among the doctoral students involved in the project were the now renowned Randall Thomas and Ken Yeang.[12]

For an autonomous and modern house

The creation and the functioning of a completely autonomous home utility unit, Pike said, was "an area in which very little research has been carried out; one must therefore begin by collecting and analyzing the separate studies on the distribution network and self-sufficient services."[13] In December 1971, he presented his ambitions to the director of the Civil Engineering Science Research Council Committee in order to obtain funding. The draft agenda, which proposed nine years of research, was divided into several phases:

- The first phase endeavored to present a theoretical and technical base that could demonstrate, compared to the existing centralized network, the potential economic validity of a house that was self-sufficient in energy. This was the study phase.
- The second phase consisted of creating a housing unit that could be industrially produced and meet comfort levels. It included the improvement of certain existing systems, the creation of appropriate equipment and a presentation model. A prototype would be built at the end of this phase in 1975: the building itself would become a laboratory for testing and finalizing the energy equipment.
- The third phase would start in 1978, once the house had become operational: a family would occupy the house for two years to familiarize the public with the idea of an autonomous house. In parallel, the research team would focus on evaluating the cost of marketing the model to determine production costs and define a sales strategy.

Let us note that the experiment concerned building an *individual* home, in a zone *not connected* to a utility infrastructure. Though there were numerous efforts to broaden the possibility of autonomy for large-scale developments in the late 1970s, many self-builders favored the small-scale framework for technical experimentation and democracy. The choice of the basic unit – the individual house – denoted a cultural, architectural and technical approach that seemed very American at first glance. For the architect Peter Cavanagh, who was close to Pike, "England is in the 1970s more American than America."[14] Pike himself was fascinated by the construction industries and engineering across the Atlantic, on which he was a true specialist. But he believed that the choice of the individual house was above all technical:

> Energy Autonomy has been praised by a number of futurologists as a stable ecological and political condition. The question, which presents itself, is that of scale: autonomy for a country, a region, a community, a single house? It seems to us that the simplest and cheapest scale on which to direct the experiment on autonomy is the individual house; we will begin with this.[15]

When the city reached its optimal size, this energy decentralization could reduce congestion in urban outskirts and encourage housing development in outlying areas.

Pike believed that no one had imagined the possible spread of such systems, even in America where research, though promising, was limited to Fuller or NASA's work. An observer of these programs, Pike was persuaded that he could improve architecture for everyone.

> A certain number of technical innovations could improve the possibility of autonomous housing if they could be finalised, mass-produced and commercialised. Such is the case for two systems already developed within the programme of spatial research.[16]

These were the fuel cell, a version of which was presented in 1967 but was not available on the market, and photovoltaic panels used by NASA in the early 1970s that were financially prohibitive for home economics. Pike was sure they had a bright future and called on engineers, entrepreneurs and manufacturers to develop this market.[17] The energy system for the autonomous house would be a combination of different renewable sources, including solar, geothermal, water collection and methane (see Figures 89a–89c).

Pike's challenge was to design a new model for the domestic utility core to attain energy autonomy in different climates, whether the rainy skies of England or in developing countries. He was very enthusiastic about the possibility of the latter:

> There is, at the world scale, an almost total absence of energy services; we must drive this research so to develop a services strategy which is alternative and adaptable. [...] The

principal objective is to imagine a house, which could be totally independent of a network and situated – within reasonable limits – anywhere in the world.[18]

Pike's position as an adviser to the United Nations for an emergency housing program in Peru, with A. M. Gear & Associates in 1971, convinced him of energy autonomy's enormous potential in the countries of the Global South, where infrastructure was almost nonexistent. Questions concerning urban sprawl and self-sufficiency in the United Kingdom were, in Pike's opinion, being quickly overtaken by challenges of another magnitude that affected the entire inhabited world: energy infrastructures.

As the herald of energy autonomy, with the desire to make this goal an architectural and urban planning priority for the twenty-first century, Pike was a catalyst, an *active* witness of his time, but he was also its *critic*: he closely observed the technical experiments of the American counterculture, without adhering to it. Randall Thomas recalls: "This project was born in that context, but it was not a project of the alternative-culture. Pike was not at all impressed by this ideology. He was an idealist but not at all a hippy!"[19]

Pike was aware of the housing experiments that asserted certain autonomy principles. The performance of projects built in the early 1970s in the United States, like Steve Baer's house, *Prototype I* by the ILS Laboratories, the New Alchemy Institute, the *Ouroboros* project and the Farallones Institute were discussed in several reports. These different sites had been visited in the early 1970s by one of Pike's collaborators, the architect Philip Steadman, who enumerated these experiments in *Energy, Environment and Building* (1975). In the majority of cases, Pike regretted the fact that the resolving of technical problems came at the expense of domestic comfort. In fact, the concepts and program developed in the *AHP* bore no similarity to these experiments, which mostly concerned self-building and community housing. In their second request for funding from the Science Research Council (SRC) in 1975, Pike and the engineer Thring stressed these differences, noting the need to technically improve these models.[20] Thring pointed out that these North American applications, "have not created autonomy in the sense that we intend: an integrated system and a total autonomy, but also of a very high performance, which respects the high level of comfort in the modern house."[21]

It was in response to this dual challenge – total autonomy and high performance – that the team, very well informed on the constructions of this period, would formulate its specific approach. Its arguments were partially supported by a critique of the urban energy network and its access mode. Access to infrastructures was perceived negatively; it had, according to Pike, "become an economic, social and political problem."[22] As for the decrease in energy resources and the increase in the population, domestic

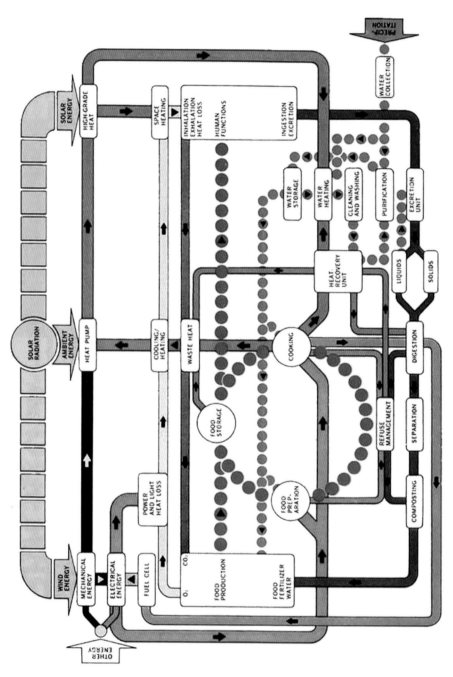

Figure 89 Alexander Pike, Integrated Services and Systems (1976)

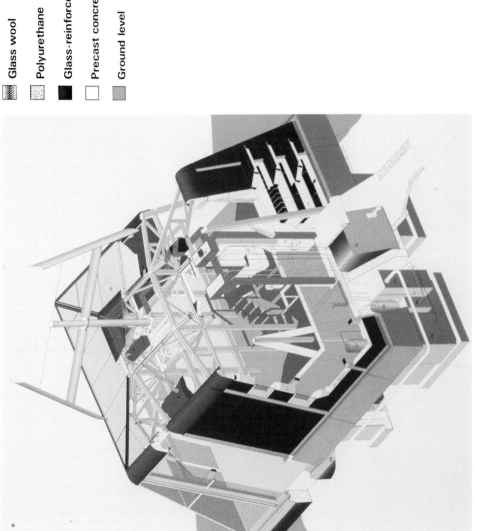

Glass wool

Polyurethane

Glass-reinforced plastic

Precast concrete

Ground level

Figure 89 Continued

needs and pollution, the network could soon become completely obsolete. For Pike, most urban planning, economic and environmental problems were caused by the constraints imposed by the network distribution system:

> It seems that these extensions of the energy network are economically less affordable than it could be with decentralisation. Their influence on the growth and health of towns is much bigger than one can believe. We are forced to accept this incessant expansion: even if this is undesirable, it has become the norm. We are in a situation where the network is simultaneously the cause and the effect of urbanity, and our hypothesis is that it is less and less legitimate […] In our studies at Cambridge, we have undertaken to analyse the real costs of the network distribution system, in order to propose an autonomous domestic energy system which is competitive.[23]

One of these objectives was therefore to disconnect from certain networks that imposed their constraints relating to size, form and density on regional development. Initially, autonomous and decentralized distribution networks could free up land and reduce property costs in peri-urban and rural areas. Taking Cambridge as a pilot zone, Thring completed a comparative study, published in the *Quantity Surveyor* and *Architectural Design* in 1972, which established cost prices for autonomous services and demonstrated their potential (see Figure 90). Though it was still not possible to totally eliminate the network, Pike stated that autonomy had to be debated and seriously considered with respect to the energy transition that would occur in the twenty-first century.

The team considered autonomy an architectural and energy approach that would have positive economic repercussions on daily life, since costs would be limited to materials and maintenance. In an ideal situation of abundant energy, Pike depicted a totally controlled and adjustable environment in line with the technical-scientific utopia of John Adolphus Etzler or Buckminster Fuller, in whom the engineer and the visionary were combined.

An iconic prototype

At the same time as Pike's experiments, various institutions also took hold of the question of energy autonomy: the SRC and the Department of the Environment (DoE) regarded the idea of autonomy – besides its experimental nature – as an opportunity to draw up an international assessment of alternative energies. In 1971, a budget of about £207,800[24] was allocated to a multi-annual program (1973–79). The following year, Pike's team obtained an initial grant of £6,000 from the SRC for a feasibility study, which was subsequently increased to £29,279 for a more in-depth

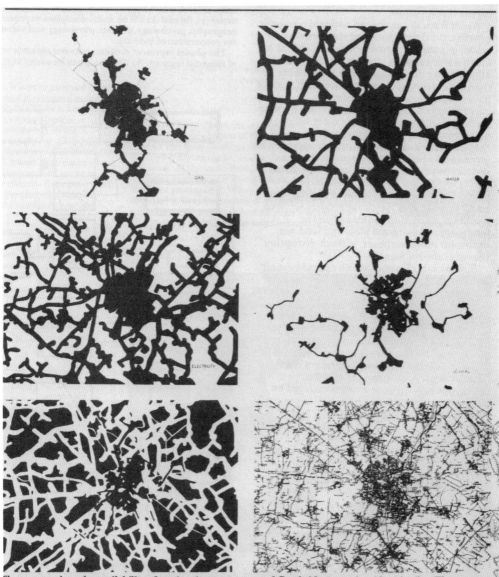

These maps show the availability of services in an area around Cambridge, covering 12 x 16 miles. The extent to which areas outside the city are covered reflects the importance of the service and the size of the community that is feasible to connect. Only 6% of the area is fully serviced, while 56% lacks all typed services but is well provided with an under-used minor road system, along which individual houses or small groups of dwellings could, if autonomously serviced, be economically sited with minimum effect on the existing rural environment. Composite map *bottom left* shows areas with no services at all   Richard Church

Figure 90 Alexander Pike, "Cambridge Studies" (1972)

Figure 91 Alexander Pike, The Autonomous House (1974–75)

development of the various elements (1973–75). The DoE provided £6,000 in 1974, which increased to £13,000 in the following year. In addition, the University of Cambridge, which had supported the researchers since 1971, gave the team a site of about one hectare to the west of the city, in 1973, to build the prototype (see Figure 91).

Gradually, the model became more refined. Pike defined it as:

[A]n autonomous system, entirely integrated, which uses the principles of recycling and regeneration, by exploiting the sun, wind, rain and other forms of ambient energy. [...] It is a house, completely independent of pipework & services infrastructures.[25]

In 1972, the form of the *Autonomous House* was definitively chosen: a cube whose south facade was inclined, a cross between a Roman tent and a technological box. Suspicious of high tech, Pike wished to avoid forms that were too futuristic in order to attract a broad public. This choice would be challenged, notably by Frazer (closer to the Architectural Association and Archigram), who wished to create an architectural object and "more eloquent" aesthetics (see Figures 92a and 92b).[26]

The wood and steel prototype had a surface area of 70 m², which was divided between two floors, plus an inner garden of 35 m² that could be closed off by mobile walls. The mobile structure allowed for many possible furniture arrangements. A wind turbine, designed to meet electricity needs, was mounted on a tower placed in the center of the building that housed the mechanical equipment:

In the centre, a service core contains the bathroom, the toilet and below the ground level, the digester and the tanks. The water recuperation system is located on the roof within the service zone. The living space is distributed around the core.[27]

Completed by the electricity system, the passive solar panel and the geothermal installation provided heating. Water was purified and stored in the tank; gray water was treated by reverse osmosis and then evaporated. A Clivus System digester produced methane from organic waste.

Combining different energy systems, this building was one of the first to be developed using computer-aided design. Research had been conducted with manufacturers and scientific institutions to produce the materials needed to build the project. Given the experiments, the construction cost could not really be quantified, but the prototype cost was estimated at about £40,000. If mass production was assumed, the model could be put on the market for a cost equivalent to that of the *Dymaxion House*, estimated at $6,500 in 1946, a little more than the cost of prefabricated houses at the time.

Its design and the equipment were extremely important for the prototype's publicity. In 1976, Pike was asked by Crosby to present the full-scale prototype at the exhibition in London, A Salute to British Genius. Theo Crosby and Alan Fletcher of Pentagram Design were responsible for the scenography and drew the

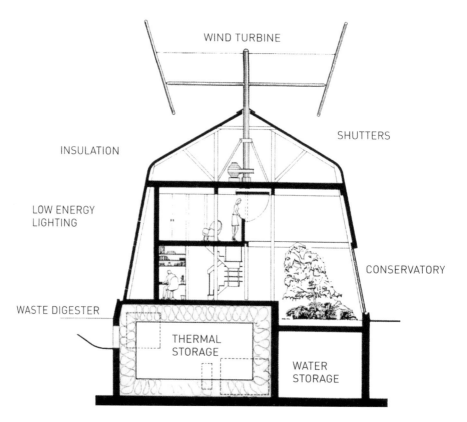

Figure 92 Alexander Pike, plans and section of The Autonomous House (1973)

plans and sections of the fully equipped model for the Homes of the Future section. One of the objectives was to present a living space containing "ultra-modern" technological equipment to the public: "it is envisaged that the quality of life which the middle class enjoy is preserved and even improved upon."[28] Working sessions were organized with Pentagram Design and the London School of Furniture (LSF), which helped to develop the furniture. If the shell of the house highlighted a new energy process, the interior had to demonstrate the high quality of life offered by this dwelling. The household equipment was designed to use less energy, but provide a great deal of convenience. The *Kitchen Unit* was presented and detailed as an equipped and compartmentalized kitchen. Specialized manufacturers would develop certain household appliances, requiring precise controls. The autonomous house also proposed a telecommunications and computer unit. This cutting-edge technology included a color television set with a teletext, telecommunications system, and telephone,[29] as well as a computer.[30] All the furniture was specially designed: wall covering and carpets would come from the Crafts Advisory Committee; the

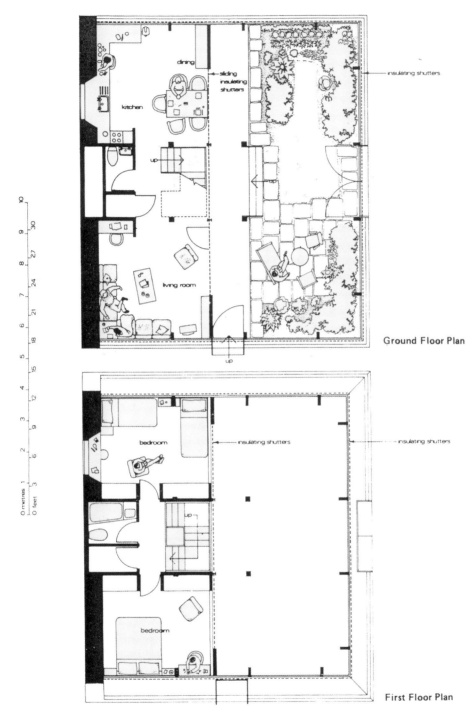

Ground Floor Plan

First Floor Plan

Figure 92 Continued

layout and furniture of the telecommunications and office space would consist of chairs, stools and worktops created by the LSF. The armchairs, kitchen table and coffee table were to be designed by Pentagram and manufactured by the LSF. This exhibition was very successful and was in part responsible for the prototype's renown.

An international media success

According to those close to Pike, an article in the American magazine *Popular Science* in August 1973 marked the beginning of the national and international dissemination and success of the prototype (see Figure 93).

> You've just had a shower, finished dinner, and are lounging in a comfortable living-room watching television – and it hasn't cost you a cent. More important, you haven't consumed any of the world's dwindling energy resources to heat the water, cook the food,

Figure 93 Alexander Pike, model of The Autonomous House (1974)

or power the light and TV. Your house is completely self-sufficient in all forms of energy needed for a comfortable normal life. This is the vision of Alexander Pike of Cambridge University.[31]

From September 1973, publications, exhibitions and conferences multiplied. The *AHP*'s success reached as far as Japan and the former Yugoslavia. Everywhere, the concept generated fascination, as shown in the titles of several articles: "The house of the future," "The house built on science," "The house that can beat fuel strikes," "The revolutionary unit," or "The decentralized unit." Pike and the model appeared a dozen times on television in the United Kingdom, Australia, Belgium, France, Italy and Germany:

> German Television and crew arrived at Alexander Pike's house a little after the Autonomous House had been presented at the Science Research Council press conference the previous week. This demonstrates the worldwide interest in the question of autonomy since it became the subject of study at the Cambridge Department of Architecture.[32]

The project became the major reference point for energy autonomy and the *Autonomous House* was certainly the most celebrated of its kind in the 1970s. In November 1973, the BBC devoted a program to the project, "Towards the Autonomous House." The journalist introduced the project as follows:

> Many people have produced plans and texts on the way in which houses ought to function energetically, some people have constructed dwellings which are partially self-sufficient, by using solar heating, etc., but none, as far as I know, have realised a completely autonomous house which satisfies the western standard of life. A group could well achieve this challenge next year – a team of architects and engineers from the University of Cambridge. They have become a kind of 'friend' for people throughout Europe and abroad who are interested by new technologies.[33]

A great deal of correspondence demonstrated the support and interest of the profession: Norman Foster, Richard Rogers, Monica Pidgeon and even, through the influence of one of his close friends, Mike Jones, Buckminster Fuller – who would be informed of the research and ready to discuss the question of the autonomous utilities core.[34] Several students did their internships or final year studies or wrote theses on the *AHP*, including Brenda and Robert Vale, who published *The Autonomous House: Design and Planning for Self-Sufficiency* in 1975. Offering an overview of energy autonomy systems, Brenda and Robert Vale's book made use of the research carried out by the *AHP* team. Pike and his team did not take kindly to this work, which became a bestseller and was translated into six languages in 1976. Pike and his team felt that too great haste had been taken with their research and that it had been popularized, but above all that the book had reduced architecture to a simple statement of ecological technical protocol, without any deep analysis of the network and technological presuppositions. The team harshly criticized the work. For John Frazer, this approach was a symptom of a certain amount of research on alternative energies:

> [I]t is this absence of aesthetic preoccupation and those ecological clichés which have regrettably won the field of architecture and environmental conception, and that has been very damaging. The Cambridge project wanted to say that something more radical was necessary and that the technical solutions would not be simple.[35]

But neither Pike nor the Vales were the only ones working in the field of autonomy. Following the first oil crisis, the concept had competition and a number of groups and institutions exploited this idea with varying objectives: many abandoned the advantages and privileges of technology, while others targeted only partial autonomy. Though it popularized this research and these technologies, this movement stole some of the credit. The aesthetic pollution (roof and facade solar panels), the low level of efficiency – even the counter-performances – of certain systems provoked criticism. Pike became increasingly careful and asserted the *AHP*'s originality in the press: "We are not eco-freaks, we are trying to establish a firm theorical framework before we start building hardware."[36] To stress their distinctiveness, the team concentrated on the problematic relationship between the infrastructure and the house and the need for total energy independence.

Autarkic Housing Project

During the 1970s, the use of terms to designate disconnection from the network proliferated: in French: "autonome," "autosuffisant," "autarcique"; in English: "autonomous," "self-sustaining," "self-sufficient," "autotechtonic," "off the grid," "autarkic." These descriptive terms were often used without any effort to precisely differentiate between them. In 1975, in order to distinguish himself from projects that used partial alternative energies, and faced with the political radicalism of certain "autonomists," Pike renamed his research: the *Autonomous Housing Project* became *Autarkic Housing Project*.

> The expression – *autonomous house* – is not satisfactory, means "self-governing" – implying that the house should take over control from the occupants – or that is intended

solely for self-governing societies. This is not our intention. The Autarkic House means self-sufficient rather than self-governing. Not intended for the small section of society which wants to "opt-out" but for the average householder.[37]

Frazer, who disagreed with what he considered to be a lack of political courage, left the project and returned to London.

The change in terminology here conceals deeper questions and challenges. Frazer defended the political underpinning of the idea of autonomy. He believed that the project had to take a more radical position. But for Pike, the challenge was primarily technical: he was afraid to speak out on the broader question of governance or self-management, which were being debated within the counterculture movement. However, though he seldom took sides on political questions, his views were not inexistent, as shown in this extract from an article:

[I]n many of the developed countries, the individual has become totally dependent on the central government, public services and social services, by adopting a passive role, which manifests itself in numerous cases by a general unease, a lack of initiative and poor spirit. It is hoped that self-sufficiency in housing can induce a greater idea of autonomy in the inhabitants and a return to the self-determination they once enjoyed.[38]

Initially written for a French review, the article was published without this passage. It seemed that this type of reflection depreciated the value of the project and was incompatible with the efforts and request for funding. John Frazer underlined this contradiction:

More the project advanced, less I was in agreement with the concept of autonomy as was being developed by Pike. He wanted to make the project conventional so that it would be immediately acceptable and seduce the mass-market. He emphasized the scientific dimension in order to benefit the most from funding. I left the project principally because I found it too institutional. I thought that it was necessary to be more radical, with a political point of view.[39]

This debate on terms raised the issue of the different orientations of autonomy and apparently situated the *AHP* in a more conformist dynamic. Moreover, it seems that by playing on this institutional and scientific register autonomy was popularized. The *AHP* was, to our knowledge, the only program of this scope funded by a government and private industry.

From enthusiasm to renouncement

Pike succeeded in captivating the British government in the 1970s through the unusual nature of the project: its technological innovation, its holistic dimension, as well as the idea of total autonomy. But the hoped-for progress during the 1973–75 period was delayed, and insufficient knowledge and experimentation made it difficult, if not impossible, to advance. In January 1975, an assessment meeting was held in Cambridge with a committee of SRC and DoE experts to discuss provisional funding for 1976–78. Above all, the jury criticized Pike's ambition to create both an autonomous utilities core and to improve the existing tools, which it considered excessive. Though a few wind turbines were available on the market at the time, the solar panels sold were not efficient enough. Pike deemed it necessary to develop a specific model. The SRC committee warned the architect and asked him to limit his plans to the available equipment and target partial autonomy. As Pike agreed to reconsider a certain number of the points raised during this meeting, the SRC renewed its support and increased it to £44,350.

Despite this funding, the team stressed that it had trouble completing the program. In 1976, bids were launched and a local contractor, Rattee & Kett, was chosen. However, in order to begin work on the construction site quickly, some elements of the technical system had to be modified. Whereas his collaborators were ready to sign and begin to adjust the model, Pike refused. No matter what the technical obstacles were to his pioneering research, Pike would never agree to reduce his ambitions. Though these experiments on new forms of energy attracted attention in the early 1970s, their application was limited and the results proved fragile and indecisive. In 1977, Pike acknowledged his difficulties: "The concept of an Autarkic house is perhaps too advanced for our economic and technical means."[40] But this was a reason for him to persist and not to give up: on the contrary, rigorous research had to be conducted over the long term. Pike called on the institutions to extend their financial support, but they refused. In 1978, the SRC did not renew his subsidy: the allocation committee deemed that the few objectives attained were insufficient. It also pointed out the proliferation of research on this subject and the difficulty, even the impossibility, of achieving total autonomy with the technical means available at the time. Pike defended the pioneering status of his project, hoping to obtain the extension of support from the SRC:

> The committee recognises that research on these questions has multiplied and considerable advances have been realized elsewhere over the last three years, but it would not be immodest to say that this progress is due in part to the result of the diffusion of our work, which was freely and generously described, published and presented internationally. Our

studies are always cited in reference [...] One must remember that no study of importance had been produced within this domain before we began in 1971.[41]

Nothing however came of it. The team henceforth functioned with fewer staff. Pike nevertheless persevered, until he suddenly died from a cerebral blood clot on 24 March 1979. He was 55 years old. The *Autonomous Housing Project* died with him. This double announcement in the press produced glowing praise, which reflected the uniqueness of the architect and his research: "The Autonomous House of Pike was the first. He has been the pioneer and was internationally recognised,"[42] "Pike had a role of catalyst, his project has provoked interest throughout the world,"[43] "His work will continue without him, he has planted the seed."[44] The prototype became an icon, and Pike acquired real renown.

The thwarted posterity of an inaugural program

The legacy of the *AHP* is, however, ambiguous. On one hand, there was silence. If the *AHP* was a major reference source, no publication or scientific article will be produced that would "consecrate" these ten years of research. It would remain in the margins of architectural history as well as the history of home technologies. The impact of national energy policies must not be overlooked, with priority given to nuclear energy in France, the United States and the United Kingdom, nor the responsibility of the lobbies in the painful emergence of alternative technologies. But what this failure to concretize Pike's research reveals is the difficulty in conducting experiments that were both technical, economic, social and urban. On a more individual level, it can be explained by the personality of Pike, who never compromised on his objectives: he accepted neither the partial connection to the network, nor the reduction in living standards or that of technical performance. This history is also that of a technological and industrial idealism without concession, whose diminished posterity is due to this "obsessive" radicalism.

On the other hand, the success of the *Autonomous Housing Project* is undeniable. Because, at the very moment when the *AHP*, too institutional for the counterculture and too utopian for the institution, was doubly marginalized, the research to which it had so strongly contributed became a full-fledged movement.

Notes

1 Stephen Games, "Open house," *The New Statesman*, 3 January 1975.

2 Donella H. Meadows, Dennis L. Meadows, Jørgen Randers and William W. Behrens III, *The Limits to Growth* (New York: Universe Books, 1972).

3 Alexander Pike and John Frazer, "Simple societies and complex technologies," *RIBA Journal*, no. 9, September (1972), pp. 377–378.

4 This professional building trades school was created in 1904 and quickly became a center of excellence in construction techniques. At the end of the First World War, it trained project managers who would work for the London County Council (LCC). As of 1941, head architect John Henry Forshaw and urban planner Patrick Abercrombie were responsible for the London reconstruction and modernization plan.

5 Pike, "Better homes."

6 *Ibid.*, p. 212.

7 *Ibid.*

8 Ron Herron would take part in the Cambridge Autarkic System, a company founded by Alexander Pike and Peter Cavanagh in 1973 as a branch of the *AHP*. Designed to promote the feasibility of autonomous systems, this technical consultancy company offered access to the *AHP*'s data bank and computer program.

9 Colin St John Wilson was an ardent defender of another type of modernism, whose principles he developed in *The Other Tradition of Modern Architecture: The Uncompleted Project* (London: Academy Editions, 1995). He was an active member of the Independent Group, in which he took part in the exhibition "This is tomorrow" (1956) at Whitechapel Gallery in London, alongside Reyner Banham, Alison and Peter Smithson, John McHale, Lawrence Alloway and Theo Crosby, among others.

10 Cf. Alexander Pike, "Energy conservation and housing form," *RIBA Journal*, no. 7, June (1978), pp. 233–238.

11 Architecture was introduced into the school at the instigation of Edward Schroder Prior (1857–1932), a renowned architect and founder of the Arts and Crafts Movement. Sir Leslie Martin, architect and member of the LCC, was appointed to the first architecture chair at Cambridge in 1956 and founded the Centre for Land Use and Built Form Studies in 1967, which took his name and became The Martin Centre for Architectural and Urban Studies.

12 An architect of Malaysian origin with a doctorate in urban ecology from Cambridge University, Ken Yeang was the cofounder of T. R. Hamzh & Yeang, an office specializing in the environmental design of tall buildings, notably in tropical milieus. He is Professor of Urban Ecology at Cambridge University and a consultant for Max Fordham LLP.

13 Pike, "Product analysis 5: Heart units," pp. 206–211

14 Peter Cavanagh, interview with Fanny Lopez, 19 February 2007.

15 Alexander Pike, "Motivations and reasons behind the proposal research program" (1972), AAP.

16 Alexander Pike, "L'habitation autonome," *Le Moniteur des travaux publics et du bâtiment*, no. 13, March (1974), pp. 99–104.

17 Science Research Council, Engineering Board, note on the meeting with the Civil Engineering and Transport Committee (21 January 1975), AAP.

18 Alexander Pike, "*Autarkic Housing Project*, summary of objectives" (July 1978), Technical Research Division, AAP.

19 Randall Thomas, interview with Fanny Lopez, 31 July 2007.

20 Alexander Pike, "Proposal for a research grant for the study of autonomous domestic servicing" (26 March 1975), AAP.

21 James Thring, interview with Fanny Lopez, 16 November 2007.

22 Pike, "Social energy alternatives for urban human settlements."

23 Alexander Pike, research note (1972), AAP.

24 In 1971, this was equivalent to two houses in an area of South London, Kensington.

25 Alexander Pike and John Frazer, "Presentation and notes on research objectives" (November 1971), AAP.

26 These questions on aesthetic choice set off internal divergences that brought to light those of the institutions. In London, the AA was much more focused on formal expression (see Archigram, Piano and Rogers). Despite the overlap between these universes, tradition and the debates in Cambridge were not those of the AA, as the historian Dean Hawkes pointed out in *The Environmental Tradition: Studies in the Architecture of Environment* (London: E. & F. N. Spon, 1996).

27 James Thring, "Toward the *Autonomous House*," BBC, 14–15 November 1973.

28 Alexander Pike, "The Autonomous House Research Programme," Technical Research Division, Architecture Department, Cambridge University, research assessment, (October 1974), p. 6, AAP.

29 Whereas Ceefax was a one-way service, Viewdata was a later emitter–receiver system with a telephone so that data could be found and received on a separate channel.

30 It was a computer terminal: DG Colouris Q, Queen Mary College.

31 David Scott, "The Alexander Pike *Autonomous House*," *Popular Science*, August (1973).

32 Rodney Tibbs, "Science: Pike dream comes true," *Cambridge Evening News*, 23 November 1974.

33 Thring, "Toward the *Autonomous House*."

34 Mike Jones, letter concerning Richard Buckminster Fuller (December 1973), AAP.

35 John Frazer, interview with Fanny Lopez, 3–5 February 2005.

36 "House of the future," *London Evening Standard*, 15 March 1974.

37 Alexander Pike, "Autarkic/autonomous" (ca. 1975) working notes, AAP.

38 This extract was taken from the original English text "Studies in autonomous housing," translated and partially published under the title "L'habitation autonome."

39 John Frazer, interview with Fanny Lopez, 3–5 February 2005.

40 Donald Forrest, note for a meeting (December 1977), AAP.

41 Alexander Pike, letter to G. Richardson of the Civil Engineering and Transport Committee of the Science Research Council, in answer to the announcement that financing would not be renewed (16 October 1978), AAP.

42 Leslie Jermyn, *The Scotsman*, 27 June 1979.

43 "Self-supporting House Project's Future Uncertain," *Cambridge Evening News*, 6 April 1979, p. 17.

44 Martin Ryle, correspondence (18 January 1980), AAP. A celebrated British radio astronomer, Astronomer Royal from 1972 to 1982, and winner of the Nobel Prize for Physics, Ryle was close to Pike and enthusiastically supported his research.

6 The self-sufficient city

Autonomy's growing popularity

In 1973, architects, engineers and urban planners began to vigorously debate the possibilities and perspectives of energy autonomy. *Architectural Design* published two issues on "Autonomous houses" in November 1974 and January 1976. The latter included a chapter from Peter Harper and Godfrey Boyle's *Radical Technology*, which devoted considerable attention to energy autonomy.[1] The authors noted:

> During the last 3 or 4 years, one of the programmes which had dominated the architectural avant-garde has been the conception and development of independent dwellings in terms of energy and food. The autonomous house has become the most familiar symbol of alternative technologies.[2]

The majority of research on autonomous housing was influenced by that of Cambridge University.

Proposals for the autonomous house were broken down into categories: "highly autonomous," "very sophisticated and expensive," "modular and compact" and "low cost." The *AHP* was placed in the first category; the *Prototype I* by ILS Laboratories (United States) and the house by Jaap 't Hooft (Netherlands) in the second; the proposals by Graham Caine (United Kingdom) and the *Ecol House* by the Minimum Cost Housing Group of McGill University (Canada) were in the third. All of them were located in the peri-urban zone.

In the late 1970s, energy autonomy in a city or region already connected to the grid remained in the realm of the future. The evolution and spread of these systems were strongly dependent on the growth of their performances. The incorporation of energy autonomy in a city or region fed by the network had to take into consideration a host of factors, notably morphological. If it was possible to envisage that the tight grid of the city could open spaces for energy collection, from installing a water tank to reinserting vegetation and agriculture, autonomy had to be adaptable to the heterogeneity of urban contexts. However, it was still difficult to assess the economic effects of such domestic micro-economies, their status (private, semi-collective, public) and their governance mode. The authors concluded that these gaps comprised the principal weakness of these studies, which were too often focused on technology. Nevertheless, although these publications called for caution and stressed these models' lack of adaptability to the urban fabric, they highlighted their potential in the event that the environmental or economic crisis worsened.

In September 1977, *L'Architecture d'aujourd'hui* proposed an issue on solar architecture that included a section on "Autonomous architecture." Recent and future operations were highlighted: "rare being totally completed works of autonomous architecture, [...] many remained in the prototype stage."[3] The author devoted part of his article to "scientific autonomy," which he carefully distinguished from "self-building":

> Formerly comprised of self-builders, a new component of the autonomous architecture trend is represented today by very official university research centers. One of the best known is the *Autonomous Housing Study*.[4]

Autonomous architecture was henceforth presented as a genuine movement, whose major reference was the *AHP*.

Among the most important publications were technical popularization works. In France, two volumes were published by Alternatives: *La Maison autonome n° 1* (1977) and *La Maison autonome n° 2* (1980).[5] Similar to *Radical Technology* in terms of composition, the content of these works was, however, less synthetic and problem oriented. In 1979, supported by the Canadian organization Ayer's Cliff Centre for Self-Sufficiency, the self-builder Nick Nicholson produced three brochures that developed the successive stages of building an autonomous house from a technical popularization angle.[6] As we can see, there were many publications of this type (see Figures 94a–94e).

Nonetheless, most of the movement's actors hailed Pike's pioneering work. The Vales themselves acknowledged their debt to him in a much later publication, *The New Autonomous House*.[7]

Energy autonomy emerged from the ecological craft industry, and all these references give an account of its expansion. In the mid-1970s, its growing popularity was accompanied by a change in program: universities and public institutions, companies and private agencies mobilized to rethink the distribution system on every scale. If the self-builders were generally focused on the individual living space or a community group, the second wave would experiment with autonomy and would shift it from the family unit to the city-region. Sean Wellesley-Miller and Day Chahroudi, Georges and Jeanne-Marie Alexandroff and Yona Friedman all took hold of this operating concept that re-examined scales and governance modes.

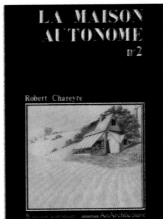 

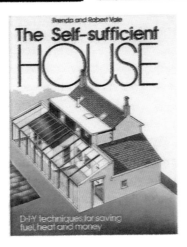

Figure 94 Selected covers of publications on the autonomous home

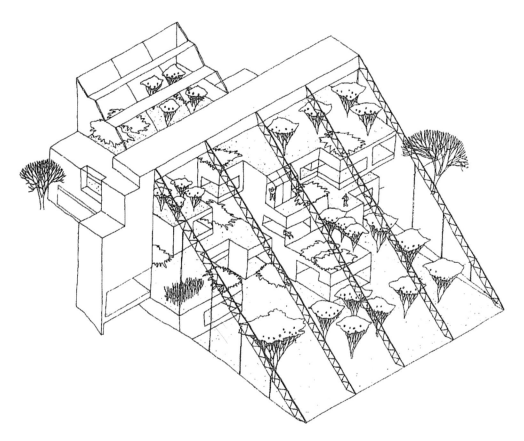

Figure 95 Sean Wellesley-Miller and Day Chahroudi, "Bioshelter Axonometry" (1974)

The *Bioshelters-Total Energy System* of Day Chahroudi and Sean Wellesley-Miller

Close to Steve Baer, with whom he conducted research at the Zomeworks Corporation, the physicist Day Chahroudi founded the Suntek Research Associates company in the early 1970s. Co-directors of the solar energy laboratory at the Massachusetts Institute of Technology (MIT) with Sean Wellesley-Miller, in 1973 they presented the concept of the *Bioshelters-Total Energy System*. These were autonomous dwellings under climatic envelopes (see Figures 95 and 96).

Their projections were based on techniques that would be developed by Suntek, like Cloud Gel,[8] the Tensegrity Climate Envelope and the Flexahedron Climate Envelope. Acting as inhabitable greenhouses in glass or noninflammable rigid plastic with a life span of twenty-five years, the Tensegrity and Flexhedron models were presented as evolutions of Fuller's geodesic domes. If climatic structures were initiated

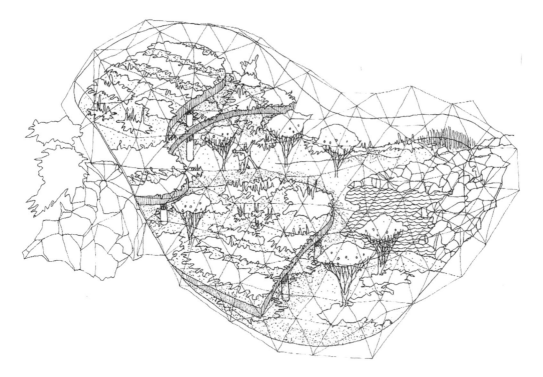

Figure 96 Sean Wellesley-Miller and Day Chahroudi, "Upper View" (1974)

by Frei Otto in Germany and Walter Bird and Richard Buckminster Fuller in the United States, Sean Wellesley-Miller and Day Chahroudi's objective was to enable the optimization of energy autonomy through thermal regulation and the creation of a microclimate, made possible by Cloud Gel.

> Let us then also imagine a building that is designed not only to provide shelter for the weather but also to provide some food, fresh water, liquid and solid waste disposal, space heating and cooling, power for cooking and refrigeration and electricity for communications, lighting and household appliances. The two ideas are different, but both are inspired by our own biological systems. The first shelters man from extremes of climate, as does his skin. The second building type emulates natural body processes and behaves as a total, almost self-sufficient system. Both schemes are possible; neither is a Utopian dream.[9]

Playing on the confusion between outdoors and indoors, the *Bioshelter* principle stressed the creation of a fertile and lush milieu. Several units were planned: these were habitat-terraces, mostly composed of superimposed planted platforms. One of

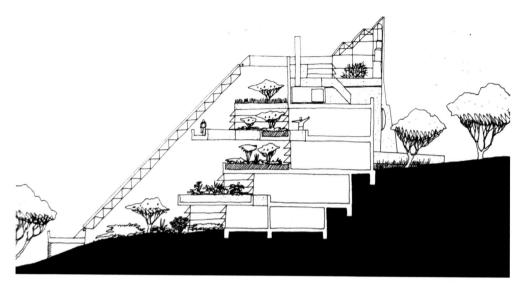

Figure 97 Sean Wellesley-Miller and Day Chahroudi, "Bioshelter Section" (1974)

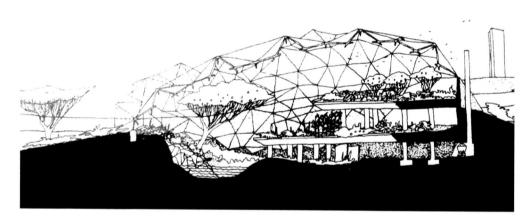

Figure 98 Sean Wellesley-Miller and Day Chahroudi, "Bioshelter Section" (1974)

the collective buildings proposed provides a glimpse of a series of terrace-gardens in an interplay of projections, each level consisted of one or two apartments (see Figures 97 and 98).

Electric cars could be charged at the foot of the wind turbine installed on the site. The line and finesse of these sketches recall the aesthetics of Fuller's projects. These spheres of efflorescent nature offered every energy convenience. Detailed diagrams explained the complete cycle: the resources used and their processing, circulation, use and conversion method (see Figure 99).

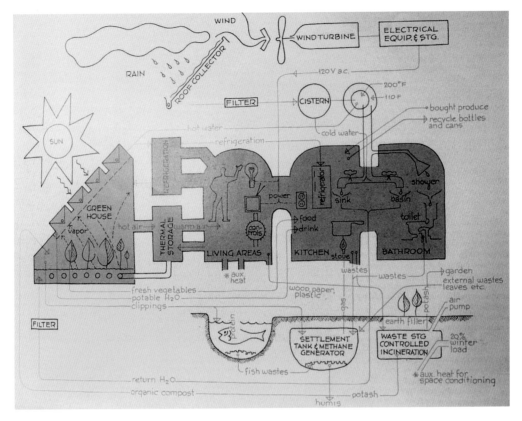

Figure 99 Sean Wellesley-Miller and Day Chahroudi, energy diagram (1974)

Like an ecosystem, the technical equipment self-produced, stored and recycled the energy required for home economics in a complex interrelationship. These projects were presented at the Aspen Design Conference in 1974.[10] They would strongly influence the members of the New Alchemy Institute, who hailed Chahroudi's coining of the term *Bioshelter*, which they used instead of "ark."[11] Among the two architects' arguments were the criticism of the supply system at the time and the proliferation of architectural experiments based on the new environmental ideals:

Some parts of the U.S., for example, southern California, are also experiencing water shortages, overloaded sewage nets and solid waste disposal problems. The ability of the natural environment to absorb the drains and loads imposed by centralised utility nets is fast approaching the limit in many parts of the world. Our first influence was the development of the concept of an autonomous house, which is very new, still very experimental and of course there is a long way to go before it becomes widespread. The idea of the autonomous house is the strongest and most radical change in concept for housing since that of the 'living machine,' to which in many aspects it is diametrically opposed.[12]

Sean Wellesley-Miller and Day Chahroudi defended the autonomy concept, which though they admitted was relatively immature, felt it had a wonderful future since they considered it as revolutionary as the *machine à habiter*. They readily abandoned the icon of the autonomous house for collective housing programs; however, despite solid technical studies, Wellesley-Miller and Chahroudi thought that the disconnection project was still in its infancy. To support it, they founded the Bioshelters company in 1977.

We have seen that the path to energy autonomy gradually progressed: first taking the form of the mobile unit, then the house, before evolving into the semi-collective habitat, as in the example of Wellesley-Miller and Chahroudi's *Bioshelters-Total Energy System*. In the late 1970s, experiments turned to the urban scale, as illustrated by Yona Friedman's proposals on autarkic city-states and Georges and Jeanne-Marie Alexandroff on the self-sufficient city.

Yona Friedman's modernized peasant civilization

In 1958, in *L'Architecture mobile*, Yona Friedman had criticized the rigidity of the infrastructure and called on architects to "free the dwelling from its networks." What should be noted, however, is the simultaneity of his reflections on the recycling of materials, energy autonomy and self-planning. Breaking with the role traditionally assigned to him, Friedman would no longer be the designer and organizer but a consultant providing structural and environmental knowledge.

It is unquestionably in *Alternatives énergétiques* (1980) that Friedman offered us his most original contribution on autonomy. Showing a radical urbanistic idealism, the author detailed his openly utopian self-sufficient city. By first re-evaluating a set of economic and political values, then launching a technological reform involving the reorientation of production and distribution methods, Friedman presented the ideal of a "modernized peasant society" that local self-sufficiency protected from the crises the international economy suffered and unemployment. In the early 1980s, Friedman took advantage of the questioning of the industrial civilization's energy consumption to imagine an energy policy founded on a new social and global policy. His narrative stressed an undetermined urbanism, with industrial, agricultural and energy production decentralized and dispersed over the landscape. He introduced autarky as the key element of a subsistence economy to fight the prejudice according to which this autarky would not be profitable. Associated with wartime or a marginal appropriation, autarky had long been kept at a distance from the energy debate. Friedman justified this disparagement as a strategy of the states and companies concerning this direct "non-profitability":

> If the consumer has the 'ludicrous' idea of producing the energy that he wants to use himself, by installing for example a micro-hydraulic plant using the little waterfall that flows into the bottom of his garden, he can be sure to have the police on his back after EDF files a complaint. Why have something for free that you can pay for?[13]

He considered at the time that the energy crisis had swayed the priority of industrial profitability, revealing the high concentration, storage and distribution costs of mass production that were insignificant when energy was inexpensive.

Decentralization had become attractive in these times of crisis, but it had to be enriched by a societal project. For Yona Friedman, the new energy orientation had economic and social repercussions; it developed a home economics program that questioned the right balance between the subsistence and the industrial economy. He imagined a mixed system, of twenty hours of work per week (under traditional conditions, paid for in money) and twelve additional hours for income in kind, consequently producing goods and services reserved for their own consumption or that of their neighbors. He believed that this would free the workers from part of their constraints and would guarantee them food and energy security that no longer depended on daily price fluctuations and job offers. Though Friedman demonstrated that this depended on the social organization of the decentralized, small-scale economy, he stressed the necessity of rethinking both technologies and agricultural and industrial strategies. Recalling the principles set out by Kropotkin in *Champs, usines et ateliers*, he supported the recomposition of a regional fabric of small raw material production units, family workshops and small factories (see Figures 100a–100d).

"It is industrial self-sufficiency that can be combined with food self-sufficiency, the two being able to be created under almost-urban conditions much more than those of the countryside."[14] Friedman questioned large-scale self-sufficiency and the necessity of combining political, social, economic and energy aspects. These reflections on urban agriculture and the "farm-to-table" movement were largely echoed in the 2000s, marked by waves of environmental and economic crises. Friedman proposed reducing the consumption of energy from centralized production by 60 percent, that of transportation by 70 percent and that of household usage by 50 percent.

> It is an economic revolution; but the concept of the almost-urban self-sufficient region goes further: it means the start of a new civilization. [...] Neither socialism nor capitalism dares

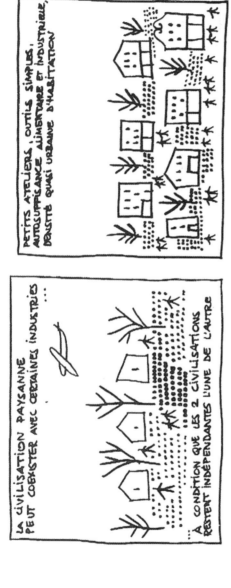
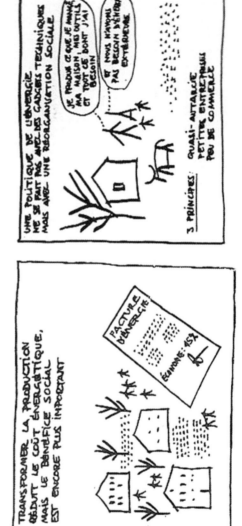

Figure 100 Yona Friedman, energy alternatives (1982)

envisage transformations that cause such a radical change and that are so very unspectac-
ular. A new energy policy (that is, a new economic and social policy) should therefore be
able to advocate and support a 'modernized peasant civilization' trend. Initially, it would
doubtlessly be important to imagine a new regional development mode to replace ours, for
example an 'agro-urban' fabric in which, in our cities and countryside, a very dense way of
inhabiting (about 5,000 inhabitants per km^2 as a national average, or even more), would
be replaced, with 'urban villages' that are juxtaposed, near each other; it would be a matter
here of small almost autarkic urban zones.[15]

As Migge imagined, autarky would mean going beyond both socialism and capitalism, but also the city and the countryside. This "modernized peasant civilization"
would be founded on the primacy of agriculture and non-market production. The
author presented many themes that were unequally treated: property, governance,
employment, education. He set out energy alternatives for home economics, from
solar panels to shared electric cars and waste recycling, which he described as small-
scale energy savings. Autarky is central in this text. Friedman gave his project an
urban and regional dimension, proposing a shift from an industrial society to a subsistence society. Friedman believed that the density of Paris could allow near autarky
in terms of food and water, following the undertaking of some improvements and new
technical systems. He asserted, however, that it was impossible to envisage these types
of transformation without conflicts with lifestyles, except if these transformations
were triggered by a verifiable shortage of food or energy. This restructuring proposed
a multiplication of "city-states" that were none other than self-sufficient urban villages
based on an agro-industrial economy.

With his modernized peasant civilization, Friedman pursued the idealism of the
preceding decade; he promoted an idyllic vision and described the didactic enthusiasm of his text as an "optimistic hypothesis." When necessity weighs heavy, he wrote,
utopias become realizable. However, Friedman's hindsight in the 1970s allowed him
to qualify his position: self-sufficiency (or autarky – the use of these terms is more
or less interchangeable here) could be partial. Friedman also stressed the idea of
process. Though he proposed beginning with the experimental development of a
small territory, Friedman refused to sweep away everything that came before. There
would be adaptations, coexistences. Friedman consequently continued in the register
of utopian planning. His approach was systemic: though he envisaged autonomy as
an opportunity for new social organization paradigms, this concept strengthened
his theses on the mobility and self-planning that were responsible for his renown.
Georges and Jeanne-Marie Alexandroff's urban planning seems more realistic and
pragmatic, and its operating applications connected different scales.

Georges and Jeanne-Marie Alexandroff: a territorial trajectory

The architects Georges and Jeanne-Marie Alexandroff[16] were key figures in the solar sector in France. Close to Jacques Michel, Félix Trombe (director of the CNRS laboratory of Odeillo) and Alain Liébard, the Alexandroffs were advisers to various public and private organizations, notably the CNRS (French national scientific research center), the CEA (French atomic energy commission) and EDF (Electricité de France). In 1967, Georges Alexandroff founded the Sofretes company, which enjoyed great technical credibility and, from 1968, marketed pumps, photocells and mini-solar power plants to export to developing countries. At the School of Architecture Paris–La Villette, Georges and Jeanne-Marie Alexandroff developed ambitious research on solar and bioclimatic architecture. EDF made them the project managers of ten solar houses (five in Aramon, in the Gard, and five in Le Havre) to test their performances and profitability. Sofretes would build the first solar building with inter-seasonal storage in Blagnac in 1978. The Alexandroffs acknowledged that it was not a great success in terms of formal innovation, while defending the importance of these creations for technical experimentation.

Unlike these modest houses, the architects developed the solar utopia, hoping to upset the energy order and institutional immobility. In the early 1970s, they advocated a prospective approach, seeing alternative technologies, and their management methods differentiated as a new vehicle of urbanism and sociability. In 1977, they criticized the minimal integration of solar energy into individual dwellings and office buildings. They proposed a utopia that combined and incorporated a new lifestyle in society. For Georges Alexandroff, the self-sufficient city "is the counterpart of the self-managing society."[17] He made a frank commitment to autonomy:

> The energy submission of urban spaces contrasted with the economic autarky of rural milieus. In discovering this subjection, the architect brings to light the tenuous, underground, unexpected but powerful links that connect his works to an energy system, itself dependent on a political and economic structure that underlies it and justifies it. It is certainly not by chance if energy production and distribution reflect the public power: centralized. Consequently, architecture, in its metabolic reality, reveals the hidden face of energy, its non-geological but political roots. The architect thus becomes aware – belatedly – that it is not a matter of indifference as to the use of energy from oil or that of electricity of nuclear origin. In using one or the other – directly or indirectly – he supports an economic circuit and therefore a political practice that he perhaps considered secondary before. It seems, in this respect, that an increasing number of architects reject the linking that their predecessors accustomed us to.[18]

Georges and Jeanne-Marie stressed the architect's responsibility and commitment in his or her approach to energy. In 1982, they published *Architectures et climats*. Based on research for the Construction Plan between 1974 and 1979, this work presented their entire practice, while offering a retrospective look at vernacular architecture archetypes and a critique of the Modern movement's approach to energy. The Alexandroffs also gave an account of their work on the different types of built fabrics: the dispersed rural milieu, the grouped rural milieu, the old urban milieu, and lastly the nineteenth- and twentieth-century suburban milieu, with its housing developments and single-home districts.

For the Alexandroffs, the low-rent housing sector presented very favorable characteristics for these integrations. He proposed rehabilitations that took on the appearance of inhabitable energy mega-machines (see Figure 101). The Alexandroffs set out the main points of his renovation program: wind turbines on terraces, whereby the electricity produced could be connected to heat pumps; large solar water heaters; the creation of climatic buffers in the form of bow windows, and the development of closed gardens for horticultural purposes. Land in Argenteuil, Antony or Fontenay-sous-Bois would thus recover its former fertility. They studied urban morphologies,

Figure 101 Georges Alexandroff, The Self-Sufficient City (1976)

considering the city as a "physical model of a specific behavior."[19] They recognized that though diffuse fabrics with low density were more favorable to active energy collection, they were a disaster in terms of space and energy savings. The dense urban area seemed to minimize the possibilities of integrating autonomy means, and this was the genuine challenge:

> In a more current manner, we find the theme of domestic autarky and the autonomous house, maximizing the relationship between the habitat and the natural milieu, and consequently energy collection and recycling capacities. However, extending the scale to a large number of autonomous units would rapidly consume space and would prove [to have] a clearly prohibitive global energy cost vis-à-vis semi-urban structures establishing their cohesion in the collective use of autonomous energy capture and storage methods on a medium scale.[20]

It is important to grasp how the image of the autonomous house was questioned by the movement's new actors: it was no longer a model, nor an ideal experimental base. For the Alexandroffs, autonomy had to "work" on the adaptability of its systems; its integrations were dependent on the various types of fabrics and buildings. The degree of autonomy sought had to be systematically assessed and energy combinations and compensations had to be created between buildings. The large areas of parking lots or commercial zones would be favored energy points, whereas the location of other buildings had very low potential. These rehabilitation projects were envisaged in the more global framework of his research on the self-sufficient city, to which he devoted himself from the early years of the 1970s (see Figures 102 and 103).

The inexhaustible abundance of energy, Georges Alexandroff wrote, "would make it possible in favorable climates to create agro-artisanal complexes and even genuine self-sufficient solar cities."[21] Wanting to develop an efficient energy capture, distribution and consumption system needed to supply an urban center, he sketched a series of resolutely utopian city views, ranging from large housing developments to office buildings. Alexandroff presented a new urban order, developing the theme of the hemicycle, the sphere, the parabola, juxtaposition and energy densification. He totally covered surfaces with linear collectors, wind turbines, Stirling engines or cylindrical-parabolic collectors. Their multiplication and structural dimension took into account the desire for energy performance and a formal technical renewal: each building would produce the energy needed for itself or its neighbors. Georges Alexandroff displayed a taste for regional development in these plans with the creation of large-scale energy sources: the wind turbine-reflecting pool, the wind turbine water tower, fields of reflective collectors or the amphitheater solar conch, which structured territories as visible points of an ecosystem (see Figures 104 and 105).

Figure 102 Georges Alexandroff, The Self-Sufficient City (1976)

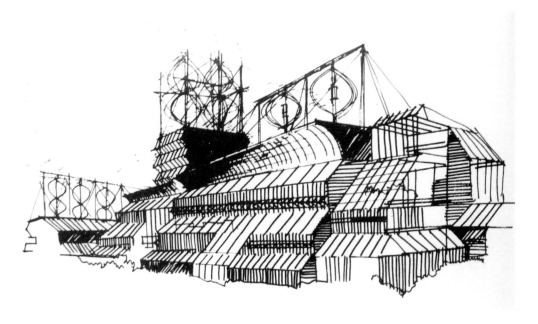

Figure 103 Georges Alexandroff, The Self-Sufficient City (1976)

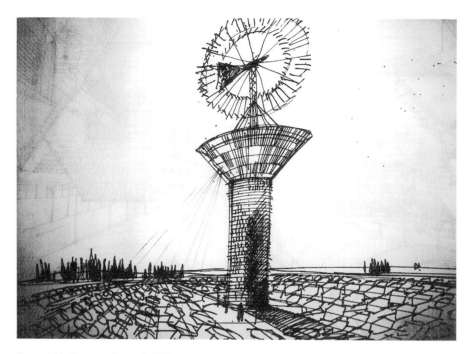

Figure 104 Georges Alexandroff, Energy Monument (1976)

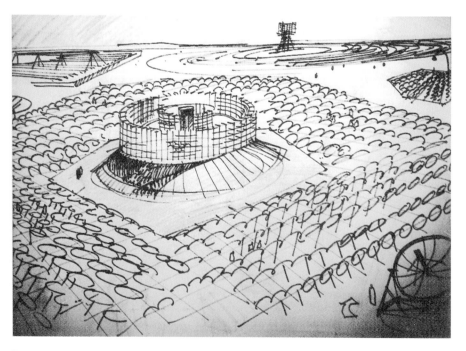

Figure 105 Georges Alexandroff, Energy Monument (1976)

These energy megastructures revealed an original, imaginary take on infrastructure. If the "traditional" urban energy network was generally invisible or concealed, this situation was reversed in his approach; the exaggeration of mechanical visibilities put this change on record. Faced with skepticism, the assertion of this monumentality saw itself as a provocation, but the authors warned: "the elements that we handle are never isolated objects, but the terms of complex and living relationships."[22] The autarkic house or group was in a certain way left behind. Based on his volumetric research, Georges Alexandroff imagined self-sufficient new towns developing in a fan shape on a circular plan, in a natural evolution of the classic urban space. The autonomy project had gone beyond its initial limits to tackle a diversity of morphological situations (see Figures 106a and 106b).

Many of the members of the energy autonomy movement laid claim to a universalist view of renewable solar, wind, hydraulic, biomass energies for the countries of the Global South. Georges Alexandroff himself developed many projects for them. The architect considered that these emerging territories were more favorable to innovation and less rigid in terms of construction and energy standards. He believed that regions of the world cut off from the networks seemed more inclined to host towns or villages that were self-sufficient. The Sofretes company would install a hundred or so pumps that functioned via thermodynamic conversion in Africa, South America, the Middle East, India and the Philippines. It also developed solar collectors in layers

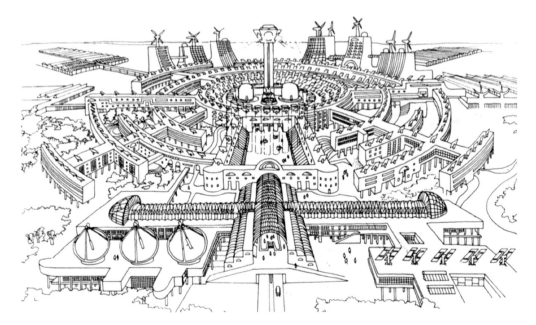

Figure 106 Georges Alexandroff, Self-Sufficient New Town (1980)

on lightweight metal structures. These infrastructures consequently delimited covered areas that could be divided up. The most important projects were the installation in San Luis de la Paz, Mexico, in 1975 and Diré, Mali, which brought up 900 m³ of water a day and provided electricity for a tourist complex. Alexandroff also planned many rural buildings and facilities, such as an autonomous hacienda in Mexico and an agricultural cooperative in Cape Verde. He equally offered proposals for emergency housing, with dismountable structures that were self-sufficient in energy. If some of these projects no longer function today, they proved their efficacy and made Sofretes' reputation (see Figures 107 and 108).

Its success was unquestionable abroad, but France did not really give this experimental company a chance. At the very beginning of the 1980s, when François Mitterrand proposed Paris' bid for the organization of a world's fair in the frame-work of the bicentennial commemoration of the French Revolution of 1789, the Alexandroffs submitted an ephemeral self-sufficient city project to the president of the Republic. They suggested that this ensemble take the form of an "ideal self-sufficient city" (see Figure 109).

Realistic and quantified, the program captivated French solar and wind turbine manufacturers and interested the ADEME (French agency for the environment and energy control, at the time the AFME), but in the end Mitterrand abandoned the idea of this world's fair. The Alexandroff's effort had been in vain. In a general climate of skepticism, and confronted with these new energy possibilities, Sofretes collapsed before being bought in 1981 by the shareholders of Total and the CEA (French atomic energy commission).

Sofrete's existence, from 1967 to 1981, corresponded to the French solar energy epic. Georges Alexandroff looked back on this failure and its context:

> One day, they pulled the rug out from under us; the director was fired and the Montargis factory, which shipped collectors, pumps and turbines all over the world, closed. We didn't have any choice! We had an important leadership role. It felt like an erosion. This history of autonomy, the solar sector, was very hard, it was a real combat. Giscard had supported solar to some extent, but above all the atom was king. I remember, under Giscard, having been involved in the 8th Plan, in the Energy-Habitat Commission. All the network's technocrats were part of it. During a session, they had concluded using the Delphi method that there was a future for solar but none for wind. Sometimes it is the private forecasting institutes, experts, who decide in complete impunity on the future of a technology! With Mitterrand, it was a disaster. Moreover, the names had been changed: it was no longer the Comes (solar energy commission) but the AFME (French energy control agency). And starting at that point, when no one said anything any longer about solar, less was done with it[23]

Figure 107 Georges Alexandroff, Hacienda, Mexico (1976)

Georges Alexandroff believes that the primary causes for this state of affairs were skepticism, the choice of atomic power and the lobbies. Throughout the 1990s, he denounced the institutionalization of this research and its lack of scope, burying the energy utopias of the 1970s. His criticism is still harsh today: "France accepted wind turbines because they are coupled to the network," "energy autonomy is blocked, "it's a genuine war of religion."[24] Georges and Jeanne-Marie Alexandroff's approach, at the crossroads of prospective and institutional research, showed all the ambiguity of the undertaking. As supported as it was censured, the disconnection project was unanimously praised for having opened a huge field of possibilities in these divergent trajectories, laying the foundations of an energy reinvention. Oscillating between impoverishment and architectural "scientification," the technical assessment was mitigated. The evaluations mostly concerned the relevance of total autonomy and the right energy scale, but also that of governance, querying the urban project that often lacked the connection between the micro- and the macro-scale.

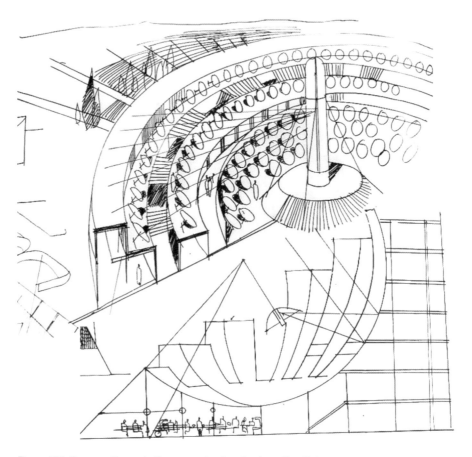

Figure 108 Georges Alexandroff, energy structure for the self-sufficient city, no date

The movement's ambiguous legacy

The positions of the protagonists of autonomy varied considerably: they mirrored their diverse concepts of architecture and objectives to be met. The ideological stance, the technical ambition, the execution cost and governance were factors of disagreement. Although we find, in most, a general condemnation of the energy monopoly and great enthusiasm for alternative energies and the development of an economy of everyday life founded on the reintroduction of biological cycles, truck gardens and farm-to-table distribution, they did not agree on either the radicalism of the political project or the means of implementation. Whereas the self-building movement laid claim to an economic liberation of the citizens through the recreation of a private autonomous sphere based on mutual aid, free association and decentralization, the second wave seemed to distrust this ideal and wished to incorporate its research into

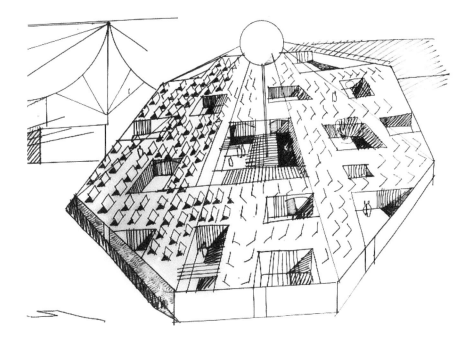

Figure 109 Georges Alexandroff, proposal for a self-sufficient city in view of Paris's candidature for the Universal Exhibition

the existing production system. Pike is one of its most striking examples. He envisaged autonomy as a technical challenge and wanted to conquer the building market. Like Pike, Chahroudi and Wellesley-Miller believed in industry and mass production: they alone would manufacture a highly developed housing model at a low cost, which required the knowledge of both specialist and avant-garde technology. In Rosell and Reynolds, mistrust could be observed vis-à-vis everything that was related to the modern building tradition, its technologies and materials. They laid claim to less developed models, favoring inventiveness and original uses. There was a revolutionary predetermination in their approach: for them, autonomy functioned like a totalizing, extensive concept that spanned the economic, political, energy, social, biological. The means of production of the modern capitalist system were contradictory by nature with the economic emancipation project. They refused to use the means of a society that had to advance.

The self-building movement advocated minimal use of the existing production system and mass-produced technological tools; an entire system of technical, economic and social relationships had to be reinvented. Faced with a practice and knowledge creating a power struggle, they undertook a reappropriation and a direct application with the least number of mediations possible. The popularization of this research both generalized and discredited these emerging technologies: the low level of efficiency and the poor performances of certain systems were criticized like the so-called "aesthetic pollutions." The political and social dimension and the analysis of power struggles induced by dependence held an important place in the texts by Michael Reynolds, the Street Farmers and Michel Rosell. In the Cambridge and MIT projects, the viewpoints were qualified: tables and energy ratios and figures primarily dominated; the challenge was first technical and industrial. If, for the counterculture supporters, energy autonomy was first a political project that materialized counter-powers faced with a system on its last legs, for Pike – as for Fuller – utopia was technological before being social. Even if a technical invention – an autonomous, accessible and efficient home system – could transform lifestyles and cause upheavals by expanding to the world scale, their modalities remained undetermined, as did, above all, their value: autonomy did not guarantee ideality. Pike did not perceive autonomy as a political concept but as a technical tool that was complex enough to also try transform it into a social utopia. As for the intrinsically subversive dimensions of such an idea – that he was certainly not unaware of – they seemed counterproductive to him: he persisted in making them responsible for the lack of institutional commitment. It was as though, in this term and these techniques, there was something implacably controversial. An apparent incompatibility can be noted between the technical challenge, the search for institutional funding and the development of a broader program that could make energy autonomy a driving force for global change. When the technical invention upsets the economic relationship created, it often turns politics upside down. It seems that disconnection makes this complex balance reel.

The theme's influence and the scope of its dissemination bore witness to the success of energy autonomy. Its technical possibilities, its economic stakes and its political perspectives were fervently debated but, despite this enthusiasm, there were very few concrete examples. Most of the projects built belonged to the most radical current: the *Ecol House*, Graham Caine's house, Reynolds's *Earthships* and Rosell's site. Their architects built vessels out of odds and ends, as rudimentary as they were refractory. Notwithstanding unprecedented calculations, Pike, Wellesley-Miller and Chahroudi, more formalists and technicians, perfectionists concerned with optimal results, persevered to the point of getting lost in technical conundrums. They have left us a major technical substratum attesting to the originality of their research, but, despite the substantial financing from which they benefited, no prototype emerged in the end. Autonomy contained this utopian potential, but due to its technical difficulties many concluded that total autonomy could not be attained. The actor-builders of the counterculture had demystified this technical impossibility on their small-scale construction projects, which though were not very efficient models, were easily accessible in terms of costs and techniques. The landscape thus presented, on one hand, projects

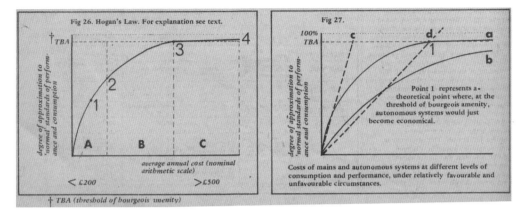

Figure 110 Ian Hogan, "Hogan's Law" (1976)

that did not garner acceptance but were built and, on the other, social utopias or high-performance prototypes that were never built because they were technically and financially inaccessible. This mitigated balance-sheet tempered initial enthusiasm at the time.

The ideal of abundant and free energy conveyed by the autonomous house revealed a certain blindness. The finished product ensured the renewal of energy needs, but the production costs of such a system must be examined. In 1973, the autonomous dwelling was expensive. In comparison, traditional utilities were economically competitive because they were for the most part amortized by the materials in place and economies of scale. The national average of annual energy costs for network subscribers was £80 in 1973,[25] whereas the annual bill for partial autonomy amounted to between £200 and £500 and over £500 for total autonomy (see Figure 110).[26] For the architect Ian Hogan, a specialist in alternative technologies:

> By spending around £1,000 on alternative technologies, any home becomes 60% self-sufficient. By spending more, say £3,000, adding a heat pump and a wind turbine for example, you achieve 80% self-sufficiency. The last 20% is the most difficult and expensive to achieve.[27]

The technical and financial difficulty in controlling this last 20 percent would be responsible for the aberrations of Cambridge's *Autonomous House* and MIT's *Bioshelters-Total Energy System*. Consequently, a mixed system with a periodic use of the network was, for Hogan, the best compromise – while awaiting other technical advances that would enable autonomous micro-networks to be created. As for complete autonomy, it was triply blocked: guaranteeing both total independence and a high standard of living was exorbitantly expensive; attempting to reduce costs while keeping to the independence objective led to a significant drop in performances; lastly, trying to reduce costs while maintaining a high performance level only permitted partial autonomy. It was in part on this observation that the ideal dimmed; only a few diehards would hold on to it.

Some researchers, however, showed that an autonomous system could, in certain cases, be more profitable than connection. All of the work that Thring carried out focused on living conditions in off-the-grid zones.[28] He demonstrated that the disconnected house would consequently be less costly than an extension of the network. Most of this movement's protagonists nevertheless agreed on the technical immaturity of a period whose investments were exclusively concentrated on developing the traditional network. For all of them, the economic efficacy of autonomy depended on progress in alternative technologies and their components' mass production. Like Alexander Pike, Peter Harper recognized that developing the standard autonomy kit for an individual house would be more economical than using separate pieces of equipment; he nevertheless thought that a cluster of houses, a building or a block was more interesting in terms of installing autonomous services. If the self-builders and Pike remained focused on the domestic unit or small community, this scale was criticized from the mid-1970s. For Wellesley-Miller, Chahroudi, the Alexandroffs and Friedman, a broader vision was necessary. Autonomy also had to be adapted to the urban fabric, by retaining and broadening its biological, human and economic interaction capacities. Enlarging autonomy's scale could optimize its results and break with the image of the solitary object. Collective or semi-collective installations led to real cost reductions and the improvement in the performances of certain systems, including sewage and wind. But how far should the sharing of utilities go? Starting at a certain scale, why not go back to centralized services?

The answers to these questions depended on the reasons why the "autonomists" chose this path. They varied: taking part in protecting nonrenewable resources, creating long-term savings, being independent, surviving in the event of a natural disaster or economic crisis, experimenting or recreating a sharing economy. However, even those like Harper and Hogan, who believed that autonomy was the best solution for outlying and unconnected zones, were reticent about its application on the urban scale. Setting aside the major upheavals that could accelerate the honing of these technologies while pushing the public authorities to encourage their development, including a rise in unemployment, an aggravation of the environmental crisis, or the necessity of a subsistence economy, they believed that energy autonomy in the city was a proposal as marginal as it was premature.

The opportunities it presented on the communal scale for semi-collective housing, however, were debated. Total or partial, autonomy on this intermediate scale seemed appropriate for giving local economies back their dynamism and reconnecting the social link between individuals. The communal level would offer more affordable manufacturing costs than the private sector and could sometimes reduce public expenditures, which increase with communal connection work. However, "the primary justification of the intermediate scale – the communal level of servicing – is not technological but social."[29] At the very start of the 1980s, even if its advantages in terms or social and environmental value were unanimously recognized, autonomy had trouble imposing itself from a technical viewpoint.

This was all the more significant as the governance and urban planning proposals were vague. For the radical movement, individuals or the jointly owned properties could deal with breakdowns and replace equipment themselves. Everything was based on the micro-scale, following the principles of direct democracy and community meetings. The shortcomings and repeated errors of common law policies on energy, housing and urban planning had proved their ineffectiveness, even their danger. Each inhabitant had to use his own initiative to engage in an autonomy process without any intermediaries. There were only two decision-making scales: home and community (the latter in the sense of grouping together the peer-based libertarian multitude). The state was doomed to disappear and society was envisaged as an immediate experience. Mutual aid and technical knowledge-sharing were to propagate their concepts house by house and block by block, in order to recreate territories of shared powers. In a simplified and abstract representation, social phenomena appeared as a result of combining individual actions. Following an approach that could be described as methodological individualism, it focused on the impact of the private on the public, of the individual on the group. If several small groups laid claim to self-determination, the implementation of a broader decision-making process was barely examined.

Inversely, the Cambridge group used the term "autarkic" to differentiate itself from the political idea of "self-governmentality." In choosing this more precise and concrete term over technical and economic sufficiency, the team hoped to distance themselves from political governance questions, which they did not really examine. Pike and the Alexandroffs, like all the members of this movement, proposed buildings whose energy structure guaranteed the supply and replenishment of water, electricity, heating and even food. More conformist and institution-based, their positioning on the policy of the city was no less ambiguous. Though they acknowledged that they were in contradiction with it, they considered that ideally a central power had to promote energy autonomy, encourage experiments and draw up global, structured and coordinated measures. The municipalities could make exceptional financing available for priority zones and pilot projects. Though the inhabitant played a major role in the project's different phases – becoming familiar with these new systems and their management – specialized technicians were indispensable in the event of breakdowns or modifications. During the initial occupancy period of the *Autonomous House*, an engineer was tasked with follow-up in order to improve the model. The system's technological complexity could not be delegated. The policy of the city had to be decentralized and the democratic nature of the local decision-making processes improved, but these tracks were not mentioned.

In Friedman, the territory was divided into a constellation of city-states, in which a host of processes and energy, economic and pedagogic systems favored autarky. With his ideal infrastructure, the architect and urban planner reinvented functionality based on a direct democracy that closely resembled the projections of the first movement. However, he went further into the different processes and the restructuring of governance. Friedman's idealistic proposal was founded on the primacy of agriculture, non-market production and radical land and industrial reform. Friedman believed that it was impossible to imagine a change of this kind without a hierarchical conflict, unless an event occurred that brought about shortages and compelled self-organization, such as war or a natural disaster. The inhabitants' involvement had to upset political proposals, whose reform programs were imperceptible on the scale of everyday life. In Friedman, technicians had the same role as architects and urban planners and were considered advisers, while the inhabitants were experts on their living environment and needs. Education and training reform would partially provide an answer to this question. The starting point of Friedman's plan for modernized peasant civilization was unemployment and the increased importance given to one's free time, which he defined as "quaternary work" (unpaid subsistence occupations such as do-it-yourself, mutual aid, gardening). This product-in-kind increased the living standards of the unemployed and helped re-establish an economic balance of proximity. Generating and combining local micro-economies, the subsistence society practiced direct democracy.[30] The example, however, was general and did not propose a genuine governance project; the change from one traditional decision-making scale to another (communal, municipal, national) was given short shrift. Though an intermediate scale emerged – Friedman estimated the city-state at a space of 20 to 30 km^2 – there were few elements on its connection with a larger administrative unit, on intra-urban balances and metropolitan frameworks. The peasant civilization would be doomed to fragmentation by the reconstitution of local powers that would transform the metropolis into a profusion of small autonomous territories. The ecological energy principles for this territorial renewal were not described in detail.

Though many efforts were made to project autonomy to much larger dimensions, it was most often the small scale that was perceived as the best place for expressing democracy. The crises in the late 1960s encouraged a rejection of planning and command. A large-scale development crisis also challenged the modernist discourse. The return of the individual showed a great desire to participate and intervene. The rejection of political centralism was conveyed by the condemning of large development projects in which the multiplication of actors, mediations, interests and governance levels brought with it a fragmentation of generally accepted intentions. One of this movement's ideological successes was the return to the scale of everyday life. But the apparent disconnection between institutional policy and concrete and localized small-scale actions does not prevent us from grasping the architectural and urban movement's contribution to energy autonomy, which is above all based on the reinvention of economic forms of proximity and the search for an intermediate level in terms of micro–macro, private–public and individual–collective. The Alexandroffs were undoubtedly the ones most concerned about urban cohesion. A relative weakness in the theoretical framework and the operational application may, however, be noted. No document consulted reveals a detailed description of the ideal city as Tony Garnier's industrial city, Howard or Migge's garden cities, or Wright's *Broadacre* dream could have been. Some ideological connection with the American bioregionalist movement gathered in the 1970s around the figure of Peter Berg is apparent.[31] But if self-sufficiency is central in Berg's vision, especially for California, the infrastructural dimension remains very abstract. Ideas had certainly been roughed out in the energy autonomy movement, but the content remained timid and formless and there was no manifesto. Governance was either reduced to its economic infrastructure or fragmented into different spheres, to the point where it would have been difficult for a society to adhere to it.

In the late 1970s, energy autonomy was still a small-scale, multifaceted utopia and reflection on the shift from the basic unit of the house to the collective reality remained insufficient. Technical questions and energy programming were, in a certain way, obstacles to thought. Friedman's autarkic city-states or the Alexandroff's self-sufficient city, however, marked an important step in the road to autonomy: from architecture, to the city and to the region. This mitigated balance sheet could not weaken the extraordinary potential of energy autonomy, which was the subject of surprising architectural concepts and far-reaching theoretical anticipations. Today, they have made "history."

Notes

1   Peter Harper and Godfrey Boyle (eds), *Radical Technology* (London: Wildwood House, 1976), pp. 135–171.

2   Peter Harper and Godfrey Boyle, "Autonomous house," *Architectural Design*, vol. 46, no. 1 (1976), p. 3.

3   Pierre Diaz Pedregal, "L'architecture autonome," *L'Architecture d'aujourd'hui*, no. 192, April–May (1977), pp. 43–44.

4   *Ibid.*, p. 56.

5   Robert Chareyre, *La Maison autonome 1* (Paris: Alternatives, 1977) and *La Maison autonome 2* (Paris: Alternatives, 1980).

6   Nick Nicholson, *Autonomous House Report, Parts 1, 2 and 3* (Ayer's Cliff: Centre for Self-Sufficiency, 1979–80).

7   "The original concept of an autonomous house was initially proposed by Alexander Pike, a professor at the School of Architecture at Cambridge University in 1971." Brenda Vale and Robert Vale, *The New Autonomous House: Design and Planning for Sustainability* (London: Thames & Hudson, 2000), p. 8.

8   Cloud Gel is a plastic or glass sheet whose composition has self-regulating properties depending on the energy received. The surface becomes opaque to block sunlight when the desired temperature has been reached, and becomes transparent again when it decreases. Cf. Elaine Smay, "Thinking window can switch off the sun," *Popular Science*, March (1984), pp. 102–104.

9   Sean Wellesley-Miller and Day Chahroudi, "Buildings as organisms," *Architectural Digest*, vol. 45, no. 3 (1975), pp. 157–162.

10 These conferences have been held every summer since 1951 and bring together designers, architects, historians and economists. Cf. Reyner Banham (ed.), *The Aspen Papers: Twenty Years of Design Theory from the International Design Conference in Aspen* (New York: Praeger Publishers, 1974).

11 John Wolfe, "The latest year of research on Bioshelters: a summary," *New Alchemy Quarterly*, no. 9, Summer (1982), pp. 7–9.

12 Wellesley-Miller and Chahroudi, "Buildings as organisms," pp. 157–162.

13 Yona Friedman, *Alternatives énergétiques, ou la civilisation paysanne modernisée: Pour une réelle économie des ressources: comment désindustrialiser l'énergie* (Saint-Jean-de-Braye: Dangles, 1982), p. 58.

14 *Ibid.*, pp. 58–59.

15 *Ibid.*, pp. 60–63.

16 Very little research has been done on this duo and it's hard to know who did what. It seems that Jeanne-Marie Alexandroff did more research, writing and teaching and Georges Alexandroff did more architectural projects and public performances. Here again the partition is very gendered.

17 F. Ro, "Les années 1970, le solaire," *L'Architecture d'aujourd'hui*, no. 308, December (1996).

18 Georges Alexandroff, "Architecture solaire: quelques perspectives," *L'Architecture d'aujourd'hui*, no. 192, April–May (1977), p. 2.

19 Alexandroff and Alexandroff, *Architectures et climats*, p. 331.

20 *Ibid.*, p. 329.

21 Alexandroff, "Architecture solaire: quelques perspectives," p. 11.

22 Alexandroff and Alexandroff, *Architectures et climats*, p. 349.

23 Georges Alexandroff, interview with Fanny Lopez, 23 September 2008.

24 *Ibid.*

25 In France in 2006, the bill amounted to €720 per household (source: Insee, "Enquête logement," available at: www.insee.fr/fr/insee_regions/reunion/themes/revue/revuehs5/revuehs5_charges.pdf).

26 Harper and Boyle, *Radical Technology*, p. 158.

27 *Ibid.*

28 James Thring, "Residential services systems," (PhD thesis, University of Cambridge, 1972); James Thring and Alexander Pike, "Cambridge Studies," *Architectural Design*, vol. 42, no. 7 (1972), pp. 441–445.

29 Harper and Boyle, *Radical Technology*, p. 162.

30 *Ibid.*, p. 129.

31 Cheryll Glotfelty and Eve Quesnel, *The Biosphere and the Bioregion: Essential Writings of Peter Berg* (London: Routledge, 2014).

7 Critical technology: a problematic development

More than a phenomenon that homogeneously broke with the energy tradition inherited from the nineteenth century, what must be grasped are the imaginary and ideological complexities of autonomy, as well as the persistence of conflicts of interest and governance that made disconnection a contested architectural and urban practice. The analysis of the results, difficulties and internal positions in the movement facilitated the understanding of its ambiguous success. This analysis must not however overshadow the external factors. The distancing of the specter of the energy crisis increased the public administration's lack of interest and the energy lobbies' marginalization of disconnection advocates. As the causes of this problematic development were often associated with its image of "critical technology," the relevance of this description would be discussed in view of its founding concepts: the self-guarantee of vital necessities and the reconstitution of an economy of everyday life.

Overcoming negative symbolism

Energy autonomy provided a glimpse of surprising spatial and social potential. Rather than a technical reappropriation, Georges Alexandroff wrote, "it is a new architectural utopia that becomes possible and is in line with the continuity of the innovations of the 1920s or even the *Ville radieuse* that architectural criticism today is striving so hard to ridicule."[1] An upheaval of architectural design and regional development was produced with autonomy; this development was until that point dependent on hyper-centralized energy production. As Alexandroff stressed, these new systems aroused a hope and a growing interest in milieus as diverse as marginal communities, scientific and academic institutions and a few governments. The prospective nature of autonomy was tangible in the recreation of an imaginary dimension of infrastructure, in which energy monuments and genuine mechanical parades expressed an idea of abundance and fertility proliferated. The idyllic visions of these energy speculations counterbalanced the negative attributes frequently paired with the autonomy and autarky concept. As popularly represented, self-sufficiency has often been reduced to

and caricatured as a little house overloaded with useless and uncontrollable technological devices. The categorical position-taking of a few fanatical autonomists forged
these views. Though they did not represent the major trend of this movement, a few
small groups assumed it. This efficiently deprecatory argument was often used to
destabilize and marginalize the practice of autonomy (see Figure 111).

Figure 111 Monica Pidgeon, "Autonomous Houses" (1976)

The cover of the January 1976 issue of *Architectural Design* took this line. Behind the gate we can see one of Pike's autonomous houses. Cows, a kitchen garden and a biogas digester complete this domestic enclosure. In the background, we glimpse a nineteenth-century vision of the dark and threatening silhouette of an industrial city and complex. The autonomous community would be nothing other than a guarantee of the protection of individual interests. The entrance gate with the warning "Autonomous property, keep out" recalls the enclosed space of gated communities, some of which moreover seceded from their original municipality to provide their inhabitants with better services, with ecology and autarky often being constituent principles of their foundation. They were generally organized on a private management mode, within which joint-ownership contracts, unions and civic meetings ensured social consensus. In these socially negative "correspondences," autonomy amounted to an architectural abdication in which the small individual house was set against the city and energy disconnection against the symbols of sharing. The architect and urban planner Peter Buchanan summed it up as follows:

> In the mid-1970s, the autonomous house, isolated and self-sufficient in its small food-producing garden, incarnated the green ideal. But today, at the dawn of the twenty-first century, the autonomous house is now perceived as socially problematic, partially due to the time and energy spent on transportation, and an increase in social isolation. Today, the green ideal is incarnated by connection and not by isolation: mixed and compact cities, multifunction districts, with all the installations nearby and strong community links.[2]

The image of the small solitary house has remained associated with the concept of autonomy, dissolving all the complexities and promises of this movement into a form of amnesia.

The symbolic echo propagated by autonomy was that of conflict: the individual against the collective, or a community against a region, a country, even the rest of the world. It was the reduced world of the monastery, the space colony or the gated community. Furthermore, technological progress often comes out of war. The military industry was responsible for dazzling advances, developing, among its war machinery, bunkers, survival kits and other minimal subsistence spaces, from the spacesuit to vital armor. The role of the FEMA (Federal Emergency Management Agency) created under the Nixon administration was to ensure the survival of citizens and the government in the event of an attack, a natural or other disaster that could cause energy structures to malfunction or break down. The FEMA-designed bunkers and vehicles were self-sufficient. The American question of "survival" clearly seems to be linked to the autarky concept. The American government considered it, in this specific case, as a tool that preserves its power. Energy independence combined with mobility guarantees survival, as Paul Virilio recalled in his work *Bunker archéologie*:

> This fixity of the infrastructure, this permanent regional development will be questioned, to the benefit of mobile, dismountable structures: the engineer's self-deployable bridge, aviation fields made of prefabricated plates, artificial 'Mulberry'-type bridges, temporary runways in rolls, etc. The dual 'all terrain' and 'amphibious' nature of certain combat vehicles is found in all the means of transport. The independence and autonomy of rolling materiel compared to infrastructures is developing, mobility and autarky are becoming keywords – taking root has become too great a risk – everything must henceforth be movable to avoid destruction.[3]

Autonomy and autarky clearly appear here as the strategic vocabulary of war. Everything had to be impermeable and unsinkable, on Earth as on Mars or in a nuclear environment. Among the handful of projects that were just sketched or drawn, without any programmatic or technical details, is the autonomous house by the architect M. Perenic in 1975, built in an unsettling lunar landscape, justifying the apprehensions of Peter Buchanan (see Figure 112).[4]

In a nihilist reduction, autonomy would have tended toward isolation and impermeability. The communitarian risk would emerge in the constant assertion of its principles and ideals faced with a hostile milieu. The radical independence project would launch an ideological conflict with the world. These secessionist builders would erect an insurrectional dogmatic model whose intransigence would be the only certainty.

Would the autonomous house be a survival machine? Would energy autarky lead to an architecture of defense, abdication, reconstruction of a world against the world? If the insurrectional deviation of this caricatural narrative was sometimes evoked to incriminate these projects, it remained very marginal. But the importance given to the infrastructure in the anarchical-autonomous movement warrants being briefly examined. Although armed battle was criticized by a number of its activists, who linked it to an "autistic logic of despair," many of them directly attacked the infrastructure.[5] Roads, railroad lines, bridges, electric power plants were nerve centers whose breakdown could paralyze the functioning of the whole society. At the beginning of a classic conflict, the infrastructure is attacked. Let us note the peremptory tone of the reflections of the "Comité invisible" on the network in *L'Insurrection qui vient*:

> In a relocated economy, in which companies operate on a just-in-time basis, in which value is derived from the connection to the network, in which highways are links in the dematerialized production chain that goes from subcontractor to subcontractor and from there to the factory's assembly line, blocking production is also clearly blocking circulation [...] The technical infrastructure of the metropolis is vulnerable [...] Sabotaging with some

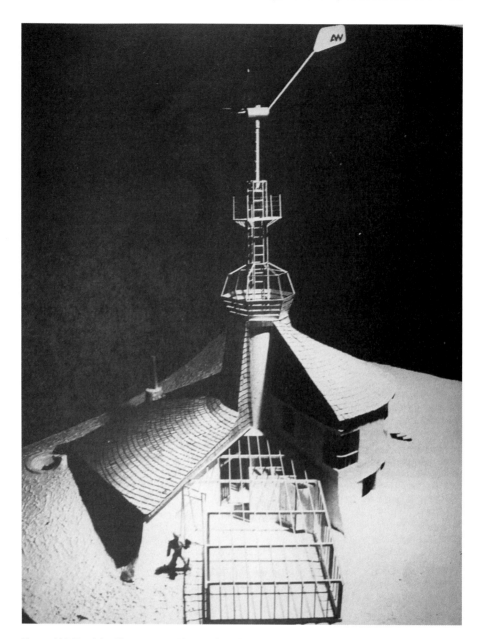

Figure 112 Pereinic, "Autonomous House" (1977)

impact the social machine implies reconquering and reinventing the means of interrupting these networks today. How can a high-speed train line, an electricity network be made unusable? […] Let us retain the following principle from sabotage: a minimum of risks in action, a minimum of time, a maximum of damage.[6]

Defending the irreversible nature of insurrectional actions, this type of activism counts as the physical blocking of the economy by the destruction or hijacking of its foundations. Its advocates see a way to give impetus to self-organization and the reactivation of micro-territories impenetrable by any authority through the deterioration of infrastructure mechanisms. Without going into further detail in the analysis of these action processes, let us point out that no proposal to replace the infrastructure has been suggested and that its annihilation seems to exist before its reinvention. No one in our study put forth a frontal attack of the network, and if there happened to be a few lines of comparable critical approaches, the action strategy clearly diverged. If, in certain self-builders, autonomy was envisaged as a negation of the infrastructure and the state, invention focused on disconnection was clearly opposed to destruction. The energy autonomy project would mark, from this viewpoint, the phase of a more lucid and constructive realism.

The strongest opposition raised by the disconnection project seems to be the questioning of public service as a symbol of the community and a sharing mode. Energy autonomy did not solely appear as a form of civil combat against a monopoly but especially against a public "monument" that had a positive distinction value. In the framework of public right, utilities are supposed to permit everyone, including those excluded from distribution structures, to access consumption. Public service is emblematic of a societal model, it is the sphere of collective functions, it is one concept of the state's role: regulator, planner, welfare provider. Infrastructure corresponds to both a power structure and a collective structure: it is the image of society's technological modernization, a symbol of republican equality. Connection became a political project whose goal was universal access to basic services, giving legitimacy to the growing support and intervention of the states, which were strengthened by it.[7]

The positive dimension of this institutionalization process was notably pointed out in Hegelian philosophy. In *Philosophy of Right* (1820), Hegel deemed it to be a necessary prerequisite of the state to overcome individual subjectivities, to move toward an "objective morality" and to create society. Public right and the public edifice were a moral and social representation. Many researchers examined the social import of the network, promoting the feeling of cohesion that it expressed.[8] They noted the rules of right shared by these members of the network, the access rituals. These same actors built a global project based on the precepts of solidarity and equality. Gabriel Dupuy defined the network as "technical equipment of urban solidarity":

> The urban technical network in the end appears as physical connection equipment and one that socially links localized elements of the urban system, acting as urban solidary equipment.[9]

Joel Tarr, like Stephen Graham and Simon Marvin, shared this definition. This solidarity was part of the concept of the city as a coherent system. The network operators guaranteed a huge amount of energy to be shared; subscription offered both immediacy, stability and belonging to the territory-network in a normative and regulatory relationship. The emancipatory potential of autarky and autonomy, whether on the individual scale or that of a small community, seemed an ideological illusion for the defenders of the image combining network and solidarity. Upholders of an interventionist state, they believed that environmental, economic or political crises were solved on the large scale, like the New Deal. The political symbolism of public service and its management, however, started to show cracks in the mid-1970s. Shaken by the combination of internal and external pressures, the model has become saturated, blurring the face of the welfare state and renewing the focus on autonomy.

The enormous effort made by the advocates of the "autonomous house," and everything they did to replace what commonly evoked war or communitarian reclusion through images of peace, shared abundance and fertile nature, must be stressed. In this light, the energy autonomy concept functioned as a creator of ideality, both to confront its negative contiguity (narcissistic and individualistic culture) and to be legitimate faced with the conceptual power of public service. The protagonists studied in this work showed no hesitation in playing – sometimes without acknowledging it – on the imaginary dimension to win trust and encourage action.

Rid of its warlike dross, the concept was recreated around an ideal of life and consumption in which the energy reinvention marked an imaginary idea of infrastructure, breaking the traditional pairing of opposites: connection-sharing v. disconnection-isolation, house v. city. From this viewpoint, energy autonomy took part in creating new connections on other territories of thought. It was also the birth of a reconciled energy landscape in which "positive" machines joined in with the climate and resources to redefine and combine other ways of inhabiting.

Mechanical parade and energy deconstruction

Mechanical visibility, invisibility or over-visibility attested to this imaginary idea of infrastructure that provided intelligible signs of urban connection or disconnection. The *Bioshelters-Total Energy System* by Wellesley-Miller and Chahroudi made use, for example, of this imperceptible technology. The systems under shells played on a total merger with the environment. Nature minimally structured by a lightweight and organic greenhouse superimposed two living stories, invisible from above. The architecture could not be differentiated from the site's vegetation; the porosity was total. One lived and inhabited the landscape, energy was dematerialized; the infrastructure was modeled nature, like the oasis. For the designers, the technical mastery of alternative energies and biological cycles made it possible to play with the milieu to the extreme and to blend into it. In certain cases, the exaggeration of mechanical visibilities asserted by this renewal was made more explicit by the accumulation of its machinery. With the Alexandroffs, solar panels and wind turbines of all sizes totally concealed the buildings; Georges Alexandroff reduced their architecture to autonomous energy structures. In his projects in Mexico, the proposals for emergency infrastructure or the visions of the self-sufficient city, the machinist deployment was clearly perceived as an interplay of aesthetics and architecture. The construction of a new infrastructure was experimented on in the imaginary sphere, in which every extrapolation was possible. This desire clearly showed through in the solar or wind monuments erected to the glory of the technological renewal. Energy was envisaged architecturally (see Figures 113 and 114).

Emilio Ambasz's megastructural project, the Center for Applied Computer Research and Programming, was just as eloquent.[10] This information center presented in 1975, which was supposed to be built on the outskirts of Mexico City, displayed an architecture-cum-spectacle for an asserted autonomy.[11] This majestic energy ensemble used both solar and wind power. Ambasz presented blocks floating on a 150 m-long pool. Depending on work requirements, they could be grouped together or separated. A wide platform bordering the pool housed the different spaces. The center's capacity was planned for 160 people. Two monumental walls framed the pool. The first, inclined, was a giant photovoltaic collector anticipating the development of solar walls. The energy obtained was to be stored in cells and used to supply electricity to the common utilities. The second was an information board enabling messages to be disseminated and research projects to be presented. The pool's water was directed to purifying tanks before flowing into the building's pipes. The two wind turbines pumped the pool's water to supply the cloud. This cloud (considered an architectural element in the model and description) slowed down the pool water's evaporation and kept it cool. Both sculptural and pastoral, Ambasz's environmental approach brought forth a new architectural rhetoric, even if autonomy was not a critical element in his production.

Let us also mention the *Self-Sufficient House* by Richard Rogers, planned in 1978 in Colorado. It was an inhabitable energy machine, a wind turbine-crane house. The architect's interest in autonomy had already been shown in the *Zip-Up House* (1968–71), but its machinery remained discreet.

A wind turbine provided electricity (2 kW) in this modular and dismountable house, which was also equipped with solar panels and a water collection system. Thirty years later, a confident Rogers declared:

> For self-sufficiency, I think we are already there. The last century was the century of elec-
> tronic technologies, carbon and oil. This century will be the century of clean technologies,

Figure 113 Emilio Ambasz, Center for Applied Computer Research and Programming (1975)

Figure 114 Emilio Ambasz, Center for Applied Computer Research and Programming (1975)

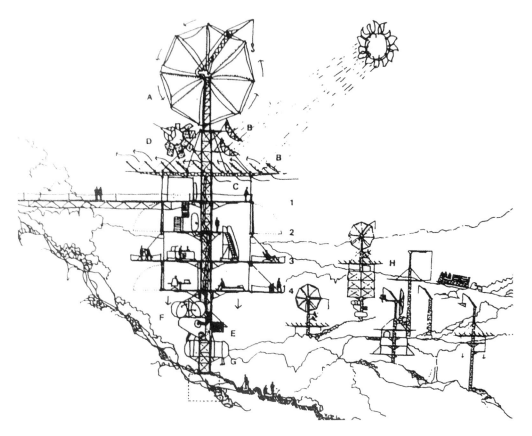

Figure 115 The Autonomous House, Richard Rogers Partnership (1978)

biotechnologies and the autonomous home. All this is partly due to climate change. Many buildings could be self-sufficient, it is now possible.[12]

From his first productions on, Rogers defended the idea that technologies and machinery change more rapidly than buildings. But apart from these futuristic anticipations, autonomy's political and social potential is what interests him: "In a democracy, architecture should express democratic ideals and egalitarian values."[13] Autonomy is one of these ideality vehicles. With the *Self-Sufficient House*, originality sprung out of this amazing wind-turbine system, and the question was not to discover if the representation was viable and how, but – as in Michael Jantzen and Emilio Ambasz – to suggest a new formalism. These architectural references brought energy to the fore. These futuristic models sowed the seeds in our imagination of a technological transition that took thirty years to come to fruition. Though the 1973 oil crisis encouraged typological mutations, the network and its infrastructures have always been an

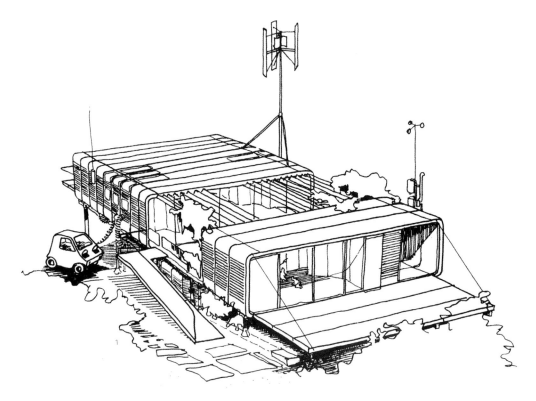

Figure 116 Zip-Up House by Richard + Su Rogers (1968–71)

enormous field of representations, as we examined above with Robida and the caricaturists of *Harper's Weekly*. A dream or reality, these infrastructure metamorphoses
show the evolutions of the postindustrial civilization.

Confronted with the difficulty in deconstructing the energy infrastructure, that
weighty industrial example, it seemed necessary to turn to fiction. The authors cited
here all made every effort to do so by using variable artifices. Rogers's house-energy
crane, the Alexandroff's solar conches and Wellesley-Miller and Chahroudi's greenhouses were mechanical parades that, by prompting a desire to inhabit otherwise in
people's imaginations, influenced technical reality.

Autonomy developed an energy fantasy enabling it to transcend the fixity and
immutability of a century-old infrastructure. The mechanics of autonomy is invisible
or expansive, lightweight, climbing, disconnecting into individual mini-machines
(Pike) or collective megastructures (the Alexandroffs); both playful, ornamental and
sustaining, the architectural and urban project was formally and theoretically enriched.
Another specific feature of this energy imaginary dimension was its exhaustive and uni-
tary intention: the ambition of the autonomous dwelling was to provide and replenish

water, heat, electricity and food. The claims of energy and food abundance were one of the greatest symbolic strengths of this concept. It is important to stress the anticipatory nature of the food question, which opened a debate on the architectural and urban project that remained on the sidelines in the mid-1970s: a debate on the city-agriculture relationship and the reintroduction of local agro-economic micro-sectors.

Energy and food abundance

Vitruvius, in the first century BCE, stressed the importance of food sufficiency, in his narrative relating the conversations between the architect Dinocrates and the emperor Alexander on the construction of a city worthy of his grandeur. The emperor's first question was on subsistence. Recognizing that supplies could not be brought by sea, Dinocrates was blamed for his lack of foresight:

> In the same way as a child without a wet nurse's milk cannot be fed or grow, a city cannot expand without its fertile countryside, have a large population without abundant foodstuffs, have its inhabitants subsist without rich harvests.[14]

Before transportation networks could ensure export and import, food production was long consubstantial with the formation and evolution of the village or urban community. If agricultural-urban projects existed throughout the history of architecture and urban planning, from utopia to reality, agriculture and the city gradually grew apart between the late eighteenth century and the twentieth century. For André Fleury, the separation was accentuated between the city-dweller's world and culture and the agricultural world and culture; the confusion between nature and agriculture constantly increased.[15] A distancing from the agricultural question clearly appeared in the Modern movement's approach, in which nature was no longer an energy or food resource but primarily a source of pleasure and landscape. Since the 1950s, agricultural development has been the preserve of large international sectors. Market gardening is no longer peri-urban, as in the example of allotments or collective gardens. They experienced a revival during war periods, openly supported by the public administration in France, which encouraged and coordinated initiatives – considered as public service missions – to feed the population. Their number would decrease in the 1960s following land requisitions to build housing developments and public facilities. If nature entered the development discourse of the 1970s, it was in the form of green zones or belts; agricultural systems were mostly excluded from urban and peri-urban natural spaces.[16]

This massive industrialization and relocation, which had reduced the agricultural population, led the actors of energy autonomy to bring the food-production question back to the forefront of both the urban and architectural project. It was one of the key points of the autonomists' program. For Yona Friedman, "in our economic context, the 'free abundance' system is more economical than that of 'possessive' property and [...] all the urban planning to come can only emerge from an economic model based on abundance."[17] Presenting a vision permeated by traces of Kropotkin's philosophy, including the benefit of shared foodstuffs and abundance, Yona Friedman as well as Graham Caine, Michael Reynolds and Michel Rosell would promote this possibility of the citizens' economic emancipation through the strengthening of food and energy autonomy. This would partially result from access to immediate natural land and energy resources, but also a cooperative network based on a direct relationship between producers and consumers. This attachment to the fertile land was perceptible from the very first experiments in the mid-1960s. The reconquest of rural territories in the form of community groups was explicitly justified by the desire for a return to sustaining nature. Then, in the mid-1970s, these concepts were gradually introduced into the city and these energy and food-producing fabrics were recreated. The *Integral Urban House* in Berkeley, *Ouroboros East* in Minneapolis and the Street Farmers in London clearly raised the question of urban agriculture, encompassing that of local activities such as access to seeds, energy and land. However, if agriculture became a cardinal social value, food autonomy remained complex and often steeped in idealism, materialized by the recurrence of certain architectural elements and tendencies. In Pike's individual house or Chahroudi and Wellesley-Miller's multi-family building, the greenhouse and interior garden could produce fruits and vegetables and the goat was a pet. In Golueke and Oswald, the enclosure was laid out for the cohabitation of four people, a cow and thirty hens. The kitchen garden was part of all these projects. Self-sufficiency and food security were systematically taken up: many publications in the 1970s were devoted to these subjects, including works by the farmers and environmentalists John and Sally Seymour.[18] They considered agriculture the basic point of the self-sufficiency project, warranting a rigorous strategy and precise expertise. The authors detailed the different production storage and harvesting techniques on the scale of the small farm, treating crop rotation and livestock production with as much precision as slaughtering and food conservation.

Despite a few naive and old-fashioned notes, these publications could be seen as attempts to reinvent farming and a peasant model at the start of the twenty-first century, by notably injecting a political and economic ideal into them. The imaginary value of a return to the land and subsistence-based home economics is very strong. It constitutes an almost mythic return to the fundamentals, to the gardens of abundance, from those of Eden (which means "fertile land" in Akkadian), Babylon or Nineveh. It is, to a certain degree, the material dream of a golden age that, from the dawn of humanity to the Neolithic hamlet[19] as well as the villages of antiquity, conveyed the illusion of a time when people lived without fear, without hunger, in abundance and security. An enclosed space, the monasteries also remain an important self-sufficiency model; they were seen as an image of the first "garden-paradise."

A representation of the ideal, the autonomous dwelling evokes, in its composition, all of these references. Its offer of shade, the abundance of the earth's nourishment (water, food, energy) and aesthetics (organization, floral profusion) would create a solid rear base against the sterility of the postindustrial world. This holistic vision expresses a state of fulfillment and peace. A self-sufficiency dream corresponds to this reassuring space: architecture, through a new technological system, provides basic needs – water, food, heat, electricity – and guarantees the perpetual replenishment of these fundamentals. But the realism and economic and political ambitions of self-sufficiency's program should not be excluded from the apparent naivety of these paradisaic and age-old meanderings, which too often marginalized the autonomy project. Invoking a "radical imaginary dimension," presenting the self-guarantee of vital necessities, the script of disconnection heralds, economically and socially, daring structural modifications. Energy autonomy's complexity then lies in going beyond the classic opposition between theory and reality; it implies a totality. Autonomy, with its diverse projects, seems to be both a form of self-government and a questioning of the imposition of consumption and production modes. It considers itself multiform in its desire to take over the power through a need-based logic. It therefore goes beyond just architects and urban planners, claiming a depth of economic and theoretical analysis. Clearly based on the revamping of an economy of everyday life (very present in the first movement, but also in Wellesley-Miller, Chahroudi, the Alexandroffs and Friedman), the idea according to which energy independence of the private space, by radically changing economic relationships, would turn an entire established power system upside down, is strongly defended without being theorized.

A vital necessities concept

The self-guarantee of vital necessities was the main idea of the 1970–80 movement. In certain authors like Pike and Chahroudi, it was a new possibility for architecture, brought about by the evolution of technologies, whose urban planning, economic and environmental effects would be shared. For others, including Caine, Rosell and Reynolds, it was the springboard for a new society. This architectural approach geared toward creating a rear base, in Proudhon's meaning of the term, that would bring about the dismantling of a few governmentality mechanisms. Energy autonomy in the private space was considered political by many thinkers. The fact that certain vital necessities were ensured by the habitation would deeply modify the citizen's economic status. With all the limits that this materialistic postulate induced, it came down to asserting that modifying the rules on dependence of the private space on networked services would consequently bring about a transformation of the public space. This argument was explicitly defended by Caine, Rosell, Jantzen and Reynolds, more implicitly by Friedman. Their vision was that of a dynamic based on the individual, schematically considering that the social phenomenon was the aggregated product of micro-behaviors. This impact consequently led to thinking that the autonomy of the private space would encourage an emancipated public space. The autonomy of the private spaces – through the restoration of its home economics – became the cardinal point of an action and emancipation philosophy. This theoretical connection was shared by several critical theory philosophers, particularly by Hannah Arendt and Jürgen Habermas, whose work brings to mind the autonomous living environment in terms of the individual–collective, private–public dialectic and its correspondences.

"The private sphere depends on the house," Habermas wrote.[20] This assertion originated in ancient Greece. The *oïkos* here designates "the house" in the sense of what is specific to each individual and is distinguished from the *polis*. "Thing common" to all the "free citizens," the *polis* was the political space where one publicly appeared, where one held dialogues to exchange ideas and carry out actions in common through "an active involvement in the world's affairs.[21] Arendt and Habermas analyzed the evolution and the state of these two clearly distinct domains: the private and the public. In *Strukturwandel der Öffenlichkeit* (1962), Habermas drew up the genealogy of the gradual interpenetration of the public and the private, which have, in our contemporary societies, reached a state of advanced confusion. As for Arendt, she clearly explained in 1958 how the private and public impacted each other and how the advent of the social sphere caused a devitalization of the domestic sphere in favor of the public sphere. Society, through a social state, became "the form in which activities concerning pure and simple survival are permitted to appear in public."[22] The private sphere burst apart; everything that it guaranteed was taken over by the public sphere. The advent of the social in Hannah Arendt converged with Foucault's concept of biopower. Both believed that modernity and liberalism were characterized by a series of mechanisms that aimed at optimizing and regulating life. This social sphere was founded on the deployment of the household's economic activities outside the private sphere via state interventionism. These logics of administration of the vital process – including utilities provided by the network – led to the domination of economics over politics. In under two centuries, these basic needs became totally dependent on technical, institutional and commercial mediators. Biological assistance made the home space mutate. The conditions of the economics of households that presided over the smooth functioning of the private sphere were henceforth outside its frame, as Habermas recalls:

The concept of economics that, until the seventeenth century, remained linked to the power and functions of the *oïkodespotes*, the *pater familias*, the *master of the house*, now takes on its modern meaning from the sole practice of exploitation whose operations are run by the profitability principle: tasks that are incumbent on the master of the house are now reduced to savings.[23]

Since that time, home economics has continued to structure itself as a market sector.

What Yona Friedman, Michael Reynolds, Michel Rosell and even Alexander Pike initiated and laid claim to was re-inverting this relationship through an ideal architectural practice that would ensure self-guaranteeing vital necessities. Technological progress is a springboard of this reconquest. By acting on the mechanics of the need-based economy, energy autonomy can be perceived as an emancipation process, echoing Habermas's statement: "It is only by being emancipated from market-driven regulations that this private sphere can be transformed into a private autonomy sphere."[24] By causing a conceptual and structural transformation of the private space, the energy autonomy movement would be a possible starting point. For example, according to Rosell:

> The first thing is that architecture must self-guarantee vital necessities. The human race must be made secure. Not to die of hunger, thirst or cold. The individual must be strengthened, nourishing homes must be created, co-research and co-implementation programs launched to reinforce autonomy wherever this is possible, in order to gradually exit the market economy. This is the process.[25]

Reynolds:

> Energy decentralization would allow each household to provide its inhabitants with everything they need to live on: energy, water, food. If every home could offer this, people would be secure and become much more invested and free. I am demonstrating at this time, in this human community that we have formed, that it is possible for each family to produce everything it needs, at least its first needs. The network grid connects people together in dependence; they are all dependent on the same thing and this makes them vulnerable. We must strengthen the individual. This is the starting point.[26]

Jantzen:

> I like the idea of not being tied to the government for my vital energy needs […] We have to develop self-sufficiency wherever this is possible and appropriate and technology enables us to do so.[27]

Friedman:

> To live in security, we must not depend on daily price and job offer fluctuations, or on
> the whims of distribution. A life more focused on the 'at home' and at the same time
> more useful (for oneself and for the community) seems to be the basis of the aspirations
> of most of us and, as odd as this may seem, it is the energy crisis (or rather the accurate
> re-evaluation of the price of energy) that seems to unquestionably take us there.[28]

The architectural project is focused on the recreation of a private autonomy
sphere. Self-guaranteeing vital necessities would amount to freeing individuals from
a part of their economic bondage. Through these practices, household consumption
would be reduced and the market sphere destabilized in one of its regulation and
collection mechanisms. Everything seemed to tighten around the private space, but
it was a starting point for many protagonists. Like Arendt, who considered that the
individual–collective dialectic was created through the individual and that an emancipated public space could be reactivated through the private:

> What prevented the *polis* from violating the private life of its citizens, what made it hold
> the limits of their fields sacred, was not respect for individual property as we understand it:
> it was that unless one possessed a house, one could not take part in the world's affairs, as
> otherwise there was no place for oneself [...]. If there was a relationship between the two
> domains, it was obvious that the family had to assume the necessities of life as prerequisites
> for freedom of the *polis*. [...] If one does not control biological necessities in the household,
> life, ordinary or 'good,' is impossible, but politics is not made for life.[29]

The evocation of this ancient idea of the *oïkos* corresponds to the arguments of certain
protagonists of the autonomy project: this private space appears as a rear base, a foundation. This converges with the theories of Proudhon and Kropotkin who proposed
first settling the question of housing, energy and food needs. This was the principal
argument of the most radical fringe of the movement that we have presented. Using
these analyses, the recreation of a private autonomy sphere could help restore politics
in the public sphere. If the economic hold is defused and the public space is cleansed
of what pollutes it, it changes status. For many, the public space was in the midst of a
crisis, but what determined it was the state of the subjects that comprised it. It would
only be in a space that the public power had not invested that the individual could
recreate a subjectivity in a position to subsequently determine an intention and a
power of action in the public. Arendt, like Castoriadis, viewed politics as the action
that constituted a free creation and "acting in common." This was in line with the
tradition of the philosophy of subjectivity, to which the autonomy project seemed to

be attached. In following this reasoning, an argument supporting energy autonomy would consist in asserting that if the public space depended on the state of the subjects who comprised it, their emancipation depended (among others) on a material autonomy (primarily energy and food) that resulted from a private organization of the vital process. As limited as this "thinking system" could be, energy autonomy would fit into it as a resumption of possession, an attempt at de-domestication, and would make it possible to create new socio-environmental balances.

A distinction can be made, however, between Arendt's advent of the social and Foucault's biopower. If both of them believed that life being made a tool serving economic purposes was characteristic of modernity, Foucault endeavored to explain the complexity of one of the most "important mutations in the history of human societies": the deep transformation of the mechanisms of power and all the ambiguity of the taking of this power that no longer directly subjugated those to whom it was applied.[30] Foucault's thinking was completely liberated from the emancipation v. domination dialectic, which was still found in the theoreticians who were critical of the Frankfurt School as well as in Castoriadis.[31] Rethinking the resistance to a positive and multiple power in terms of the vital, Foucault's approach marked a turning point. It was perhaps in following this more skeptical, less doctrinal thought process that energy autonomy ought to be viewed, by considering it from a vital necessities angle. Insufficiently conceptualized by its protagonists, energy autonomy questions one of the major issues of modern times. The self-guarantee of vital necessities as the object of a domestic architecture would ultimately comprise a return to life itself. But the autonomy project, despite these theoretical and pragmatic aspirations, would have very little resonance and few supporters in the environmental discourse in the late 1970s.

The 1980s: energy autonomy in the margins of environmental policies

The similarity of Grumman's Lunar Module and the *Ecol House* in Montreal showed an experiment that on the one hand was at the cutting edge of technology (high yield, efficiency, enormous budgets), and on the other, at its margin (low yield, limited budgets, recycling). Apart from the obvious difference in programs and means, this comparison questioned the realism of autonomy for architecture. Whereas certain skeptics set out its technical impossibility, others saw in it an institutional desire to reduce it, in the collective imagination, to an accumulation of equipment that was both expensive, complicated and cumbersome. If, from a technical viewpoint, energy autonomy was possible, it would seem that it could not be generalized in architecture; the question of the challenges and systems of instrumentality caused by this technological renewal were brought to the forefront at the time. As we have seen, in 1976, when the owners in the Lower East Side in New York installed solar collectors and a wind turbine on the roof of their building to produce their own electricity, serious legal conflicts broke out with the electricity company. Mostly reticent about the experiments that focused on a disconnection from the network, environmental policies were drawn up at the antipodes of the initial claims of those who set this awareness in motion. Whereas the sustainable development idea would receive its official imprimatur, national and international energy issues and strategies would systematically ignore the power of structural economic and social modifications derived from a decade of experiments on the question of autonomy, illustrating the persistence of the network's hold and the scope of the large technical system.

In 1980, when the effects of the energy crisis were dissipating, the energy autonomy movement was struck a few fatal blows. The lack of financial support for research, the priority given to nuclear power, the economic and political changes, the exhaustion and discredit of the theme emerged as so many reasons justifying its lack of vitality. In the United Kingdom, the United States and France, many programs were drastically cut back and numerous institutes closed down. In the United Kingdom and the United States, the link between the flagging of research and the arrival in power of neo-liberal leaders must be relativized in that during these same years the socialists arrived in France. In the 1970s, the French Atomic Energy Commission (CEA) had become a genuine industrial and financial group playing on competition and profitability. In 1973, the oil crisis made it necessary to take a different look at energy problems. It was the end of cheap energy. France, with few fossil resources, looked for a future for itself. The French nuclear program was supposed to be the answer. In 1975, an "architecture plan" was launched by the state and EDF with the participation of several architects, among them Jean Willerval, Pierre Dufau, Paul Andreu, Jean Demailly and Jean Dubuisson. Brought together in a college of architects involved in the nuclear question, under the direction of Claude Parent, they created models and built nuclear power plants.[32] The idea for French nuclear institutions – but more broadly European and American ones – and the large partner firms was to "generalize the nuclear power plant, to make it a model infrastructure, even to mass produce it.[33] An architectural wager emerged and was materialized in the reinvention of the landscape around these new energy monuments (see Figure 117).

With the emergence of the electro-nuclear sector, the degree of state control and centralization reached heights never before attained.[34] As of 1980, the cost of so-called traditional energies decreased. Alternative energies did not survive the "all-nuclear."[35] The fact that the specter of the energy crisis had receded favored the energy lobbies' marginalization of disconnection supporters. The architecture-energy experimentation field visibly shrank. International competitiveness and the sudden

Un nouvel état du paysage.

Figure 117 Claude Parent, "Nuclear Power Plant" (1975)

arrival of market mechanisms in the energy sector – until that point mostly devoted to planning – would fundamentally modify the role of public regulation at the time. The lobbies saw to it that environmental regulations and tax proposals were dismembered. Too alternative energy breaches would be sealed, their principles transformed and reintegrated. The economist Jacques Percebois, a specialist in renewable energies, denounced in the late 1970s the responsibility of the "strategy of the states and large nuclear and oil companies."[36] Public research organizations, nationalized companies and private manufacturers played the game: Total and Elf took majority holdings very early on in American companies that made solar cells or in the sector of other renewable energies. Simultaneously, the large energy providers proved that electricity and gas were the ideal complements to solar and wind energies, provided that they were in a network. The states and the lobbies' strategy was therefore limited to a minimal change in acquired habits, in the framework of a modus vivendi of association with the dominant energy distribution system. Renewable energies would only be a supplement to, in the end, endorse the dominant system. It does not seem exaggerated to assert that total energy autonomy and disconnection experimentation were never publicly encouraged.

In France, the public authorities and the various organizations made no real effort to attempt to cost other types of energy policies; this point was stressed on many occasions in the Papon, Schloesing and Mesmin reports of the Finance Commission (1977).[37] These shortcomings did not prevent local initiatives. This was the case of the Alter project, launched by the Garep (Groupe aquitain de recherche en économie physique [Aquitaine Group for research on the real economy]) in 1975 and the Groupe de Bellevue, which brought together researchers from different disciplines.[38] They launched territorial research on renewable energies and the "issue of limits." The group, "struck by the timidity of energy prospective in France," envisaged publishing a scenario on transition leading to a "modern self-subsistence" system whose phases would be spread out until 2050. By gathering together the instruments of exploratory prospective and creating a model of the real, physical basis of the economy on a piece of land in a rural canton, their goal was to locally develop an application of macro-economic models for a "free energy prospective." The lack of financing forced them to suspend their research, but the evocation of this ambitious project is enough to point out local dynamism in respect to the inertia of the organizations officially in charge of conducting an innovative energy policy.

In *Energy Autonomy: The Economic, Social and Technological Case for Renewable Energy* (2006), Hermann Scheer reintroduced and supported the same type of project. The German economist and legislator called for the establishment of a priority strategy for its development, criticizing the attachment to the principle of large international networks and offering a summary of the history of the immobility of

European governments in the late 1970s. If the specialists in scientific forecasting explained in detail, on several occasions starting in the 1970s, "that renewable energies could under certain condition meet all energy needs, whether in the United States or Europe, all of them have in common being systematically ignored in the energy debate, including by the competent environmental institutions."[39] In France, a few experimental constructions were financed, but the number of these investments seemed ludicrous compared to the nuclear program envisaged in the successive plans. Despite favorable conclusions, "the researchers do not obtain any serious aid from the public authorities."

> In 1981, bankruptcies in the solar companies are multiplying and EDF is opposed to solar power in the name of nuclear power with the complicity of the Agence française pour la maîtrise de l'énergie (AFME).[40]

The determination to favor the nuclear sector for electricity production in France marked the interruption of the Thémis (Odeillo) experiment in 1986. The energy provision liberalization movement launched in the late 1970s in the United Kingdom and the United States in the electricity sector (liberalization that also became, in 1996, the rule in the European Union) did not change anything. On the contrary, it strengthened and consolidated the positions of fossil fuels and nuclear energy. This liberalization facilitated the position of the oligopolies and monopolies in the entire conventional energy sector. It would seem that the state's disengagement permitted the establishment of a global and private planned energy economy. Using comparative studies, Scheer dissected the machinery of the energy system and brought out the paralysis of the previous thirty or so years and called for a large-scale reorientation: He made the following accusation:

> The guardians of the temple of the energy institution not only want to maintain the oligarchy of the sellers and keep the infrastructure set up for this purpose running at full capacity, but also to preserve their social role and the technological ideology they have built.

Scheer denounced the governments' total dependence on the large multinational energy groups and the states that were henceforth "the assistants and protectors of an energy sector whose role as a fourth power was recognized."[41] Speaking as a government official, Scheer criticized the deceptive consensus and the fundamental conflict between the atom and renewable energies, denouncing the protection of a "mega-network" centered on fossil and nuclear energies whose intertwining was both technical, economic, social and political. He demonstrated with a host of examples how the established powers often prevented the rollout of this technological renewal despite many attempts.[42]

The Solar Conspiracy (1975) by the sociologist John Keyes, or more recently *Le Choix du feu* (2007) by the social anthropologist Alain Gras, also described how this rapid development was blocked: the purchase of small companies by the large groups that then closed them, and subsidies granted to renewable energies that were always several times smaller than those given to nuclear and fossil energies. As we have seen, the governance of the territory depends on controlling the networks. Many authors viewed the network idea as a key to explaining the most complex phenomena, notably those governing the evolution of contemporary capitalism. In *Le Territoire aménagé par les réseaux*, Pierre Musso further demonstrated the power of the connection masters:

> Those who control (and will control in the future) this networks-territories-utilities connection will have considerable strategic power: one can speak of the 'sovereignty of connections.' The regulation and operation of networks comprise the new sites of power: they move, on one hand, from national to local and to Europe and, on the other hand, from the political to the economic and the financial.[43]

In fact, those who were in a position to influence the networks-territories-utilities trio have the power to act on the economic system and through a ricochet effect on the organization of the entire society. The network implies a complete system – an operator, regulations, an economic model, consolidations, mergers, acquisitions – the whole forming oligopolies led by the financial markets and institutional investors. The major international utility operators imposed themselves as the masters of the globalized economy. The American essayist Jeremy Rifkin also established the replacement of the markets by the networks.[44] All these references demonstrate the continuity, since the nineteenth century, of an energy orientation and governmentality, as well as the shift from a "mega-machine" to a "large technical system" showing a strengthening of the network and, as a corollary, its capacities to incorporate all types of energies – including the renewables – without any structural modification.

The environmental policies of the 1980s would be geared toward the "mega-machine." This idea, introduced by Lewis Mumford in *Technics and Civilization* (1934), could be considered the acknowledgment of a historic technical model. Alain Gras also considered the Industrial Revolution a decisive moment when, between "the different technical paths imaginable – including those of renewable energies – the Western countries finally chose fire (fossil energies)" as the main power source, consequently neglecting other energy possibilities. He re-examined the idea of the mega-machine,[45] describing the socio-technical features of its evolutions, from the creation of flow management centers to regulators, then controllers: "All this brings about the transformation of this mega-machine into a very powerful organizational structure that I call the technical macro-system, whose network is nothing but the infrastructure."[46] From the mega-machine to the macro-system, a curious entity that seemed to elude any control emerged. Alain Gras was, however, against the idea of an autonomous evolution of technologies that would impose themselves on humanity. The author believed that there was no historical determinism of technical progress but rather a convergence of factors that orientated, and still orient, structural choices.

But if technical fatality is a fabricated myth, the "non-neutrality" of certain systems seems quite real. The debates on the autonomous evolution of technologies and the neutrality of its production and distribution systems were examined, notably by Lewis Mumford, Jacques Ellul, Cornelius Castoriadis, and more recently by Langdon Winner and Alain Gras and Jean-Paul Deléage in France. Though viewpoints diverged on the autonomous evolution question, all of them called for abandoning the idea of its neutrality. Technology was not simply an instrument that can be used to serve different purposes. In this sense, energy autonomy confirms the non-neutrality of the large-scale network, a structural element of the technical macro-system. Alternative energies were gradually associated with, and then incorporated into, this technical macro-system during the 1980s, whereas energy autonomy and disconnection were sidelined. However, the approaches that attempted to make the ecologic movement inseparable from broader political and social issues, notably including the autonomy question, must not be ignored. This was the ambition of *De l'écologie à l'autonomie*, which grasped these issues with a great deal of insight, anticipating the turning point that energy would take in the 1980s with energy policies that promoted sustainable development. The authors, Cornelius Castoriadis and Daniel Cohn-Bendit, showed that on the basis of identical infrastructures, opposite social models could not exist:

> The problem is not so much the fact that the means of production belong to a power but rather that these means of production and these infrastructures incorporate the entire program and the entire history of capitalism since the nineteenth century. The question is therefore not simply one of the necessity of a new energy choice (fossil energies, renewable energies, hybrid systems) but how the technological then the economic and political whole of society is viewed.[47]

The problem was not energy in itself as much as its physical, technical and organizational structure: the network and its infrastructures. From the political ecology viewpoint, Castoriadis and Cohn-Bendit encouraged an imaginary leap and the relocation of energy provision sources in parallel with the deconstruction of macro-systems, to shift, tomorrow, from ecology to autonomy. In this framework, renewable energies could become the vehicle of another kind of organization, combining actions and reflections that foreshadow a new societal institution. Starting from energy auton- omy would greatly expand the environmental question by redefining lifestyles and traditional consumption and governance modes. It would one of the possible starting points. In their conclusion, the authors questioned and warned those who thought of renewable energies as a technology that is "unadjustable" to the macro-system and to one of its characteristics: centralization. The 1980s would moreover mark the advent of this integration and the dilution of certain energy autonomy principles through the institutional ecology filter (see Figure 118).

Tightly holding the reins of an entire economy, the dependence model resisted. The controversial question of the 1970s on the limits of growth did not cause any change in direction.

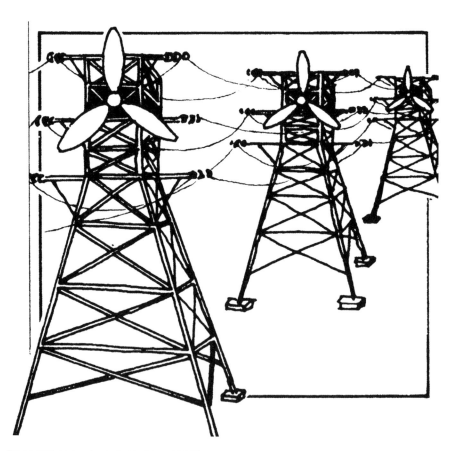

Figure 118 Networked wind turbines (1976)

From autonomy to ecology: the contradictions of sustainable development

The 1970s, marked by the Club of Rome report, the Stockholm conference, and the creation of the United Nations Environment Programme (UNEP) and its extensions, led to new cooperative attempts to protect the environment. The world energy crisis in 1973 created conditions that were more favorable than ever to the development of energy autonomy. Despite all these positive aspects, the opposition paradoxically remained strong. In 1980, after a decade of great enthusiasm worldwide on the environmental question and its economic corollary, the term "sustainable development" appeared for the first time in a publication of the International Union for the Conservation of Nature and Natural Resources titled *World Conservation Strategy*. It would be given its official imprimatur in the Brundtland Report in 1987.[48] This problematic idea would guide every discussion and action, encouraging an odd cohabitation: protection-environment-economic growth. A reconciliation between economic development and ecological balances began with sustainable development. Despite the inadequacy of the objectives set and met, these meetings and conventions aimed at international cooperation did not erase the accuracy of certain analyses and the honesty of the efforts undertaken, which set off international reflection on limits and transitions. It is not at all our purpose here to explain the origin of the term, or to present the content or internal contradictions of these reports known worldwide, but rather to observe how this sustainable development command threatened to become the environmental phase of an energy regulation process that originated in the nineteenth century.

However, despite their good intentions, the charters and protocols did not succeed in activating a genuine dynamic. Negotiations failed, notably on what compensation would be paid to poor countries for their participation in the collective effort. In terms of energy, there were encouragements right from the start. We can thus read in the Brundtland Report: "Planners must find ways of relying more on supporting community initiatives and self-help efforts and on effectively using low-cost technologies." There was no lack of questions on fairness and interest, as well as doubts on the Western consumption model. However, in the sections on energies, there were many encouraging calls for research and experimentation, without clearly challenging energy infrastructures or bringing up autonomy, whether partial or total. It should moreover be pointed out that the European countries, depending on their cultural and political traditions, did not have a uniform commitment to alternative energies. Though we cannot draw general conclusions, we can, however, make a few observations.

The pressure of the industrial lobbies and the refusal of most of the countries to sign economically restrictive agreements led to very weak results (despite Kyoto, global carbon emissions have increased fourfold since the 1990s). These difficulties were confirmed by the obvious failure of the Copenhagen summit, which cast doubt on the sustainable development concept while the fervent media incantations did not succeed in clarifying ambiguities. The first term dominated the second. The economist Serge Latouche, dissecting the semantics and demystifying the paradox of this expression, criticized "the inconsistency of the project and the ineptness of the term."[49] If economists, environmentalists, philosophers and biologists, since the 1973 oil crisis, demonstrated on many occasions that respecting the major ecological balances partially depended on challenging our economic growth model, the governments launched, under the "sustainable development banner," an environmental mega-machine that caused a degree of unease. This adjective has won over many sectors since the 1990s: sustainable economy, sustainable agriculture, sustainable landscape, sustainable urban planning and architecture … Bruno Villalba also questioned this virtuous dynamic and found a major semantic limit:

'Sustainability' must not simply be confused with what is sustained, what endures *over time*; it is more perceived as what provides a meaning to what one wishes to perpetuate; this presupposes that this duration is associated with an analysis of the conditions (political, economic, social) that bring forth a compromise on the end results of the duration. If the city must endure, be maintained as a livable and viable entity, how can it produce a social consensus that is shared by the largest number of people, taking environmental constraints into account? In this viewpoint, sustainability incorporates a temporal dimension and a dynamic dimension – in that it endeavors to create a balance between the centrifugal tensions of the social sphere, the economy and the environmental domain. Sustainability arises from a methodology whose purpose is to establish a self-reproducible balance.[50]

In the economy-social-environment compromise, we can observe the symbolic dominance of the third element, while the first two were favored by energy autonomy defenders in the 1970s. Hermann Scheer defended autonomy as an economic and social springboard for energy transition, stating that this would be "the most profound and wide-ranging structural economic change since the beginning of the industrial revolution."[51] Scheer counted on a slow propagation that would break up the uniformity of the traditional supply and consumption structures. He encouraged the public powers to take over the electricity and gas networks through regional or municipal management companies. The economic emancipation of the individual was highlighted:

Imagine that more and more owners of independent homes are moving in this direction – and that they are even doing so in the end, because it will have become a natural social attitude. People would be rid of the worries of rising energy prices.[52]

Using an analysis of the contemporary period's environmental policies, Scheer came down in favor of energy autonomy at every scale, but provided no details on the idea or its antecedents and did not address the question from the viewpoint of urban planning or architecture. This independence primarily focused on the states' relationship with the large international energy groups. This essay, devoted to the contemporary situation of worldwide energy governance, offers however a relevant assessment of what the author called "fossil and nuclear autism." Nonetheless, Scheer's positioning remains ambiguous since he defended the consensus with the current energy sector, while criticizing the governments' inertia and approving a secession strategy. Given its influence, he considered that only a collaboration seemed possible at the present time. However, we have seen that many actors rejected this consensus, since it consisted in asking for improvements from those who would immediately financially profit or derive power from them. Meanwhile Scheer did not take into account the recovery and capacity of renewable energies to be incorporated into the territorial technical system. The major energy and institutional stakeholders were often in a hurry to determine the most efficient form of electricity produced by solar or wind incorporated into the network and its marketing by the public or private sector. The decline of the environmental utopia and energy autonomy unquestionably dates from its institutionalization.

Infrastructure diversity faced with the large technical system

The submission of alternative energy systems to the networks began in the 1980s. Renewable energies often present the same institutional and physical centralization characteristics as nuclear and fossil energies. Technocratic and bureaucratic tools were redirected to the protection of the environment without, however, criticizing or reshaping dependence on the centralized system.

In the early 1990s, the implementation of Agenda 21 and the launch of the European Conferences on Sustainable Cities and Towns (with the Aalborg Charter, drawn up in 1994) activated mobilization on every institutional level, making urban environmental action more concrete. This impetus notably took the form of the creation of eco-districts, initially in northern European cities, whose progress in this domain no longer needs to be demonstrated. These districts are the now celebrated BedZED in England, Vauban in Germany, Hammarby, Björkhagen and Västra Hamnen in Sweden, EVA Lanxmeer in the Netherlands, Ørestad in Denmark and the Austrian districts of Voralberg and Güssing.

Today, there is a consensus in favor of hybrid systems of extensive networks and more localized forms of self-sufficiency or micro-grids. Rather than advocating the autonomy of units or groups of buildings, most European public–private partnerships focus on the sustainability of buildings that are connected to the electricity network and that balance energy demand in real time. The smart grid appears to promise new ways of optimizing this relationship, and with these possibilities in place, questions about the future of energy seem to revolve around interconnection: How do you hook up these small technical systems to the large technical system? How can renewable energies become included in large technical systems?

But the question that is raised – most obviously for electricity – is that of network scale. On what scale should autonomy (and therefore the network) be considered: on the scale of a building, a block, a region? And how far should interconnectivity go?

Paradoxically, it is now the threat of disconnection following blackouts or brown-outs during peak hours that ensures the survival of the big electrical networks. The majority of public–private European partnerships are, for example, keen to emphasize the resilience of interconnected buildings that are linked to the centralized electricity network. In France, for EDF (the French public energy supplier), being disconnected is equivalent to being invisible to the network during peak hours: this is a problem since the smart grid is designed to optimize and balance the various interconnections in line with the fluctuating relationship between demand and supply. Accordingly, micro-grids are invited, and sometimes obliged, to be connected to the super grid. In France, in Brittany, Kergrid Building (Smart Award 2013), for example, is "devoted to its network."[53] At the same time, the Pas de Calais-Picardie region hired the American futurologist Jeremy Rifkin to develop a master plan that put regional autonomy at its center. How can these competing visions coexist? Which systems of service management will emerge?

If self-sufficiency is still justified in environments devoid of any infrastructures, it is much harder to make a similar argument in areas already supplied by the network. In a French town outside Nantes, the power struggle by the Abalone group for a complete disconnection of its building from the EDF network shows how difficult it is for total autonomy to be imagined or realized. In this case, the demand for autonomy was seen by EDF as an act of defiance toward existing public services. The energy consensus and the defenders of the historical model, however, prefer the hybrid system, partial support and lightening of the network, backed by a series of laws and markets. In France, a group of institutions and circulars attempt to provide a framework for these future practices, but this kind of energy regulation still looks like a badly cut suit. Micro-electricity networks are asked, even forced, to connect to the super grid. Micro-grid, smart grid and super grid are the keywords of a new com-plementary energy structure that strives for maximum connection. The large-scale reticular system continues to support international or intercontinental economic and spatial projections. One example is Desertec, which is planning the creation of an electricity network that would supply North Africa, Europe and the Middle East using renewable resources in the North African desert. OMA's (Office for Metropolitan Architecture) Roadmap 2050 has similar goals: *Eneropa* is a renewable energy network interconnected on the European scale.[54] The map of Europe is thus renamed according to its regions' energy potential (see Figures 119 and 120). Ireland and the western half of the United Kingdom become Tidal States, Biomassburg emerges in the east, while Portugal, Spain, Italy and Greece have been renamed Solaria. The London Underground map used as a model shows the importance of these interconnections for such a vast network.

In France, at the Grand Pari(s) consultation launched in 2008, the energy question showed signs of reviving a certain pragmatism. Rogers's team proposed restructuring the compact city around multifunctional metropolitan frames, some including energy cells (see Figure 121). These are technical energy and resource production centers incorporated into the urban or peri-urban fabric. Waste incineration can generate heat and electricity, and biomass waste is used to produce methane. These energy poles are micro-networks, partially connected to the large systems. Laying claim to a hybrid approach, architecture and infrastructure are recreating a post-carbon urban landscape. The LIN architects urbanists team, led by Finn Geipel and Studio 09 and directed by the Bernardo Secchi–Paola Viganò tandem, also proposed resegmenting and recycling the infrastructure grid to make it flexible and create new interactions. In the framework of the research program ("Ignis mutat res. Think of architecture, the city and the landscape through the energy angle") Paola Viganò's team worked on resources, focusing on the recycling of gray energy and self-sufficiency. Also in the framework of this consultation, Philippe Potié, Djamel Klouche and Florian Hertweck's team concentrated on energy potential and self-sufficiency in cross-border regions. The urban and territorial project is structured around new energy-industrial polarities. Resource catalogues, energy mapping and reticular topography are tools indispensable for a new X-raying of the territory. But the question that is raised – in the most obvious way for electricity – is that of network scale (see Figure 122). A hierarchy and degree of connectivity can be seen in the terms *primary*, *secondary* and *auxiliary* network. On what scale should autonomy (and therefore the network) be considered: that of a building, a block, a region? And how far should interconnectivity go?

Today, micro-grids are proven to be technically and environmentally viable on the scale of a neighborhood, a city, even a region or an island. Examples include the district of King's Cross in London, the town of Woking in England, the Marcus Garvey Village in Brooklyn (and other micro-grid projects in New York state).[55] Micro-grids are also an alternative in rural areas like Feldheim in Germany or Murek and Güssing in Austria.[56] Each of these examples – in different time frames and contexts that go beyond the framework of our analysis – have sought to shift the

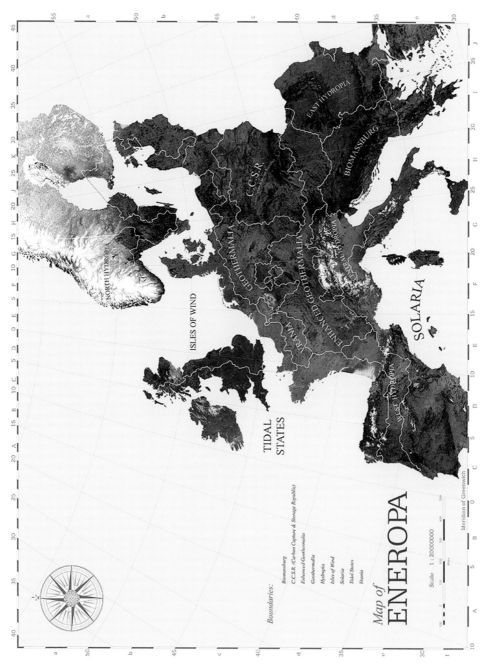

Figure 119 OMA, "The European Renewable Energy Network" (2011)

Figure 120 OMA, "Energy Network for Eneropa" (2011)

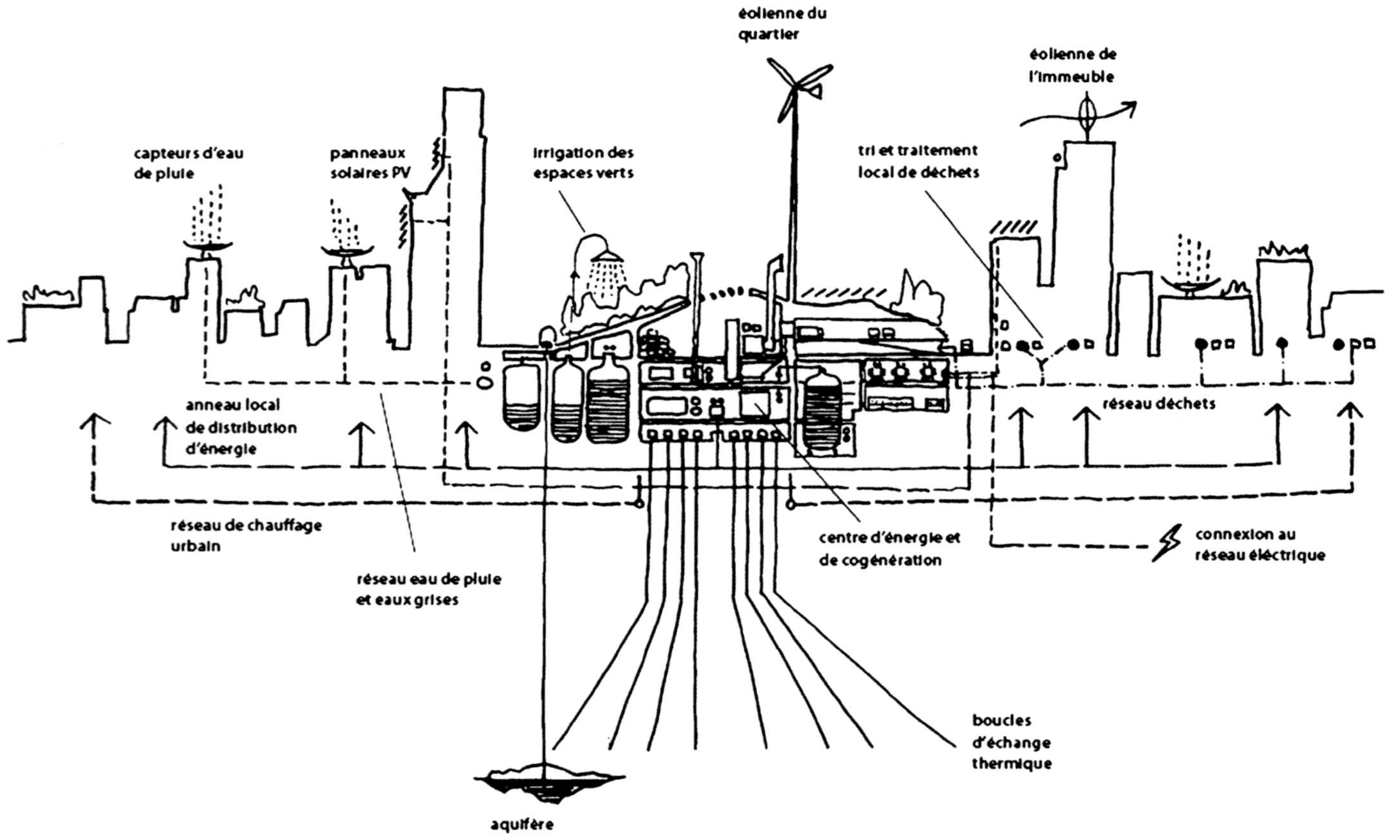

éolienne du quartier

éolienne de l'immeuble

tri et traitement local de déchets

réseau déchets

connexion au réseau électrique

Irrigation des espaces verts

centre d'énergie et de cogénération

boucles d'échange thermique

aquifère

panneaux solaires PV

réseau eau de pluie et eaux grises

capteurs d'eau de pluie

anneau local de distribution d'énergie

réseau de chauffage urbain

Figure 121 Richard Rogers, Urban Energy Hub (2009)

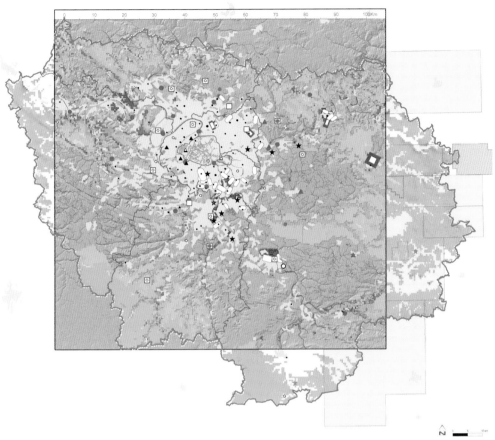

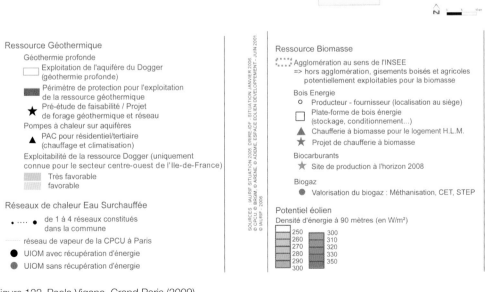

Ressource Géothermique

Géothermie profonde

☐ Exploitation de l'aquifère du Dogger
(géothermie profonde)

■ Périmètre de protection pour l'exploitation
de la ressource géothermique

★ Pré-étude de faisabilité / Projet
de forage géothermique et réseau

Pompes à chaleur sur aquifères

▲ PAC pour résidentiel/tertiaire
(chauffage et climatisation)

Exploitabilité de la ressource Dogger (uniquement
connue pour le secteur centre-ouest de l'Ile-de-France)

▨ Très favorable
▨ favorable

Réseaux de chaleur Eau Surchauffée

•····• de 1 à 4 réseaux constitués
dans la commune

······ réseau de vapeur de la CPCU à Paris

● UIOM avec récupération d'énergie

● UIOM sans récupération d'énergie

SOURCES : IAURIF SITUATION 2005. DRIRE-IDF : SITUATION JANVIER 2006
© CPCU. © BRGM. © ARENE. ESPACE ÉOLIEN DÉVELOPPEMENT - JUIN 2001
© IAURIF - 2006

Ressource Biomasse

⌐···¬ Agglomération au sens de l'INSEE
=> hors agglomération, gisements boisés et agricoles
potentiellement exploitables pour la biomasse

Bois Energie

○ Producteur - fournisseur (localisation au siège)

☐ Plate-forme de bois énergie
(stockage, conditionnement...)

▲ Chaufferie à biomasse pour le logement H.L.M.

★ Projet de chaufferie à biomasse

Biocarburants

★ Site de production à l'horizon 2008

Biogaz

● Valorisation du biogaz : Méthanisation, CET, STEP

Potentiel éolien

Densité d'énergie à 90 mètres (en W/m²)

	250		300
	260		310
	270		320
	280		330
	290		340
	300		350

Figure 122 Paola Vigano, Grand Paris (2009)

management in line with the goal of self-sufficiency, and many have succeeded. [57] The idea that traditional energy infrastructures can play a minor supporting role in projects like these has made headway in both the countries of the North as well as the South.

The conflict over scale is far from resolved – and in any case takes different forms, but the structural foundations of a 'modern' energy system are clearly shifting in line with the following trends. With a diversification of productive energy resources and systems, small technical or individualized supply systems are emerging that overlap with existing large networks. Now situated in relation to each other in new eco-systemic configurations, water, waste, sanitation and electricity service networks are no longer considered as wholly separate arrangements, but are routinely interlinked and complementary. These kinds of energy transition involve innovative partnerships and new decision-making processes between energy managers, public authorities and civil society, all of which generate and reflect new social and economic issues concerning service management and governance.

In this perspective, hierarchies could be reversed; the major electricity network would remain highly structured but could become secondary for supplying certain sectors in which it would basically be a solidarity reserve depending on needs. On each borough sector or energy territory (defined according to the common good, productions and needs), the exchange ratio between private networks (whose energy production/consumption ratio would aim at being optimal) and the national network could be redefined in a new solidary relationship (insufficiency, too heavy load current, risk of a blackout). Unlike the augmented technical macro-system (smart grid) which thinks of the effacement or autonomy of certain parts of the electricity system as an adjustment variable of the major network, the micro-network would make the optimization of the small scale the priority of a technical system whose scope would be extendable.

From this point of view, being autonomous now means being disconnected from the large-scale normative historical model and being able to build a utility system on and across other scales. Disconnection is not a matter of imagining energy provision without the network but is, rather, a matter of reinventing the network along with other modes and moments of connection. On one hand, energy futures are envisaged as a continuation of the historical tradition of large-scale connection; on the other hand, the potential of distributed, decentralized and self-sufficient systems is still strongly defended. New questions bridge between these debates. For example, are there full and partial forms of self-sufficiency, and if so, what does this mean for the extent and depth of interconnection involved? Who ensures the management of these interlinked services? Who pays? Faced with the unpredictable cost of energy transitions over the next ten years, real dilemmas are emerging at the city scale, where there is a choice between investing in networks, or pursuing greater levels of autonomy on the scale of more and less extensive real estate projects.

Despite being marked by vacillations, disconnection is making its way, marking an extraordinarily contemporary structural modification of power. Rid of its negative symbolism and its dogmatic weightiness, autonomy offers the possibility of reinventing the management of vital processes, structural economic modifications and the reactivation, on the scale of a shared daily life, of imaginary and experimental forces. Reversing beliefs and technological programs inherited from the nineteenth century, mobilization is stressed to reflect on and coordinate infrastructural restructuring, to revitalize local systems and to propose new partnerships between civil society, the public authorities and the private sector. Long squeezed between a communitarian archaism and technological futurism, the revivals, continuations and rebounds of energy autonomy ask us to reconsider the relevance of this theme in the twenty-first century. With a bright future ahead of it, it establishes new steps for the rollout of a concept that has irresistible dynamism.

Notes

1   Alexandroff, "Architecture solaire: quelques perspectives," p. 10.

2   Peter Buchanan, *Emilio Ambasz: Casa de retiro espiritual* (Milan: Skira, 2005).

3   Paul Virilio, *Bunker archéologie* (Paris: Centre Pompidou, Centre de création industrielle, 1975), p. 54.

4   Pedregal, "L'architecture autonome," p. 46.

5   Bernard Nadoulek, *L'Iceberg des autonomes* (Paris: Kesselring, 1979), p. 186.

6   Comité invisible, *L'insurrection qui vient* (Paris: La Fabrique, 2007), pp. 115, 101, 100.

7   Olivier Coutard and Géraldine Pflieger, "Une analyse du rôle des usagers dans le développement des services de réseaux en France," *Entreprises et histoire*, no. 30, September (2002), pp. 146–152.

8   Stephen Graham and Simon Marvin, *Splintering Urbanism: Networked Infrastructures, Technological Mobilities and the Urban Condition* (London: Routledge, 2001).

9   Gabriel Dupuy, "Villes, systèmes et réseaux. Le rôle historique des techniques urbaines," *Les Annales de la recherche urbaine*, no. 23–24 (1984), pp. 231–241.

10 Born in 1943 in Argentina, Emilio Ambasz is an architect and professor. A graduate of Princeton University, he was director of the design sector at the MoMA in New York from 1970 to 1976 and directed the exhibition "Italy: The new domestic landscape" in 1972. In the 1970s, he developed green megastructures in which he merged the site and the buildings.

11 Emilio Ambasz, "Center for Applied Computer Research and Programming: Ultimately a flower barge," *Progressive Architecture*, vol. 56, no. 8 (1975), pp. 76–79.

12 Richard Rogers, interview with Fanny Lopez, 21 May 2008.

13 Richard Rogers, "Sustainable City," BBC, Reith Lectures (February–March 1995).

14 Vitruvius, *Les Dix Livres d'architecture de Vitruve, corrigés et traduits en 1684 par Claude Perrault* (Brussels: Mardaga, 1979), p. 29.

15 André Fleury, "L'agriculture dans la ville, projet urbain?," conference paper, 40th ISOCARP congress, Switzerland, 2004.

16 *Ibid.*

17 Friedman, *L'Architecture mobile*, p. 86.

18 We should note the recent republications of John Seymour, *The New Complete Book of Self-Sufficiency: The Classic Guide for Realists and Dreamers* (London: Dorling Kindersley, 2003) and *The Concise Guide to Self-Sufficiency* (London: Dorling Kindersley, 2007).

19 Mumford's Neolithic hamlet depicts a lost golden age. He described these autonomous villages, surrounded by kitchen gardens and farmland, as an example of a permanent association between groups of humans, nature and animals. Cf. Lewis Mumford, *The City in History: Its Origins, its Transformations, and its Prospects* (San Diego, CA: Harcourt Brace International, 1968).

20 Jürgen Habermas, *The Structural Transformation of the Public Space* (Cambridge: Polity, [1962] 1989).

21 Hannah Arendt, *The Human Condition* (Chicago, IL: Chicago University Press, 1958).

22 *Ibid.*, pp. 30–31.

23 Habermas, *The Structural Transformation of the Public Space*, p. 15.

24 *Ibid.*, p. 149.

25 Michel Rosell, interview with Fanny Lopez, 14 June 2009.

26 Michael Reynolds, interview with Fanny Lopez, 15 November 2009.

27 Michel Jantzen, interview with Fanny Lopez, 17 January 2008.

28 Friedman, *Alternatives énergétiques*, p. 52.

29 Arendt, *The Human Condition* pp. 67–68.

30 Foucault, "Les mailles du pouvoir," p. 1013.

31 See Philippe Caumières, "La pensée de l'autonomie selon Castoriadis au risque de Foucault," in Sophie Klimis and Laurent Van Eynde (eds), *Cahiers Castoriadis* (Brussels: Facultés universitaires Saint-Louis, 2006).

32 Claude Parent, *L'Architecture et le nucléaire* (Paris: Le Moniteur, 1978) and *Les Maisons de l'atome* (Paris: Le Moniteur, 1983).

33 See Jean-Claude Debeir, Jean-Paul Deléage and Daniel Hémery, "À la recherche d'une issue: genèse et contraintes du nucléaire," in Debeir, Deléage and Hémery, *Une histoire de l'énergie*, pp. 261–337.

34 Michel Damian, "Les temps nucléaires" (PhD thesis, University of Grenoble II, 1983).

35 Cf. Hermann Scheer, *Energy Autonomy: The Economic, Social and Technological Case for Renewable Energy* (London: Routledge, 2006), p. 70.

36 Jacques Percebois, *L'Energie solaire: Perspectives économiques* (Paris: Centre national de la recherche scientifique, 1975), p. 99. See also: Jacques Percebois, "Energie et théorie économique: un survol," *Revue d'économie politique*, vol. 111, no. 6 (2001), pp. 815–860.

37 "It will be repeated that [the new energies] will not be able to provide significant results in the future and that they can only represent at best 1% of our consumption. It is true that the efforts made in their favor can only end in mediocre results," Schloesing Report of the Finance Commission (October 1977).

38 Groupe de Bellevue, *Projet Alter: Esquisse d'un régime à long terme tout solaire* (Paris: Syros, 1977).

39 Scheer, *Energy Autonomy*, p. 70.

40 F. Ro, "Les années 1970, le solaire," *L'Architecture d'aujourd'hui*, no. 308 (1996).

41 Scheer, *Energy Autonomy*, p. 159.

42 In 1978, Wolfgang Palz, head of the Renewable Energies Division at the European Commission, defended the idea that renewable energies were much better prepared for marketing than nuclear energy. Wolfgang Palz, *Solar Electricity: An Economic Approach to Solar Energy* (Paris/London: UNESCO/Butterworths, 1978). The applications of the recommendations issued by the G8 Renewable Energy Task Force in 1999, the "global Marshall Plan" in 2004 and the successive conferences in Kyoto, Rio and Johannesburg remained weak in comparison to the declarations formulated.

43 Pierre Musso, *Le Territoire aménagé par les réseaux* (La Tour-d'Aigues/Paris: L'Aube/Datar, 2002), p. 12.

44 Jeremy Rifkin, *The Age of Access: The New Culture of Hypercapitalism, Where All of Life is a Paid-for Experience* (New York: J. P. Tarcher/Putnam, 2000).

45 Mumford, *Technics and Civilization*, p. x; Gras, "Les réseaux, les machines et la mégamachine," p. x. See also Serge Latouche, *La Mégamachine: Raison techno-scientifique, raison économique et mythe du progrès* (Paris: La Découverte/Mauss, 1995).

46 Gras, "Les réseaux, les machines et la mégamachine," p. 149.

47 Cornelius Castoriadis and Daniel Cohn-Bendit, *De l'écologie à l'autonomie* (Paris: Seuil, 1981), transcription of the conference "De l'écologie à l'autonomie" held at the University of Louvain-la-Neuve on 27 February 1980.

48 World Commission on Environment and Development, *Our Common Future* (Oxford: Oxford University Press, 1987).

49 Serge Latouche, "L'imposture du développement durable ou les habits neufs du développement?," *Mondes en développement*, vol. 31, no. 121 (2003), pp. 23–30.

50 Bruno Villalba, "L'utopie sociale de la ville durable," *EcoRev': revue critique d'écologie politique*, no. 27, July–August (2007).

51 Scheer, *Energy Autonomy*, p. 86.

52 *Ibid.*, p. 77.

53 Personal correspondence with Fanny Lopez, 19 January 2015.

54   In 2009, the European Climate Foundation launched the "Roadmap 2050" study to encourage proposals on drastically reducing CO_2 emissions by 2050. Rem Koolhaas and OMA were among the consultants.

55   Fanny Lopez, "Keep the lights on! La décentralisation énergétique à Londres," in Gilles Lepensant (ed.), *L'autonomie énergétique en Europe* (Paris: Inalco, 2017), pp. 30–52. Translated as "Micro-grids in London: a new device for urban capitalism?," in Gildo M. Santos and Nuno Madureira (eds), *Electric Energy in History: Social, Economic and Cultural Issues* (Newcastle: Cambridge Scholars Publishing, 2018).

56   Laure Dobigny, "Le choix des énergies renouvelables: socio-anthropologie de l'autonomie énergétique locale en Allemagne, Autriche et France" (PhD thesis, Université Paris I, 2016); Laura Dobigny, "Absence de représentations ou Représentation d'une absence? Pour une socio-anthropologie de l'énergie," in S. Poirot-Delpech and L. Raineau (eds), *Pour une socio-anthropologie de l'environnement, Volume 1* (Paris: L'Harmattan, 2012), pp. 149–164; Laura Dobigny, "L'autonomie énergétique: acteurs, processus et usages: De l'individuel au local en Allemagne, Autriche, France," in M. Dobré and S. Juan (eds), *Consommer autrement: La réforme écologique des modes de vie* (Paris: L'Harmattan, 2009), pp. 245–252.

57   Olivier Coutard and Jonathan Rutherford, "Vers l'essor de villes post-réseaux: infrastructures, changement sociotechnique et transition urbaine en Europe," in Joëlle Forest and Abdelillah Hamdouch (eds), *Quand l'innovation fait la ville durable* (Switzerland: Presses Polytechniques Universitaires Romandes, 2015), pp. 97–118.

8 Electricity micro-grids: a tool for the energy transition?

Since the beginning of the 2000s, the recomposition of service networks has questioned the emergence of a new hierarchy of electricity systems.[1] The changes in the scale of production, even in distribution, are modifying urban and regional energy futures. Communities, inhabitants' collectives, citizen cooperatives, companies, historic or emerging service operators have undertaken strong initiatives in favor of a relocation of energy systems. The infrastructural transition presents a large diversity of technical, political and scalar responses today; there are new elements and additions, but also coexisting elements and hybridizations.[2] The share of decentralized renewable energy is being discussed on the international, national, regional and municipal scale and the micro-network has appeared as a recurring reticular figure. There are many projects in the United States, in New York in particular, but also in London[3] in the United Kingdom, whereas in France, these micro-networks have been tightly restricted in the framework of the law on individual and collective self-consumption after a dispute in which Enedis brought proceedings against the ValSophia company for a micro-network built in the Sophia Antipolis activity park.

The large historic distribution operators are attempting to keep their hands on this historic competence by developing smart grids whose principle is to envisage local micro-productions as an import–export reserve in the energy market to benefit the balance of the large distribution network. If energy production is a reappropriation issue, low- and medium-voltage distribution has become one as well. Consequently, the micro-network is perceived by a growing number of real estate developers, municipalities and inhabitants' cooperatives as an energy transition tool and a lever of the local economy, beyond questions of resilience or the saturation of the existing networks. In terms of collective action logic, these micro-networks can be promoted as much by corporate strategies directed toward financial profit as by citizen initiations that often take the form of an association or cooperative. Whether they are a top-down or bottom-up initiative, private or public, micro-networks often develop where liberalization of the energy market and deregulation have been the strongest, showing in these dense urban contexts radically different, even contrasting projects, as is the case in New York and London.

By analyzing energy decentralization through the angle of the micro-network technical object incorporated into urban projects, whose scale is often the neighborhood, this chapter queries the spatial effects of the infrastructural changes underway.

The growth of micro-networks

According to the International Energy Agency (IEA), the number of micro-networks already or being installed is increasing rapidly in many regions of the world, and this deployment is motivated by very different factors. Micro-networks can meet an electrification need in remote regions or territories that are poorly equipped or unequipped in electricity infrastructures: islands, like that of Bornholm island in Denmark, mountain refuges or zones without any electricity.[4] They can also be envisaged as supply alternatives for communities that want to secede from traditional operators; their profiles and the reasons that guide them are very diverse: communities of survivalists, anarchists or more liberal groups, but communities like rural communes or more urban areas can also follow this path.[5] This was the case of Frieamt and Jühnde in Germany, Mureck and Güssing in Austria and the community of communes of Le Mené in France, whose empowerment trajectories were analyzed by Laure Dobigny, an anthropologist whose specialty is technical sectors.[6]

In the United Kingdom, the town of Woking,[7] not far from London, has taken this path since the mid-1990s, and to attain a certain energy autonomy installed and interconnected over eighty micro-networks to circumvent regulatory obligations limiting connection to the residential.[8] In these projects, initiated by municipalities or counties, connected to a citizen mobilization, micro-networks, self-sufficiency and/or energy autonomy are considered able to strengthen local development.

It is also in the territories where distribution networks have recurring vulnerability problems, as in the state of New York, that micro-networks are increasingly envisaged as a credible alternative. They are then presented as a means of optimizing the existing distribution network by decreasing congestion through a transfer of electrical charges to their independent system.

A micro-network is an energy system that can function autonomously and has the capacity to balance supply and demand to maintain a stable service on a defined territory. Micro-networks are of variable sizes. They are defined less in terms of their size than by their degree of interconnection to the large network (nil, partial- or partial+); their necessity and their context (reliability and efficiency of the existing networks, energy shortage situation, multi-energy reflections, energy savings, weather risks). In the vast majority of cases, the micro-networks are interconnected to the large network.

Electricity autonomy, partially or totally reached onsite, is therefore compatible with interconnection. The systems that cannot function in "island" mode are not identified as micro-networks. For example, many smart grid demonstrators such as the Confluence districts in Lyon, the Issy grid or Batignolles in Île-de-France, are more defined as a decentralized production that is complementary to the network. Moreover, backup systems in hospitals or data centers that serve very specific and limited electrical charges in the event of a charge interruption on the large network, could be considered micro-networks, but it may be said that they belong more to the categories of simple backup systems.

Legal and financial structures differ between the micro-networks due to variable economic and energy factors. What all the micro-networks share, however, is the need to optimize both energy consumption and production to reach the client's objectives on savings, resilience, reliability and durability. The development of micro-networks is growing, but they remain confronted with curbs and challenges of many types (often superimposable), such as rules or regulations unfavorable to infrastructural diversity, the volatility of energy costs as well as uncertainties on financial investments, and the issue of interconnection and interoperability.

On the scale of a region or a state like New York, micro-networks can comprise a kind of energy Meccano of territorial solidarity. They make it possible to rethink the efficiency, durability and resilience of the large network by inverting electricity hierarchies. Unlike Europe, the American distribution networks have weaknesses caused by a shortage of historic investments in favor of their repair and modernizations, aggravated by the opening of competition but also by natural disasters that have caused major breakdowns. After the damage inflicted by Hurricane Sandy in 2012, electricity micro-networks became a central concern for energy actors in New York financially supported by the state's Department of Energy.[9] They are perceived as an efficient means of lightening the transmission networks known in New York for their fragility and meeting a growing demand that increasingly favors peaks.[10]

The Micro-Grid Initiative, created in 2012 by the Smart Grid Consortium, made it possible to conduct a study aiming at itemizing the micro-networks in the state of New York. A project tender was also launched in 2015 – the New York Prize – to favor the development of micro-networks in zones considered priority because they periodically have problems.

The private micro-network: a new tool of urban capitalism

Marked by the liberalization of the energy market in the 2000s, the cities of New York and London have catalyzed the issues linked to energy relocation, complexification and the interplay of economic, political and social actors. The micro-network market has heavily developed on the American West Coast, supported by a very liberal context but also a climate risk, in which electricity autonomy is considered a solution resilient in the event of a disaster or breakdowns. Private luxury real estate development companies have specialized in the field and taken hold of micro-networks to guarantee their clients electricity autonomy "whatever happens."

This is notably the case of Hudson Yards, which is both the largest urban development project underway in New York City and also the largest private real estate project ever built. Located between the Hudson River and Penn Station, bordered by the famous High Line, this commercial and residential development includes about 5,000 apartments with hotels, cultural and educational facilities, five office towers, over 100 stores, as well as restaurants, public spaces and heating and electricity micro-networks. Two tri-generation electricity plants will produce 14.5 MW onsite: 13.3 MW (located above the sales surface) and 1.2 MW (at 10 Hudson Yards). A heating network connects the largest tri-generation plant to all the buildings. Five buildings supply additional thermal energy (redundancy and backup) by means of boilers and chillers. The electricity micro-network can operate in complete autonomy, but there is an interconnection to the electricity network and backup service supplied by ConEd. The Hudson Yards Microgrid Company (HYMco) designed the technical systems, leases and operates the micro-networks as a kind of energy manager. The autonomy of the micro-network is an argument for marketing the apartments: "You have security, you'll always have energy," but it is also a way for the HYMco energy company to develop a new competence in energy maintenance and management (see Figure 123).

In the framework of public services reform in New York, a certain number of zones on the electricity networks were identified as the most vulnerable, which were often sectors where energy precariousness accentuates already high social precariousness. The Brooklyn–Queens Demand Management program, created by ConEd, is considered a pilot project. It is a part of the city that has long been neglected and that is being re-urbanized (or gentrified) today with the gradual arrival of new inhabitants and activities, which has also help to create a peak in electricity demand. Rather than investing as was traditionally done in new production infrastructures, the incentive policy of the state of New York has enabled ConEd to invest in decentralized production and distribution systems of which the Marcus Garvey Village project is one of the most emblematic examples. It is a housing project that the landlord co-designed with ConEd. Apart from the energy renovation of the buildings, an electricity micro-

Figure 123 Hudson Yard under construction from the High Line (2018)

network was created to enable optimization of peak power reduction. At peak intensity, 400 kW are produced by solar panels and 400kW by a fuel cell. Lithium-ion
batteries of 300 kW were installed to handle storage (see Figures 124a–124c).

This project is part of ConEd's Non-Wires Alternatives Program, and the company
is remunerated for the interconnection, the installation costs and the maintenance of
the network, and guarantees backup service (the macro-network is insurance-related).
In the long term, however, this system could threaten ConEd's financial balance
because the company is obligated to maintain low rates in exchange for the interconnection of decentralized electricity sources. If these decentralized sources multiply,
the operator's historic business model will have to radically change, all the more so
as new actors like real estate developers and new energy companies try to position
themselves to recover these market shares linked to the production, distribution and
maintenance of these new decentralized electricity systems.

Among the urbanism plans that have made the energy decentralization question
a priority, that of London is rather unusual, because it has witnessed several decentralization strategies coexist in a strong liberal context. In 2007, the proactive public
policy of the Greater London Authority was notably illustrated by the Decentralised
Energy Program that aims to have 25 percent of the energy consumed produced by

Figure124 Marcus Garvey Village (2018)

Figure 125 River Light apartments designed by the Richard Rogers agency (2017)

"decentralized sources" by 2025.[11] The River Light residence is one of these pilot projects, designed by the Richard Rogers agency and delivered in 2016 for the St James Group real estate developer (see Figures 125a–125d).

Six 12- to 20-story buildings are rising on the banks of the Thames. The program includes 806 apartments, a daycare center, restaurants, bars, as well as a few commercial spaces. In the basement there is a parking garage; half the area is occupied by an energy installation designed, installed and managed by SSE Enterprise Utilities, a private company that is helping the developers solve the "complex energy issues."

The system consists of a cogeneration plant, gas-fired boilers and geothermal heat pumps. The gas-fired boilers are 90 percent efficient and the cogeneration 40 percent.[12] The efficiency of the cogeneration plant is minimal to the degree that there is no ambition to produce electricity onsite. Regarding current energy prices, the developer Eddie Pinchin acknowledges that it is less profitable to operate the local geothermal and cogeneration production system than to connect to the traditional electricity network that remains less expensive. Moreover, the new buildings of this operation are well-insulated, which increases thermal comfort and induces a reduction in heating needs. This example illustrates a certain energy opportunism in the developers in the sense that the installation has made it possible to capture financing and to take part in the city's energy policy. But the technical system has not been optimized in order to maintain the economic model and the control of their operation's energy bill. For these private developers, the question of extending the heating network is not really a subject: who would pay for the connection cost?[13] If major objectives were proposed on the national scale, the strategic vision on the metropolitan scale remains fragile, in view of the profusion of operations with very different ambitions. At River Light (as at Greenwich Peninsula), the developers are co-building an energy management model vis-à-vis the objectives that they set in the framework of the return on investment of their operations. This is very different from the remunicipalized electricity network of Woking, where the operator Thamesway (a public–private partnership created by the municipality) handles the management of decentralized installations, and where the benefits from energy savings are reinvested in new projects initiated by the town, connected to civil society.[14]

It is somewhat different at King's Cross, where a private electricity network was installed to better incorporate local production. It is interconnected to the public network to export the surplus and import if necessary. This old heterogeneous industrial fabric of 27 hectares gave way to a residential and activity district that offers some 316,000 m² of offices, 2,000 housing units[15], 46,400 m² of businesses and leisure facilities, a hotel and schools. This new urban area acquired a heating network and a private electricity network that is based on three cogeneration systems operating on gas and inserted underground in the heart of the block. There are two 2 MWe cogeneration plants and three 10 MWth boilers. A 2 MWe cogeneration motor will complete the system to meet a possible rise in demand. The fuchsia-colored turbine[16] of the cogeneration plant, located on the ground floor of a group of housing units, is open for visits (see Figures 126a–126c).

Eighty percent of electricity needs and 100 percent of hot water and heating needs of the district are ensured by this technical system. Wind turbines mounted on the roof, photovoltaic panels, geothermal pumps and thermal solar panels complete the system. The electricity network "only" connects local businesses, offices and a few large facilities like the hospital, because the regulations limit connection to the residential. For the engineer Allan Jones, president of the International Energy Advisory Council and international expert on micro-networks, the evolution of regulations in favor of connection to the residential is a major issue of decentralization and the transformation of the energy sector.[17]

Even if the new urban development projects are producing decentralized energy, none of them can really consume the electricity produced onsite and the sale to the network must be done by an electricity supply company that has a specific license.[18] There are currently numerous reflections on the evolution of regulatory tools to favor and supervise the development of private networks, but they remain inaccessible for small real estate operations. For Peter North, as for Allan Jones, the main incoherence in the decentralization policy remains the dominant position of the Big Six who maintain strong lobbying on connection rates.[19] Faced with national regulations, micro-networks have trouble existing. And in the energy market, new actors are making their appearance with colossal means. This is the case of the large data center operators who have entered energy production and the development of private micro-networks. If their strategy is somewhat opaque and remains totally secret, we can ask ourselves if some of the GAFAM (Google, Apple, Facebook, Amazon and Microsoft) companies might have the ambition of becoming major actors in a more decentralized energy market, and especially if this orientation will also benefit the population.[20]

GAFAM in the loop: the self-sufficient micro-grid or sharing

Microsoft and Facebook's involvement in the micro-grid program is a revelatory sign of this interest in energy autonomy.[21] Apart from the countries of the Global South where the rolling out of this market is envisaged, it is on their land that the digital giants are testing and installing this type of infrastructure.

Since 2013, Microsoft has been co-financing a data center park in Colorado, whose ambition is to produce an electricity micro-grid and 200 MW onsite. The micro-grid will function as autonomously as possible through a gas-fired cogeneration plant, a photovoltaic plant and fuel cells deployed on the site. This installation will enable data center operators to set up there by connecting to the micro-network with

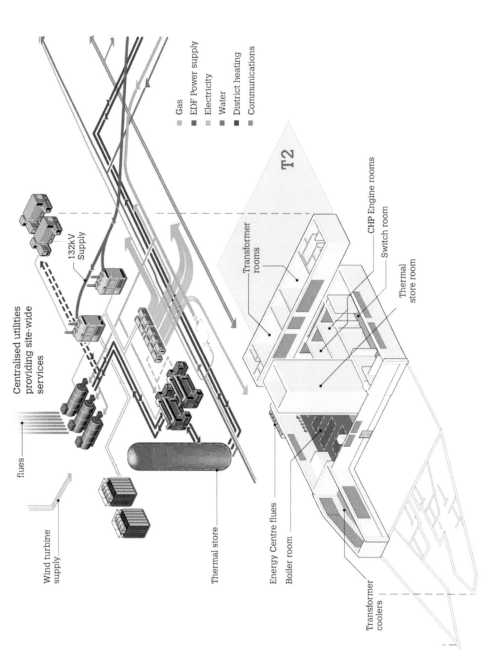

Figure 126 King's Cross development and integrated energy centre (2017)

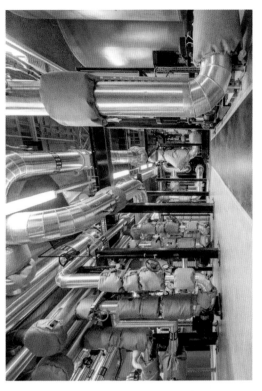

Figure 126 Continued

the possibility of connecting to the traditional electricity network as a complement or in case of problems on the micro-grid. Consequently, the hierarchy of the electricity system is inverted: the onsite systems are the primary source of electricity for basic functioning and the traditional network becomes a backup system. The capitalistic power of the GAFAM enables them to do energy experimentation that few other actors can match. This high-tech energy enclave brings to mind a sort of energy-digital gated community for the sole profit of the sector's industrialists. Microsoft is involved in a similar project for its corporate headquarters in Redmond, Washington, and the company envisages energy autonomy on its campus.

Certain actors, such as energy companies, are specialized in accompanying the implementation of design standards and the operation of an electricity infrastructure that would permit electricity autonomy. This is notably the case of Uptime Institute, which encourages the operators to produce onsite to increase their electricity auton-omy so that it is the principal energy source for the data center, the network being considered an "economical alternative." The data center operator would consequently have control over the maintenance and operation of the generators vis-à-vis the distribution network, whose client it is.

On the scale of the building, there are many examples of nano-networks – for instance, the New York Times Building, a 52-story skyscraper, completed in 2007 and designed by the architect Renzo Piano. A nano-grid was installed on the building's scale, partially supplied by a cogeneration system. Two natural gas-fired generators supply 1,400 kW of continuous electricity to the data center. The specific nature of this installation is that it is continuously used as the main energy source. Diesel fuel motors and the distribution network provide backup and redundancy for this system. Hot water heated by the motor provides heat in the winter and also cools by means of an absorption chiller in the summer. Unlike the nano-network that can constitute an electricity backup system on the scale of a building (interconnected or not to the traditional network), micro- or mini-networks are rolled out between several build-ings on variable district scales. A desire of the government to go from nano to micro, which is considered more energy efficient and more relevant in terms of sharing, can be remarked in strategic planning documents.

Examples of sharing (micro-, even macro-network) on urban or regional scales on the initiative of GAFAM are multiplying. Microsoft and the electricity operator Black Hills installed shared gas-fired backup generators in Wyoming. This installation that serves the Microsoft data center as a priority will also be used by the community during peak periods on the network. When Microsoft began to negotiate with Black Hills for the construction of its 200 MW data center in Cheyenne, several problems arose. The first was that of the electricity availability requested, which was too high for the electricity supplier whose electricity came mostly from coal-fired plants. The construction of a new plant of this type to supply the data center would have required major financial investments and did not correspond to the energy balance that Microsoft wanted to give its installation. Black Hills and Microsoft therefore made a deal: the data center would be equipped with gas-fired backup generators that could be started up to relieve the peaks on the local electricity network by giving it electricity during peak hours. The data center would then become a peak-period power plant, using cleaner gas-fired generators, in exchange for which Black Hills would buy electricity on the market and convey it to Microsoft if there were gaps in production. Microsoft benefits from a negotiated rate (when Microsoft's charge exceeds 35 MW). This rate is intended for large industrial clients that use at least 13 MW of electricity, have a large quantity of backup energy onsite and are ready to ask the electricity company to access this energy source to compensate for shortages due to peaks.

In the state of Oregon, a co-built initiative between the energy operators and the data center operators has shown the important role of these new actors that are intensive energy consumers on the energy market. The Portland dispatchable standby generation is a smart grid designed by Portland General Electric (PGE). The principle is to remotely mobilize diesel oil-fired backup generators, with eighty-six generators in total corresponding to thirty-five clients. Among them are data centers (six for Via West, two for TATA and one for ODAS) as well as hospitals, factories, universities, banks and food warehouses. The interconnection of these generators makes it possible to have a reserve of 121 MW dispatchable by PGE to handle part of these mandatory emergency resources. There is a sharing between the different actors and what they call a win–win operation because PGE supplies the diesel oil and handles maintenance of the generators for fifteen years. Furthermore, during monthly tests, the energy produced is recovered by the network. In the different examples presented, the question is one of sharing dormant emergency capacities by connecting them to each other or sharing them to lighten the electricity network. The problem, however, lies in the use of diesel oil as the primary energy, which reduces the virtuous impact of the sharing approach in terms of the carbon footprint.

As for the network's entire infrastructure, alternative infrastructures correspond to the institutional, large-scale and commercial version. These alternative infrastructures are often managed by associative or cooperative structures, by citizens and enthusiasts, aiming to broaden access to them as much as to create a technical reappropriation of the infrastructure, even its transformation in terms of scale and operation.

Territorial empowerment and the reconfiguration of governance systems

Brought together since 2011 in a European federation, the cooperative movement appears as a privileged form of taking back power on the energy networks. However, the electricity micro-network initiatives in dense urban zones remain marginal in view of a European regulation that is still not very favorable to them. The ambition of creating shared management of the electricity network as well as the means of energy production has mobilized a strong citizen movement in Germany, notably in Berlin where two cooperatives – Berliner Energietisch or Berlin Energy Roundtable, and Bürger Energie Berlin or Citizen Energy Berlin – were created with a view to structuring a local energy democracy. Each cooperative adopted a different strategy. Berliner Energietisch took the legislative route.[22] In drafting a law and submitting it to a citizen referendum, the group tried to force the Berlin Senate to municipalize the local electricity network and create a public energy service that would handle the production of a 100 percent renewable energy and invest in energy efficiency, savings and renovation measures for buildings (notably for low-income households). Bürger Energie Berlin participated in the European invitation to tender (organized by the Berlin Senate) to buy the next concession of the energy network.[23] In his article "Struggle over Berlin Energy Transition: How Can Grassroots Initiatives Affect Local Energy Policy?" (2015), Thomas Blanchet showed that, despite their relative failure, the mobilization generated by the cooperatives had a strong influence on energy planning tools and took part in the reorientation of public policies on the energy transition.[24]

Among the emblematic initiatives of electricity remunicipalization is the city of Nottingham, which in 2015 created its own energy supplier, Robin Hood Energy, by buying a license to supply electricity from Ofgem (Office of Gas and Electricity Markets). But examples remain rare, even if there have been more than 600 community groups that launched themselves into energy production in the United Kingdom since 2008.[25] Between 2010 and 2017, their number increased by 40 percent. The cooperative Repowering London (RL) is one of these initiatives. Created in 2011 by Agamemnon Otero, it has intervened in large low-income housing projects in the heart of weakened urban fabrics in which economic, social and energy precariousness is high.[26] In an asserted perspective of empowerment, RL accompanies the inhabitants in the implementation of energy-saving projects and local production favoring a social economy of solidarity and proximity. One of the main actions of the struggle against economic and energy precariousness uses low-tech solutions to increase thermal comfort and make savings, and solar panels on the roofs of building to produce electricity and lower the consumers' bills.

It was in Brixton in 2012, in the housing project district of Loughborough, that the first cooperative solar energy project, Brixton Solar Energy 1, was launched. It was quickly followed by other initiatives: Brixton Solar Energy 2, Brixton Solar Energy 3 and Brixton Solar Energy 4. Brixton Energy Solar 1 was the first urban installation of solar panels in the United Kingdom initiated and owned by the inhabitants.[27] Consequently, RL saw its first energy cooperative successfully emerge (see Figure 127).

Figure 127 Elmore House district, Brixton (2016)

The long roof of the somewhat rundown Elmore House was covered with solar panels (37.24 kW of installed power). The project attracted 103 investors and made it possible to collect £58,000 in less than a month. A few buildings farther, it was the roofs of the five blocks comprising *Styles Gardens* (Brixton Solar Energy 2) that were equipped (45 kW). A little farther, it was the four buildings of Roupell Park (Brixton Solar Energy 3) (52.5 kW). In 2012, Lambeth Council, the district's owner, authorized the installation of solar panels on the roofs after several consultations with the residents of the area and the real estate management of Loughborough. The cooperative is appealing for communication because of its organizational principle, the social link and the educational missions it develops (see Figure 128).[28]

In the summer in Brixton, when each installation captures the maximum sunlight, each production could fill the needs of between seventy and eighty households. But it is impossible to provide a direct electricity supply to the apartments. The electricity produced is therefore sold to the supplier Good Energy. The households are the first beneficiaries of the social fund, financed by the project's revenue whose rate for the government's purchase is guaranteed for twenty years. In 2015, a new cooperative

Figure 128 Repowering London, the roof of Elmore House equipped with solar panels, Brixton (2016)

Figure 129 The buildings of Banister House (2017)

was created at Banister House, and a power of 102 kW was installed in solar panels on fourteen roofs of this 1930's social housing district (see Figure 129).

If, in terms of energy production, autonomy is relatively low, there is a demonstration of the efficacy of a social investment model. At Banister House, four people were elected directors responsible for the project's follow-up and management, twenty-five young people benefited from a remunerated thirty-week internship,[29] and six people were hired to install solar panels. The Repowering London projects cited are not micro-networks. The Brixton cooperative, like the Banister House project, have the overall ambition of accompanying and mobilizing the inhabitants of these districts around thermal comfort (by undertaking small projects to fight against energy losses) and to reduce energy bills by selling to the electricity company the energy produced by the solar installations on the roof (for which the cooperative of each district handles the follow-up and technical maintenance) (see Figures 130 and 131). But the limits of collective self-consumption in the United Kingdom restrict the cooperatives, whose energy production scope remains minimal. In fact, the promoters of decentralized energy are beginning to realize that "resale rates" are not a long-term solution and that regulatory reform would make it possible to better profit from the economic, social and environmental advantages of decentralized energy.

The situation is different in the United States, notably in the state of New York, where the development of micro-networks is strongly supported by the government and a certain number of cooperatives have appropriated this tool. This is particularly the case of Co-op City which developed one of the largest micro-networks for residential use in the world. It is a Bronx neighborhood, where for the last few years a mini-network has supplied thermal energy and electricity to apartments, as well as thermal energy to six schools and a group of businesses (see Figures 132 and 133).

The urban project was built in the mid-1960s. It is composed of thirty-five residential towers (about 50,000 inhabitants) and other buildings. Initially, a heating and cooling micro-network system had been installed but there was no electricity micro-network. It was the blackout that occurred in August 2003, at the very moment when the urban renovation project for the neighborhood was being discussed, that convinced the landlords to initiate electricity production onsite. In 2008, the buildings' energy renovation was therefore paired with a total revamping of the existing installation with the arrival of a cogeneration plant, which was installed thanks to financing by the government, landlords and the city's historic operator ConEd along with the Housing and Urban Development Agency. The two turbines (gas-fired of 12.5 MW and steam of 13 MW) had an electricity production capacity of 38 MW. A real estate and energy management company, RiverBay Corporation, manages the micro-network and represents the needs of the community that was constituted in the form of a renters' cooperative. This installation has enabled electricity to be produced

Figure 130 Workshop on solar panels, Vauxhall (2017)

Figure 131 Banister House, solar installation (2017)

Figure 132 Co-op City neighborhood in the Bronx, New York

Figure 133 Cogeneration plant of Co-op City in the Bronx, New York

at a low cost for its residents (whose bills decreased) and to sell surplus electricity to the network during periods of low demand onsite. The funds generated by the sale of electricity make it possible to reimburse the loans made to execute the project and to invest in other collective projects.

The cooperative plans to add 5 MW of photovoltaic solar capacity and to extend the electricity service to the neighboring school and shopping centers. A water purification station is also being studied to convert wastewater into gray water and to produce methane from some of the fermentable waste for the cogeneration plant that is biomass-convertible. In view of its electricity autonomy that is now around 90 percent, and the new installations to come, the cooperative would like to sell its surplus on the wholesale electricity market so that it can undertake and co-finance a certain number of projects in the neighborhood. To do so, it turned to the New York Independent System Operator (NYISO), because to sell electricity, over 2 MW must be offered and the entity must have a licensed or aggregator status. In regard to competition, the tension between NYISO and ConEd is very strong.

> As for the backup tax [that the micro-network pays the operator of the large network] why is it one-way? The micro-network pays the electricity operator, but the operator also uses the micro-network [to supply electricity]! Where is the reciprocity in this? With a relaxation of this tax, a convincing economic argument can made for disconnecting the Co-op City micro-network. With a system with almost 100% redundancy, this would make it possible to save 2 million dollars a year, and the large network would then lose the advantages it gets from Co-op City.[30]

The cooperative is trying to reform the regulations because it considers that it pays too much for the service expenses invoiced by ConEd.[31] For the cooperative, ConEd gets many advantages out of this interconnection since the cooperative supplies it with available peak capacity during the summer heatwaves. This example of a micro-network supported by public financing is an illustration of an energy community highly structured in a co-governance: landlords/renters linked to the initiative of urban renovation concerned with fighting economic and social precariousness.

Interconnection and infrastructural diversity: opening the models

In France, the restrictive definition of "closed networks" like that of "interior networks" shows a determination, supported by the CRE (Energy Regulation Commission) and the DGEC (Energy and Climate Department) to contain these initiatives. The law on self-consumption, enacted in February 2017, now makes it possible to consume, onsite, the electricity produced there, and authorizes the sharing of production between one or more producers and consumers.[32] The micro-production of electricity "pockets" is now regulated and self-consumers can choose the quantity and type of energy deployed, but, for the moment, distribution and regulation as well as management remain the protected competence of Enedis. The usage rates of public electricity networks for self-consumption remain a tricky subject, whose evolution the CRE plans,[33] to encourage local productions, resale and interconnections.

A European directive on closed networks will be launched soon and will be expressed in French law. Evolutions and the local energy pilot project idea that combines production, local consumption and "smart" or real-time management are underway. And the large distribution network will play a major role on one hand in terms of backup and on the other in the voltage/frequency balance. Apart from the technical and regulatory dimension, the question of socio-technical changes is essential, as shown by the movements of energy management remunicipalization that seem relatively ambitious in terms of citizen involvement and revenue transfers in the local economy.

Micro-networks appear as a relocation and regulatory technical tool of a new age of networks, the actors involved, in the same way as the technical-economic models and their viabilities being extremely varied. Linked to local energy trajectories, these logics involving the superimposition or replacement of existing networks are rarely duplicable and depend on very different strategies. Among the main trends, we can observe systems that can be a form of mutual and competitive exclusion (gated electricity community in luxury real estate operations) as well as initiatives on restructuring the energy community in rural, dense urban or more peripheral zones – for working-class neighborhoods or the co-op housing of the upper middle class – whose base is cooperative principles that are a matter of the social and mutual aid society. In the city, this dual movement is particularly visible: whereas citizen groups are turning the page of privatization to undertake the remunicipalization[34] of essential services or are organizing into cooperatives, new privatization movements are positioning themselves on mini-networks through private investments in order to organize collective self-consumption and recover the added value that it creates, sometimes far from the interests of consumers. Consequently, the quest for self-sufficiency (when needs are covered by productions) and the relocation of physical flows do not automatically align with an energy autonomy project that encourages more participatory governance modes, a social economy of proximity, or a change in practices and protection of the environment.

Unlike technical macro-systems that serve all the territories without using their own resources, with standard technical elements, technical micro-systems make use of available resources or those that can be captured onsite as a priority. Consequently, if energy relocation is a reproducible principle, the energy systems specific to a site are not transferable as if it were the LTS (large technical system) that stretched its network.

From the perspective of development and encouragement of the installation of technical micro-systems, we must clearly realize that each technical reality implies a relationship system (governance), an operational functioning (technical) and a metabolic chain (energy-resource-environment) specific to the territory where it is to be sited. The geographic level of sharing, and the degree of autonomy of certain service loops (total or partial) in the same way as interconnection, are a nonreproducible strategic conundrum. Heterogeneity and infrastructural diversity dominate the landscape. Micro-networks or technical micro-systems can be connected to each other. This interconnection relationship is envisaged between different entities: the building, the block, the district, the city, the region, all forming a kind of energy Meccano of territorial solidarity.

Unlike the augmented technical macro-system or classic smart grid that thinks of the optimization of peak power reduction or the autonomy of certain parts of the electricity system as an adjustment variable of the large network, the micro-network makes optimization on the small scale the priority of a technical system whose scope is extendable.

Two ideologies are in direct opposition. On one hand, the defenders of the historic network advocate the incorporation of renewable energies into the existing technical system through the smart network in a macro-infrastructural technological and cultural continuity. On the other, a change in paradigm and a technical and social rupture are emerging that is occurring through the experimentation of new technical systems that are as autonomous as possible from the large existing networks. In this case, each unit must maximize its production capacities and optimize its management in order to ensure its operating autonomy and to redistribute the surplus in the local or national energy mesh. Local energy pilot projects are developing with rather different use models, but that will often, nonetheless, be connected to the network for security reasons in the event of an incident and for stabilization problems concerning power quality. The two approaches will not be in opposition; they will be complementary.

For electricity, the micro-network examples of Woking, the King's Cross district, Marcus Garvey Village in Brooklyn and even Co-op City, demonstrate the reality of relocated electricity networks that can, however, be reconnected to the large network if need be. Consequently, the viability of the macro-systems is not threatened as such. On the contrary, the increase in the energy efficiency of the large existing networks, notably of transmission lines, remains necessary to ensure exchanges, but their extension is less so.

In this chapter, the examples of electricity micro-networks follow two project schemes. The first group concerns a top-down decentralization: it is directive energy steering that is at work in the urban projects initiated by large public and private operators in development and service networks as in London in the King's Cross district, River Light and Hudson Yards in New York. Real estate developers ensure energy management in these projects through heavy economic investments; each development operation now has its own cogeneration plant integrated into and connected to hundreds or thousands of apartments (sometimes with private micro-networks), without the inhabitant communities being involved in the energy project or that the resilience of the models installed be guaranteed over the long term. In this case, the installation of energy decentralization systems does not act as a political empowerment factor, unlike citizen initiatives, notably cooperatives. It is the second group of projects, more bottom-up, that are based on practices and uses like Repowering London or Co-op City in the Bronx, or remunicipalizing initiatives for the electricity network of Berlin or Hamburg. Infrastructures are being transformed and the change affects as much extracted resources that are transformed and distributed as much as the scale of technical objects or the public – or publics – of infrastructures.[35]

A change of paradigm is underway: the social ideal of the large infrastructure as an edifice of public service, which combined economy of scale, technical reliability and quality service for the largest number of people, has been destabilized since the 1990s by the private capital of the liberal economy.[36] The centralized technical object is prey to new assemblies and displacement of what constituted its value. The revamping of public service based on the commons,[37] remunicipalization or de-privatization movements on municipal or regional scales are multiplying, and should not be seen as a return to falling back on localism.[38] Consequently, local micro-productions and other citizen relocation initiatives appear as a desire to reinject the public based on the local. In this perspective, hierarchies could be reversed, the large electricity network, while remaining very structuring, could become secondary for the provision of certain sectors in which it would primarily become a reserve of solidarity depending on needs. As John Dewey asserted in 1927, the public of infrastructures is not an immobile and predefined mass of citizens, but a community of interest, a part of which is increasingly involved in the search for a more collective and economical governance of natural resources. This is how we can read the opposition against the development of large infrastructure projects that are at the heart of the politicization of ecological questions. The battles that are being waged on the "zones to be defended" – that of Notre-Dame-des-Landes or Bure (in France) – spatialize with great clarity, complexity and necessary radicalism the challenge of the young twenty-first century: a recovery of the territory as opposed to the convulsive movements of the modernizing infrastructural project, a new airport or a center for burying nuclear waste.

Notes

1 For a further development of a number of the examples in this chapter, see Fanny Lopez, *L'ordre électrique, infrastructures énergétiques et territoires* (Les Acacias: Edition MétissPresses, 2019).

2 Sylvie Douzou, Marc Guyon and Simon Luck (eds), *Les territoires de la transition énergé-tique* (Paris: Lavoisier, coll. EDF Socio-économie de l'énergie, 2019).

3 Lopez, "Keep the lights on!," pp. 18–33.

4 See Sylvie Jaglin or Martina Schäfer's work on the South regions: Martina Schäfer (ed.), *Micro Perspectives for Decentralized Energy Supply: Proceedings of the International Conference, April, 23rd to 25th, 2015, Bangalore* (Berlin: Technische Universität Berlin, 2015).

5 Simon Marvin and John Rutherford, "Controlled environments: an urban research agenda on microclimatic enclosure," *Urban Studies*, vol. 55, no. 6 (2018); Philip Vannini and Jonathan Taggart, *Off the Grid: Re-assembling Domestic Life* (London: Routledge, 2015).

6 Dobigny, "Le Choix des énergies renouvelables"; Dobigny, "L'autonomie énergétique," pp. 245–252.

7 Jonathan Rutherford and Olivier Coutard, "Urban energy transitions: places, processes and politics of socio-technical change," *Urban Studies*, vol. 51, no. 7 (2014), pp. 1353–1377.

8 Regulations limit the connection of a private network to the residential network; it is not authorized to exceed 1 MW (about 1,000 households). Regulations also limit the export and resale of electricity to the national network at 5 MW, or only 2.5 MW if the production is linked to domestic production. Sean Randal, interview with Fanny Lopez, 9 October 2015.

9 But not only New York: multiple projects exist in many states. This is the case of the Stafford Hill micro-network (Rutland, Vermont), solely supplied by solar energy and batteries, or Berrego Springs (San Diego, California), which both provide electricity autonomy to emergency shelters.

10 The Micro-Grid Initiative has around twenty members, including the Department of Energy of the state of New York, IBM and ConEd. Let us recall that 60 percent of the electricity of the state of New York is consumed in the New York metropolitan regions, while 40 percent of the electricity is produced there.

11 Greater London Authority, *Decentralised Energy Master Planning: A Manual for Local Authorities* (London: GLA, 2011).

12 Eddie Pinchin (project manager at St James Homes), interview with Fanny Lopez, 12 October 2016.

13 *Ibid.*

14 See Energie-Cités, "Private Wire Systems for Delivery to Tenants" (2003), available at: https://www.c40.org/case_studies/de-centralizing-energy-generation-in-woking-uk-slashed-the-citys-co2-emissions-by-82.

15 On average, £10,000 per square meter. Benoît Dufour (project supervisor for Argent, London), interview with Fanny Lopez, 13 October 2016.

16 The motor was colored in this way to support breast cancer research and a collection of funds took place around the motor exhibited in the district before it was installed in the building.

17 Allan Jones, interview with Fanny Lopez, 13 October 2016.

18 As for the purchase rates, out of 205 authorized electricity suppliers, there are only 10 obliga-tory FIT (Feed-in Tariffs) licensees and 18 voluntary FIT licensees. See Ofgem, "FIT Licensee Contact Details," available at: https://www.ofgem.gov.uk/environmental-programmes/fit/contacts-guidance-and-resources/fit-licensee-contact-details (accessed 25 January 2021).

19 Peter North, interview with Fanny Lopez, 14 February 2016.

20 Cécile Diguet and Fanny Lopez, *L'impact spatial et énergétique des data centers sur les territoires* (Ademe report, Paris: ADEME, 2019), available at: https://www.ademe.fr/impact-spatial-energetique-data-centers-territoires-l (accessed 25 January 2021).

21 https://www.greentechmedia.com/articles/read/facebook-microsoft-mobilize-50-million-for-renewable-energy-microgrids (accessed 25 January 2021).

22 Christine Kühnel (member of the Berliner Energietisch cooperative, Berlin), interview with Fanny Lopez, 21 October 2016.

23 Arwen Colell (member of the Bürger Energie cooperative, Berlin), interview with Fanny Lopez, 21 October 2016.

24 Thomas Blanchet, "Struggle over Berlin energy transition: how can grassroots initiatives affect local energy policy?," *Energy Policy*, vol. 78, March (2015), pp. 246–254. See also: N. Rochol and R. Bolton, "Berlin's electricity distribution grid: an urban energy transition in a national regulatory context," *Technology Analysis & Strategic Management*, vol. 28, no. 10 (2016), pp. 1182–1194.

25 P. Capener, *Community Renewable Electricity Generation* (2014), available at: https://www.gov.uk/government/uploads/system/uploads/attachment_data/file/274746/20140108_Community_Energy_Modelling_FinalReportJan.pdf (accessed 25 January 2021). In France, 165 participatory renewable energy development projects were listed in 2016. Since the electricity production and distribution landscape is different in the United States to Europe (three large electricity networks, more fragile distribution lines and stronger market deregulation), we can observe similar reappropriation dynamics with about 1,000 cooperatives.

26 Repowering London (RL) was created in 2011 with the status of volunteer organization (IPS for Industrial Provident Society) and obtained the status of cooperative in 2013 (Community Benefit Society). RL, which now has five employees, mostly operates with public funding.

27 R. Hopkins, "Les coopératives de Brixton Energy, Londres," in R. Hopkins (ed.), *Ils changent le monde! 1 001 initiatives de transitions écologiques* (Paris: Seuil, 2014), pp. 35–37.

28 Sumitra Gomer (urban planner, Lambeth Council, London), interview with Fanny Lopez, 15 March 2017.

29 One of them, Victoria Omobuwajo obtained the Solar Power Portal Award, following which she registered for a Master's degree in business studies.

30 K. Horne, J. Strahl and M. Bebrin, *Community Microgrid Case Study and Analysis Report*

(New York: Navigant Consulting, 2015), p. 37, http://nyssmartgrid.com/wp-content/uploads/CommunityMicrogridCaseStudyandAnalysisReport_2015–08–133.pdf. p. 40.

31 These service expenses include: connection modalities, the accounts and measurements of the production injected into the network and the consumptions extracted from them, the calculation of the portion to be divided between each building, the management modalities and possible surplus, its valuation on the market, data management.

32 Self-consumption can be individual or collective, total or partial. Collective self-consumption is defined by the fact of grouping several producers and end-users together, linked to each other in a legal entity whose extraction and injection points are located downstream of a low- or medium-voltage substation (L315–2, art. 9).

33 The calculation formula of the TURPE (public transmission system access tariff) is re-evaluated every four years.

34 In Europe, see the examples of Hamburg, Nottingham, Woking.

35 S. J. Collier, J. C. Mizes and A. Von Schnitzler (eds), "Public Infrastructures/Infrastructural Publics," *Limn*, no. 7 (2016).

36 Graham and Marvin, *Splintering Urbanism*.

37 Nicole Alix, Jean-Louis Bancel, Benjamin Coriat and Frédéric Sultan (eds), *Vers une république des biens communs* (Paris: Les liens qui libèrent, 2018).

38 Gilles Jeannot, "Les communs et les infrastructures des villes," in C. Chatzis, G. Jeannot, V. November and P. Ughetto (eds), *Les Métamorphoses des infrastructures: Entre béton et numérique* (Paris: Peter Lang, 2017), pp. 341–350.

Index